Dear Mauro,

with best wishes.

BUSINESS GROUPS IN EAST ASIA

Business Groups in East Asia

Financial Crisis, Restructuring, and New Growth

Edited by
SEA-JIN CHANG

OXFORD
UNIVERSITY PRESS

OXFORD
UNIVERSITY PRESS

Great Clarendon Street, Oxford OX2 6DP

Oxford University Press is a department of the University of Oxford.
It furthers the University's objective of excellence in research, scholarship,
and education by publishing worldwide in

Oxford New York

Auckland Cape Town Dar es Salaam Hong Kong Karachi
Kuala Lumpur Madrid Melbourne Mexico City Nairobi
New Delhi Shanghai Taipei Toronto

With offices in

Argentina Austria Brazil Chile Czech Republic France Greece
Guatemala Hungary Italy Japan Poland Portugal Singapore
South Korea Switzerland Thailand Turkey Ukraine Vietnam

Oxford is a registered trade mark of Oxford University Press
in the UK and in certain other countries

Published in the United States
by Oxford University Press Inc., New York

First published 2006

British Library Cataloguing in Publication Data
Data available

Library of Congress Cataloging in Publication Data
Data available

Typeset by SPI Publisher Services, Pondicherry, India
Printed in Great Britain
on acid-free paper by
Biddles Ltd, King's Lynn, Norfolk

ISBN 0-19-928734-1 978-0-19-928734-5

1 3 5 7 9 10 8 6 4 2

Preface

This book examines the nature and extent of business groups in East Asian countries and their restructuring subsequent to the 1997 Asian Crisis. The crisis significantly affected the nations discussed in this book. Interest rates and exchange rates skyrocketed. Banks and other financial institutions quickly became insolvent, and heavily indebted industrial firms, many of which were affiliated with the business groups in this region, went bankrupt. Unemployed people filled the street. The crisis affected Thailand, Indonesia, Malaysia, and Korea most directly, but other East Asian countries that depended heavily upon intraregional trade were also hurt by the crisis. Western commentators have argued that debt-ridden, family-controlled business groups were largely to blame for the crisis and should therefore be dismantled immediately. These arguments are not surprising, given the visibility of these organizations. In fact, the IMF and the World Bank demanded draconian measures for restructuring of business groups in return for relief funds.

In the eight years since the crisis, there has been little documentation of whether the restructuring of these groups has occurred or business groups are extinct. To answer these questions, I assembled a group of distinguished experts on business groups in East Asia for a conference that took place in September 2003 at Seoul. The conference was jointly sponsored by the Institute of Business Research and the Asia Business Center, both at Korea University, my home institution. This book emerged from that conference. The chapters on business groups in eight East Asian countries that were contributed by these experts show in great detail how national differences can influence business groups' responses to changing institutional environments.

The Asian Crisis was almost a natural experiment, as it showed how the reactions of businesses in affected countries to a common shock varied according to these countries' economic, political, social, and cultural environments. A theme that emerges from these chapters is the robustness of the business group structure. Despite adverse conditions, most business groups did not immediately collapse. Some groups went bankrupt, but most survived, and some prospered. In addition, East Asian nations embarked on very different trajectories to this external shock. The Asian Crisis affected the interrelationships among the sociocultural environment, the state, and the market of each country quite differently and had distinct effects on the operations of these countries' business groups. Taken together, the contributors' insights demonstrate how East Asian business groups' practices, as well as their past and future prospects, are influenced by specific institutional contexts.

Yet East Asian business groups face an uncertain future. Foreign investors' influence has increased substantially since the crisis, as East Asian governments had to accommodate their demands to keep attracting foreign capital. Governments supervise banks more closely and have loosened restrictions on mergers and hostile takeovers, further strengthening the discipline of the market. Various entry barriers that had inhibited foreign multinationals from competing in national markets were lifted, exposing business groups to intensified foreign competition. Under these new conditions, business groups in East Asia should reconfigure their business structures and adjust their corporate governance systems to regain momentum for further growth. Individual contributors concur that business groups will continue to be important vehicles for the sustained future growth of this region.

This book would not have been possible without the assistance of several individuals and organizations. I would like to thank ex-Dean Jangro Lee of the Institute of Business Research and Professor Mansoo Shin, Director of the Asia Business Center, both at Korea University, for providing funding for the conference. John Lafkas copyedited the entire manuscript to make it seem as if one author wrote all the chapters, and also provided detailed comments on individual chapters. I benefited from discussions with my colleagues at the London Business School, where I spent my sabbatical while preparing this manuscript. I would also like to thank three anonymous readers for the Oxford University Press, who provided very valuable comments in enhancing theoretical contribution to this volume. David Musson, my editor at the Oxford University Press, and his fellow staff members encouraged me as I prepared the manuscript and did a wonderful job of turning it into a book. Last but not least, I would like to thank the authors of these chapters, all great scholars in the field, who sent me their contributions in a timely manner and endured my demands for repeated revisions. Great books require hard work. I am sure we all are very proud of what we have achieved jointly.

Sea-Jin Chang

Seoul
March 2005

Contents

Contributors

Christina Ahmadjian is Professor of Management at Hitotsubashi University Graduate School of International Corporate Strategy in Tokyo. From 1995 to 2000 she was on the faculty of Columbia Business School. She received her BA from Harvard, MBA from Stanford, and Ph.D. from the University of California at Berkeley. Her research interests include business groups, corporate governance, and institutional change in the face of globalization, and her primary focus is on the Japanese economy. Her papers have been published in journals including *Administrative Science Quarterly*, *American Sociological Review*, *Organization Science*, and the *California Management Review.*

Chi-Nien Chung is Assistant Professor in the Department of Management and Organization at the NUS Business School, National University of Singapore. He received his Ph.D. in sociology from Stanford University in 2000. He currently studies business groups in East Asia, with a focus on how institutional changes mediate the relationships between strategy, structure, and performance. He has published in *Journal of Management Studies*, *Organization Studies*, *Developing Economies*, and *International Sociology.*

Sea-Jin Chang is Professor of Business Administration at Korea University. He used to be a faculty member at the Stern School of Business of New York University. He had visiting appointments at Stanford, INSEAD, and London Business School. He received his BA and MA in economics from Seoul National University, and Ph.D. in strategic management from the Wharton School of the University of Pennsylvania. He is primarily interested in the management of diversified multinational firms. His current research focuses on understanding the process of creating operating synergies among diversified lines of business and building a strong local organization after foreign entry. His research has been published in journals such as *Strategic Management Journal*, *Academy of Management Journal*, *Journal of Business Venturing*, *Journal of Management Studies*, *Review of Economics and Statistics*, and *Journal of Industrial Economics.* His recent book, *The Rise and Fall of Chaebols: Financial Crisis and Transformation of Korean Business Groups* (Cambridge University Press, April 2003) explores the strategies Korean business groups have pursued, examines various aspects of their structures, and assesses their performance.

Edmund Terence Gomez is Associate Professor at the Faculty of Economics and Administration, University of Malaya. He has also held appointments at the University of Leeds (England), Murdoch University (Australia) and Kobe University (Japan). The books he has published include *Politics in Business: UMNO's Corporate Investments* (Forum, 1990), *Malaysia's Political Economy: Politics, Patronage and Profits* (Cambridge University Press, 1997), *Chinese Business in Malaysia: Accumulation, Accommodation, Ascendance* (University of Hawaii Press, 1999), *Ethnic Futures: The State and Identity Politics in Asia* (Sage, 1999), *Chinese Business in Southeast Asia* (Curzon, 2001), *Political Business in East Asia* (Routledge, 2002), *The State, Economic Development and Ethnic Co-existence in Malaysia and New Zealand* (CEDER-UM, 2003) and *Chinese Enterprise, Transnationalism and Identity* (RoutledgeCurzon, 2004), and *The State of Malaysia: Ethnicity, Equity and Reform* (Routledge-Curzon, 2004).

Donghoon Hahn is Professor of International Studies at the Catholic University of Korea. He received his BA and MA in economics from Seoul National University and Ph.D. in economics from Peking University. His research interests include Chinese firms and economic system. His research has been published in diverse journals such as *Issues and Studies* and *The China Review.* His most recent studies have resulted in two books, namely *Enterprises and Economy of China* and *The East Asian Economy.* He also used to work for the investment banking division of Ssangyong Securities Company.

Alberto Daniel Hanani is a senior faculty member at the Magister Management Program of the University of Indonesia. He is also the head of the Laboratory for Mangement Studies in the same university. His research interests are mainly in competitive-cooperative strategy and Indonesian corporate diversification strategy. In addition, he used to be in an executive board position of a medium-size general insurance company, and also member of four non-executive boards which all belong to the same business group in Jakarta. He also writes regularly on Indonesian main business newspapers and weeklies. He used to present papers in some international management conferences, among others: Family Business: Indonesian Mid-size Company Model (2003); Competition and Cooperation: A Paradox Approach (2002); and Indonesian Business Conglomerates: Roles and Challenges in the Future of Indonesian Economy (1999).

Keun Lee is Professor of Economics at Seoul National University, with a Ph.D. in economics from the University of California at Berkeley. He was formerly Lecturer in Economics at the University of Aberdeen, Scotland, and a research fellow at the East West Center, Hawaii. His current research topics include corporate governance and growth, industrial policy, and innovation and technology policy in East Asia. In these fields, he has published many articles in such journals as, *Industrial and Corporate Change, Journal of Comparative Economics, Research Policy, Economics of Planning, Cambridge Journal of*

Economics, *World Development*, *Asian Economic Journal*, and *China Economic Review*, as well as two monographs entitled, *Chinese Firms and the State in Transition* (M. E. Sharpe, 1991), and *New East Asian Economic Development: Interacting Capitalism and Socialism* (M. E. Sharpe, 1993). He was awarded the 28th Maekyung Economist Prize for his article published in *MOCT-MOST*, and was listed in the *Marquis' Who is Who in the World* (1997).

Ishtiaq Pasha Mahmood is Assistant Professor at the NUS Business School, National University of Singapore. He obtained his B.A. in economics from Oberlin College and his Ph.D. from Harvard University. Before coming to NUS, he worked as an analyst at Gemini Consulting in Chicago and as a management consultant with Levitan & Associates in Boston. His current research is on managing innovation in the Asian context. Specifically, he examines how institutional aspects influence the interface between business groups and innovation. His research has appeared in journals such as *Academy of Mangement Journal*, *Management Science*, *Academy of Management Review*, *Research Policy*, and *The Journal of Economic Behaviors and Organization*. Dr Mahmood won the Haynes Prize in 2001, awarded annually by the Academy of International Business in recognition for the best paper by researchers under the age of forty.

Piruna Polsiri is a lecturer at the Department of Finance, Dhurakijpundit University, Thailand. She received her BBA in international transportation management from Thammasat University, Thailand, and MBA in finance from the University of Texas at Arlington. She was recently granted her Ph.D. in finance from the University of Melbourne, Australia. Her research interest is in areas of corporate finance and corporate governance. She is currently working on two main topics, namely corporate governance of banks in Thailand and corporate restructuring of Thai business groups.

Lai Si Tsui-Auch is Associate Professor at Nanyang Business School, Nanyang Technological University of Singapore. She obtained her B.Soc.Sc. from the University of Hong Kong, and MA in telecommunications, and Ph.D. in sociology-urban studies from Michigan State University, USA. Before joining NTU, she worked as research scientist at Technological University of Berlin and Wissenschaft Zentrum Berlin für Sozialforchung (WZB), Germany. Her current research focuses on business groups, trust and distrust in organizations, and bureaucratic rationality. Her research papers have been published in journals such as *Organization Studies*, *Journal of Management Studies*, *Management Learning*, *Journal of Asian Business*, *International Sociology*, *International Journal of Urban and Regional Research*, *Development and Change*, and *Gazette*. She has also published numerous book chapters including two that appear in the *Handbook of Organizational Learning and*

Knowledge which won the Terry Book Award at the Academy of Management annual conference in 2002. She is currently a member of the Editorial Board of *The Qualitative Report* and Editorial Advisor of the Development Bank of Japan Reports.

Yupana Wiwattanakantang is Associate Professor at the Center for Economic Institutions (CEI), Institute of Economic Research, Hitotsubashi University, Japan. Her research interests are in the area of corporate finance and corporate governance with the focus on emerging economies and Japan. Dr Wiwattanakantang has published her research papers in international journals and books. Her recent paper 'Connected Lending: Thailand before the Financial Crisis' (with Chuthathong Charumilind and Raja Kali) is forthcoming in the *Journal of Business*. Three of her research papers have ranked in the top ten most downloaded list of the SSRN in 2001, 2002, and 2003 respectively. In addition to teaching corporate governance at the graduate school of Hitotsubashi University, Dr Wiwattanakantang was invited to teach corporate governance in East Asia at the Master of International Economics and Management Program (MIEM), SDA Bocconi University School of Management in Milan. She has also served as an ad hoc referee for the *Journal of Corporate Finance*, *Journal of Financial Research and Services*, and *Pacific Basin Finance Journal*. Her consulting experience includes working with the Asian Development Bank Institute on a project investigating the corporate governance of banks in East Asia. Dr Wiwattanakantang was educated at Thammasat University (BA and MA) in Thailand and Hitotsubashi University (MA and Ph.D.) in Japan.

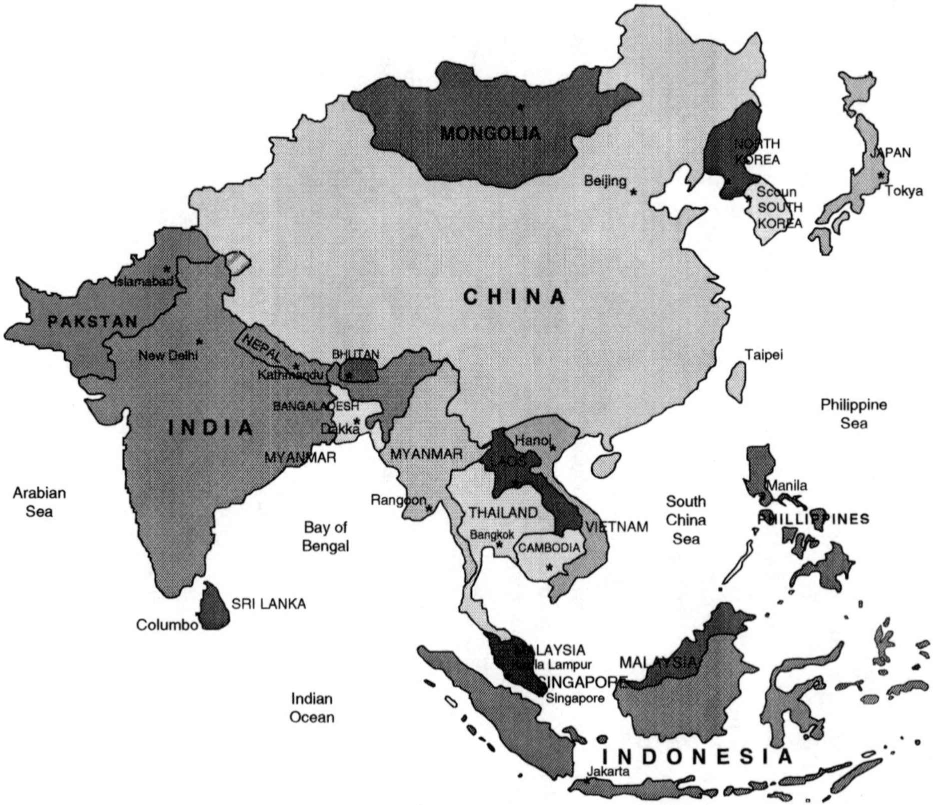

MONGOLIA
NORTH KOREA
JAPAN
Beijing
Scoun
SOUTH KOREA
Tokya
Islamabad
CHINA
PAKSTAN
New Delhi
NEPAL
BHUTAN
Kathmandu
Taipei
Philippine Sea
BANGALADESH
INDIA
Dakka
Hanoi
MYANMAR
MYANMAR
LAOS
Manila
Arabian Sea
Rangoon
THAILAND
South China Sea
PHILLIPPINES
Bay of Bengal
VIETNAM
Bangkok
CAMBODIA
SRI LANKA
Columbo
MALAYSIA
Kuala Lampur
MALAYSIA
SINGAPORE
Singapore
Indian Ocean
INDONESIA
Jakarta

Map of East Asia and Vital Statistics

	Population(million)	Area(1,000 km^2)	Per capita income(US$)	Exchange rate(per US$)	Inflation(%)	GNP growth rate(%)
Japan	127	377	34,510	103.13 yen	−0.14	2.34
South Korea	49	98	12,020	1,043.80 won	3.60	5.14
Taiwan	23	36	13,320	32.22 NT$	1.61	3.16
Singapore	4	0.7	23,918	1.64 S$	1.71	3.88
Thailand	65	514	2,190	38.96 baht	2.73	4.60
Malaysia	24	329	3,780	3.95 ringgit	1.42	4.42
Indonesia	239	1,919	810	9,319.64 rupiah	6.20	3.72
China	1,299	9,596	1,100	8.28 yuan	3.90	8.36

Sources: World Bank and IMF.

Notes: 1. Population as of 2003.

2. Per capita income are in 2003 US dollars.
3. Exchange rates are as of December 31, 2004.
4. Inflation and GNP growth rate are defined as the average annual changes in the consumer price index and GNP, respectively, during 2000–3.

1

Introduction: Business Groups in East Asia

Sea-Jin Chang

1.1. EXTENT OF BUSINESS GROUPS IN EAST ASIA

Business groups exist throughout the world.[1] Conglomerates in the Western hemisphere, 'keiretsu' in Japan, 'grupos economicos' in South American countries, and 'business houses' in India are only a few well-known examples. Although their exact features differ from country to country because of distinct economic, social, and cultural environments, they have important similarities. Most notably, business groups pursue unrelated diversification under centralized control.

Business groups are important to many East Asian countries' economies. In Korea, for instance, the top thirty business groups, known as chaebols, accounted for 40 percent of Korea's output in the mining and manufacturing sectors and 14 percent of GNP in 1996. In Thailand, Malaysia, Singapore, and Taiwan, business group affiliates (henceforth referred to as affiliates) that were listed on these countries' stock exchanges accounted for 24.3, 24.9, 39.6, and 56.2 percent, respectively, of these exchanges' total market capitalization in 2002. Further, many East Asian business groups have a significant international presence. Appendix 1.1 lists affiliate firms that were included in *Business Week*'s Top 200 Emerging Market Companies and Global 1,000 Largest Companies based on market capitalization in 1997 and in 2003. Large East Asian business groups are engaged in various kinds of direct investments, mergers, and acquisitions throughout the world, and compete directly with other large Western corporations in *Business Week*'s Global 1,000 listings.

But East Asian business groups face an uncertain future. Since the 1980s, foreign creditors and investors have become more important to East Asian economies. The sudden outflow of foreign capital out of the region in 1997, known as the Asian Crisis, significantly affected business groups in East Asia. During this crisis many business groups went bankrupt, as did the financial services firms that lent them money. Following the crisis, foreign creditors and investors have demanded that business groups have more transparent operations and stronger corporate governance. At the same time, as governments in East Asia have loosened trade barriers and as many bankrupt local firms were sold to foreign investors after the crisis, business groups have become subject to intense competition in both domestic and international markets.

This book examines the nature and extent of business groups in Asian countries and changes to these groups since the crisis. In the rest of this chapter, I first sketch out how a comparative institutional framework is useful for understanding business groups. Since the Asian Crisis provides a unique opportunity to assess the institutional environments of East Asian countries, I use this framework to examine briefly the causes of the Asian Crisis and subsequent changes in institutional environments since that time. Finally, I summarize the contributors' chapters on business groups in eight East Asian countries. These chapters show in great detail how national differences can influence business groups' responses to changing institutional environments. Taken together, the contributors' insights demonstrate how East Asian business groups' practices, as well as their past and future prospects, are influenced by specific institutional contexts.

1.2. A COMPARATIVE INSTITUTIONAL FRAMEWORK

A comparative institutional perspective regards a nation's pre-existing arrangements, particularly those among the nation's sociocultural environment, its state government, and its market, as the path-dependent context that guides how individual actors and governments respond to roughly the same external constraints (Whitley 1992, 1999; Evans 1995; Orru, Biggart, and Hamilton 1997; Guillen 2001).[2] In other words, it conceives of countries as operating on a complex set of variables that differs from one country to another. Different institutional contexts encourage different forms of business and market organizations to become established, and any changes in these environments will naturally affect the distinct characteristics of firms and markets that have developed interdependently with them. Countries thus embark on very different trajectories when a common external shock occurs. The Asian Crisis affected the interrelationships among the sociocultural environment, the state, and the market of each country quite differently and had distinct effects on the operations of these countries' business groups. Figure 1.1 summarizes the framework employed in this book.

First, East Asian business groups are embedded in the countries where they operate (Granovetter 1995; Evans 1995; Orru, Biggart, and Hamilton 1997).

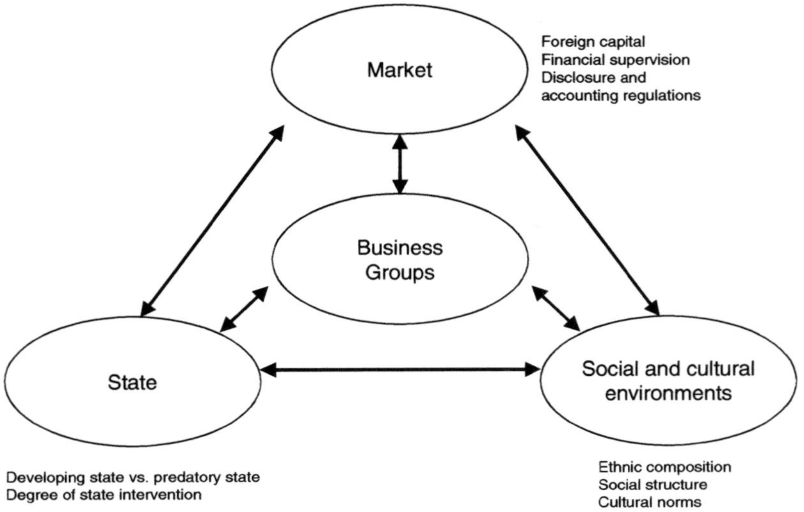

Figure 1.1. The comparative institutional framework of this book

Strachan (1976) observes that business groups have three characteristics: (*a*) a great diversity of enterprises in a group; (*b*) pluralism—the groups comprise a coalition of several wealthy businessmen and their families; and (*c*) an atmosphere of loyalty and trust normally associated with family or kinship groups. Granovetter argues that what distinguishes business groups from a collection of firms under common financial control such as American conglomerates is the social solidarity and social structure among component firms. He argues it is important to examine how identifiable 'axes of solidarity' like region, political party, ethnicity, kinship, and religion are. Different chapters in this book will highlight the relevance of these axes, especially kinship and ethnicity, to the formation and evolution of business groups in specific nations.

For instance, different evolutionary patterns of Japanese, Korean, and Taiwanese groups might reflect the history and culture of these groups' respective countries, which are characterized by Orru, Biggart, and Hamilton (1997) as communitarian, patrimonial, and patrilineal, respectively. Similarly, Whitley (1992, 1999) demonstrated how histories, cultures, educational systems, the organization of labor unions, and the prestige hierarchy of occupations in Northeast Asian countries resulted in different management structures and practices, and different forms of business and market organizations. On the other hand, ethnic divisions affected the growth and restructuring of business groups in Southeast Asian countries. Many business groups were supported by their national governments, which wanted to promote indigenous capital at the expense of Chinese immigrants, who often formed their own business groups to secure ethnic solidarity (Gomez and Jomo 1999). In South Asian countries, foreign capital was another important axis of solidarity. Access to local resources and political favors was crucial and foreign investors formed alliances with the government and local elite, which Evans (1979) referred to 'dependent development.'

Second, the state has influenced the creation and growth of business groups, as well as national differences among these groups. It has done so by favoring some industries and firms with subsidies, loans, and high import duties. Most East Asian countries pursued an unbalanced growth strategy by focusing their resources on a few sectors that their governments deemed 'strategic' (Hirshman 1958; Gerschenkron 1962). Given the paucity of well-established capitalists, governments often used business groups as vehicles to 'catch up' with more industrialized nations. For instance, the state played a critical role in forming business groups in Japan, Korea, and Singapore (Johnson 1982; Amsden 1989). The state also helps set up governance structures and rules of exchange among domestic and foreign economic actors (Campell and Lindberg 1990; Fligstein 1990). Some Southeast Asian governments' policies, which explicitly favored indigenous capitalists over ethnic Chinese, often intertwined their interests with those of business, resulting in corruption and cronyism (Evans 1995).[3] Through these actions, the state provides businesses with incentives to undertake specific actions, and it determines the relative power of managers and different classes of investors. As the country chapters shall emphasize, families that have founded business groups frequently have had power far exceeding the relative size of their investment in these groups. This power is in part a function of states' policies towards business groups.

Finally, markets are relevant to a comparative institutional perspective. Economists often regard business groups as resulting from market imperfections prevalent in developing countries. According to Leff (1978), business groups perform several functions in such nations. First, they provide access to capital and information, neither of which flows naturally in underdeveloped markets. Second, the unrelated diversification of business groups provides an alternative to portfolio diversification when markets for risk and uncertainty are absent. Third, vertical integration provides a solution to the problems of bilateral monopolies and oligopolies that stem from imperfect intermediary goods markets. Khanna and Palepu (1997) argue that business groups replace poorly performing or nonexistent economic institutions (e.g. banks or external labor markets) that are taken for granted in developed countries. For example, it is unnecessary to create an internal capital market if the banking system is well developed. There is also no need to rely exclusively on an internal labor market if there is a sufficient supply of highly skilled labor outside the business group. Yet because several East Asian countries are in the early stages of economic development, there are ample opportunities for business groups to create value by internalizing mechanisms normally performed by markets. Although the Asian Crisis and the subsequent bankruptcies of firms and layoffs of workers affected the labor and intermediate goods markets in East Asian countries, we pay particular attention to capital markets because in the aftermath of the Asian Crisis, the restructuring of banks and the enforcement of stronger corporate governance systems substantially changed the operations of the capital markets in a relatively short time.

Our focus on sociocultural environments, governments, and markets in the respective countries is useful for understanding why business groups are prevalent in East Asian countries. It also helps us understand similarities, as well as differences, in how East Asian business groups both capitalized on the conditions that caused the Asian Crisis and reacted in the aftermath of this crisis. Campbell's comprehensive framework (2004) of institutional change[4] suggests we have to understand how major actors, or 'institutional entrepreneurs' in his terminology, perceive their problems, generate possible solutions, find opportunities to change, and adopt eventual courses of actions. He emphasizes major actors because although institutional change is often triggered by exogenous factors such as a crisis or war, such shocks can be reinforced by internal friction among actors who feel contradictory incentives and seek new institutional arrangements. During such periods, existing institutional processes, cultural frames, and social beliefs constrain the options available to these actors (Dobbin 1994). He argues that institutional changes thus tend to be evolutionary rather than revolutionary.

As the country chapters will emphasize, most large business groups have cultivated similar relationships with the governments of their home countries in order to secure preferential treatment. Business groups' ability to maintain such cozy relationships with governments after the crisis, however, varied greatly across both countries and groups. At the same time, governments' abilities to perceive problems and initiate appropriate restructuring programs varied greatly. In some crisis-affected countries, governments gave in to the demand of foreign investors and creditors to initiate some irreversible institutional changes to improve governance and transparency. In other countries, such changes have been thwarted by cultural and ethnic conflicts. In countries that were not directly affected by the crisis, governments felt less urgent need for change and have implemented weak restructuring programs.

1.3. THE ASIAN CRISIS

The Asian Crisis hit several countries in the region, including all the 'Tiger Economies'. The crisis started in Thailand, where the baht plummeted in July 1997. It spread from there as unstable foreign exchange rates caused an exodus of foreign capital (see Figure 1.2). Indonesia and Malaysia were soon affected. In November, Korea, which had been regarded as an exemplar of economic development, succumbed to the crisis. Singapore, Hong Kong, Taiwan, and Japan, with their stronger financial systems and high levels of foreign reserves, survived the contagion, while China, with its closed economy, was not affected by the crisis.

East Asian countries had several structural weaknesses that made them vulnerable to the crisis. Globalization of financial markets, especially in regard to inflows of short-term capital, created an environment ripe for currency speculation. In the past, East Asian governments tightly regulated foreign sources of capital and guaranteed these funds would be repaid. When they liberalized their economies in the 1980s and 1990s, they removed such restraints. Table 1.1 shows some important trends. First, the inflow of foreign capital jumped in the 1990s as East Asian economies became more integrated into the global economy. Second, most of this inflow was in the form of short-term speculative funds, rather than long-term foreign direct invest-

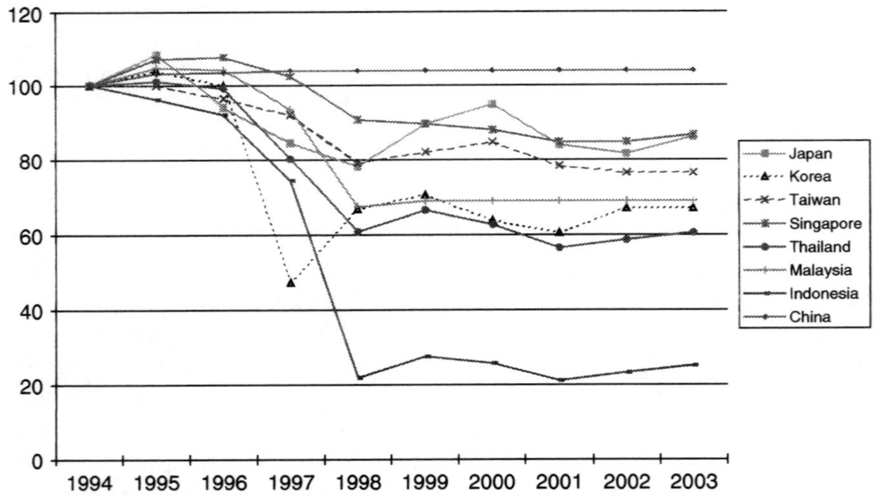

Figure 1.2. Fluctuation of exchange rates 1994–2003 (1994 = 100)
Source: IMF, *International Statistics Yearbook*, 1994–2003.

Table 1.1. Inflows of foreign capital, 1994–2003

Portfolio Investment

Year	1994	1995	1996	1997	1998	1999	2000	2001	2002	2003
Japan	64.53	59.79	66.79	79.19	56.06	126.93	47.39	60.50	−20.04	81.18
Korea	8.71	14.61	21.51	13.30	0.77	7.90	12.69	12.22	5.37	22.65
Taiwan	2.90	2.72	3.25	−1.20	1.80	13.91	9.55	11.13	6.64	30.34
Singapore	0.11	−0.24	0.98	−0.45	0.78	3.52	−1.83	0.47	−0.76	0.36
Malaysia	−1.64	−0.43	−0.26	−0.24	0.28	−0.89	−2.14	−0.66	−0.83	2.49
Thailand	2.19	4.08	3.58	4.59	0.33	−0.10	−0.54	−0.52	−0.69	0.30
Indonesia	3.87	4.10	5.00	4.67	−0.24	−1.86	−4.55	−2.97	0.14	−0.59
China	3.92	0.71	2.37	7.84	0.09	−0.69	7.31	1.24	1.75	8.44
Total	84.59	85.34	103.22	107.70	59.87	148.72	67.88	81.41	−8.42	145.17
Total excluding Japan and China	16.14	24.84	34.06	20.67	3.72	22.48	13.18	19.67	9.87	55.55

FDI Investment

Year	1994	1995	1996	1997	1998	1999	2000	2001	2002	2003
Japan	0.91	0.04	0.21	3.20	3.27	12.31	8.23	6.19	9.09	6.24
Korea	0.81	1.77	2.32	2.84	5.41	9.33	9.28	3.52	2.39	3.22
Taiwan	1.37	1.55	1.86	2.24	0.22	2.92	4.92	4.10	1.44	0.45
Singapore	8.55	11.50	9.30	13.60	7.69	16.06	17.21	15.03	5.73	11.40
Malaysia	4.34	4.17	5.07	5.13	2.16	3.89	3.78	0.55	3.20	2.00
Thailand	1.36	2.06	2.33	3.89	7.31	6.10	3.36	3.89	0.95	1.86
Indonesia	2.10	4.30	6.10	−2.63	−1.87	−1.79	−1.91	−0.24	1.22	2.25
China	33.70	35.80	40.18	44.23	43.75	38.75	38.39	44.24	49.30	47.07
Total	53.14	61.19	67.37	72.50	67.94	87.57	83.26	77.28	73.32	74.49
Total excluding Japan and China	18.53	25.35	26.98	25.07	20.92	36.51	36.64	26.85	14.93	21.18

Source: IMF, *International Statistics Yearbook*, 1994–2003.

ment. Between 1994 and 1996, the volume of portfolio investment to East Asian countries, excluding Japan and China, more than doubled—from US$16.14 billion in 1994 to US$34.06 billion in 1996. In addition, short-term commercial bank loans from foreign sources increased sharply. Thus, East Asian economies were extremely vulnerable to short-term fluctuations of foreign capital. Reflecting the exodus of speculative funds from the region, the inflow of portfolio investment dwindled to US$3.72 billion in 1998, less than 11 percent of what it had been in 1996.

Second, this inflow of foreign capital caused a credit boom, which in turn caused asset price inflation and prompted increased consumption and imports. East Asian economies became overheated, and their governments failed to cool them down.[5] Heavy inflows of foreign capital were channeled to real estate markets in Thailand, Indonesia, and Malaysia, creating asset bubbles. The general economic downturn in the global market slowed down exports, and the financial performance of firms in crisis-affected countries deteriorated sharply. In addition, the yen's depreciation in the 1990s eroded the export price competitiveness of most East Asian countries and aggravated their current account deficits. These countries' exchange rates did not depreciate, however, because foreign capital kept coming in. Suddenly, vacancy rates for commercial real estate and firm bankruptcies increased, and financial institutions began to be strapped for capital. Moreover, the private sector financial institutions had borrowed foreign funds without hedging their foreign currency risk.

Third, the inflow of foreign capital was not wisely spent. Some companies used cheap money on projects that were economically unviable. For example, Korean chaebols diversified into unrelated business areas. Most East Asian countries lacked the strong corporate governance mechanisms that might have prevented such investments. These countries relied mainly on their banking systems, rather than equity and bond issues, for financial intermediation. Banks in these countries were unable, however, to provide adequate governance. In short, financial liberalization was unaccompanied by adequate supervision, vastly increasing risk as more foreign money competed for less creditworthy borrowers. Krugman (1998b) pointed out that the existence of 'moral hazard' was prevalent in all Asian countries affected by the crisis.

When foreign investors realized these structural weaknesses, they began to withdraw their investments and loans. Soon, the net capital flow was reversed by more than US$100 billion.[6] Corporate performance in Indonesia, Korea, and Thailand had declined significantly since 1995. As a result, the debt to equity ratios of firms in those countries rose sharply. Currency devaluations of 30–80 percent aggravated firms' debt service burden and resulted in massive bankruptcies. In turn, when employees lost their jobs, they reduced their consumption, which caused more bankruptcies. Corporations that barely avoided bankruptcy cut out investment and reduced employment. East Asian countries that were not directly affected by the crisis, such as Japan, Singapore, and Taiwan, also experienced recessions due to reduced opportunities for trade (see Figure 1.3). Only China, which remained a closed economy, was not affected by the crisis. The contraction of economies and the resulting unemployment problems turned a financial crisis into an economic crisis, and eventually into a social and political crisis.

Korea, Indonesia, and Thailand received large support packages from the International Monetary Fund (IMF). Malaysia, which did not receive any support from the IMF, weathered the crisis by controlling inflows/outflows of foreign capital and depreciating its currency. The IMF demanded that countries receiving assistance adopt draconian measures of restructuring in return for the relief funds. It wanted to restore investor confidence and to fundamentally restructure these economies' financial and corporate sectors. In order to achieve the first goal, it raised short-term interest rates and ushered in a floating exchange rate regime, which was publicly criticized as triggering more bankruptcies and insolvencies.[7] To achieve the second goal, the IMF pushed the governments to restructure their corporate sectors.

Business groups' heads reacted differently to the crisis. Many failed to strengthen their corporate governance systems. Some reorganized, but others

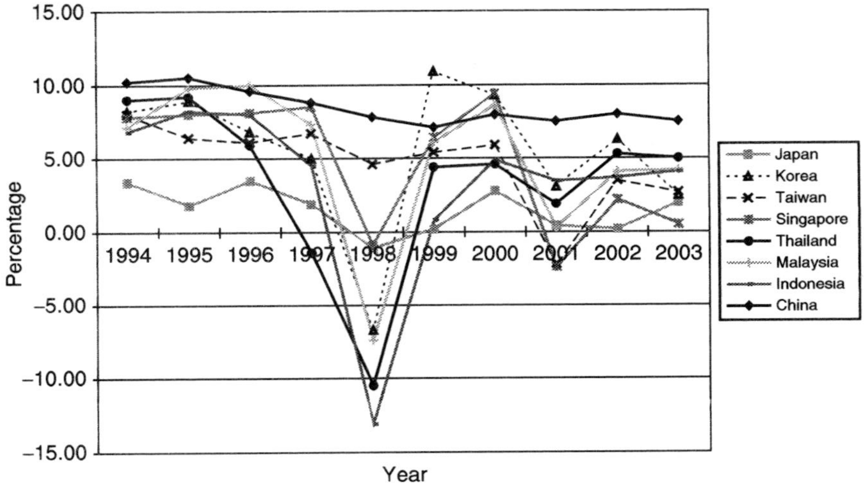

Figure 1.3. GDP growth rates, 1994–2003

Source: IMF, *International Statistics Yearbook*, 1994–2003.

expanded their businesses and diversified further. For instance, some large chaebols, such as Samsung, LG, and SK, grew bigger after the crisis, while many smaller groups divested many of their businesses. In some countries, heads of business groups lobbied the government for preferential treatment for bailouts or restructuring. For instance, postcrisis restructuring in Indonesia merely resulted in families who were better connected to the government assuming control.

By 2003 most East Asian economies had recovered. In the countries hurt most by the crisis—Indonesia, Thailand, Korea, and Malaysia—foreign reserves increased and currencies and interest rates were stable. The combination of fiscal and monetary policy stimuli, and an economic boom in western countries, contributed to the recovery. Singapore and Taiwan's economies were strong. China's economy expanded rapidly. Japan had not, however, recovered from its decade-long recession.

1.4. THE POSTCRISIS CHANGES IN BUSINESS ENVIRONMENTS

1.4.1. Banks and Corporate Restructuring Programs

Prior to the crisis, East Asian countries experienced phenomenal growth. This growth would not have been possible with retained earnings alone. Demands for capital far exceeded domestic supplies. In most East Asian countries, governments allocated capital through industrial policies, export promotion policies, and sometimes through affirmative action favoring indigenous capital. The resulting banking systems relied on tacit government approval of large loans to sectors and firms that were backed by government policies. Financial supervision by regulatory agencies was also inadequate to guarantee the soundness of the system. Since governments implicitly guaranteed bank deposits, banks felt no incentives to monitor the performance of loans and manage risk.

There were many other structural weaknesses in the financial sector. Ineffective bank regulation and supervision and poor accounting and disclosure diminished transparency. For example, many family-controlled business groups in Indonesia and Malaysia owned banks. They used the banks' reserves as if these funds belonged to them and extended credit to their own affiliates. Nonbank financial institutions, especially in Korea and Thailand, often lacked adequate discipline. They could borrow foreign capital and loan it to domestic borrowers that were politically connected or were affiliated with the same business groups.[8]

Right after the crisis, many financial institutions in Indonesia, Korea, Malaysia, and Thailand were severely distressed or insolvent. The ratio of nonperforming loans to total loans exceeded 40 percent in Thailand. Governments in Korea, Malaysia, and Indonesia had to infuse public funds into technically bankrupt banks. They guaranteed all deposits, transferring private liabilities into government liabilities. Government-owned asset management companies acquired nonperforming loans at discounted prices. Thailand closed two-thirds of its finance companies, while Korea closed two-thirds of its merchant banks. Indonesia closed many banks and placed others under government supervision.

Other East Asian countries initiated somewhat different reforms. Some injected massive public funds into commercial banks to keep these institutions solvent. Malaysia restructured its banking industry through mergers and acquisitions. China accelerated its enterprise restructuring and financial sector reform and increased the capitalization of its state-owned banks. Overall, banks in East Asia became larger through mergers, while their governments set up better means for monitoring the soundness of these banks.

For most East Asian firms, the crisis was a disaster. Their foreign-currency-denominated debts increased sharply due to exchange rate depreciation. Their foreign and domestic creditors demanded immediate repayment of debts. As their domestic economies went into deep depressions, they increasingly found it hard to service debts. Firms, especially highly leveraged ones, soon faced bankruptcy. The ways that crisis-affected countries used to restructure debts for private corporations were similar to those used by financial institutions. This massive upheaval created both opportunities and threats. Some business groups went bankrupt, but others expanded by acquiring failed businesses.

1.4.2. Corporate Governance Reforms

Weak corporate governance mechanisms in East Asia also precipitated the crisis. Firms in East Asian countries relied mainly on bank financing. Securities markets were not well developed since they required a more sophisticated institutional and regulatory infrastructure. Financial firms were not regulated sufficiently, and many East Asian governments allocated capital, further undermining the development of banks' lending function. The interlocking ownership and other interrelationships between banks and corporations also reduced market discipline. Other supporting institutions, such as credit rating agencies and regulatory agencies were not yet fully developed.

Right after the crisis, the need to address shortcomings in supervision, regulation, accounting, auditing, and legal standards was widely emphasized. Each crisis-affected country adopted measures to improve loan standards. Korea, for instance, redefined loans past due from 180 to 90 days late, and began using the forward-looking method to define loan loss provision. These countries also improved their supervision of banks.[9]

Lax enforcement of investor rights has also been pointed out as a weakness of East Asian economies (Johnson et al. 2000). There are several ways to improve investor protection. Transparency can be enhanced through more stringent disclosure requirements that are based on international accounting and auditing standards. Monitoring institutions such as credit rating agencies can be created. Most East Asian governments realize they need to adopt such measures to ensure access to adequate supplies of foreign capital. Table 1.1 shows that inflow of foreign capital in East Asia restored its precrisis level. As East Asian countries are more integrated into the global economy, they will become more subject to the influence of foreign capital. For instance, foreign ownership increased to nearly 40 percent of Korea's total market capitalization. The increased presence of foreign investors has led to greater minority shareholder activism, another significant structural change that has influenced the behavior of listed companies.

1.4.3. Intensified Global Competition

Business groups now face more intense domestic and international competition. In the past, East Asian governments aggressively blocked imports and protected their domestic markets. Since World War II, the General Agreement on Tariffs and Trade (GATT) helped remove tariff barriers and other nontariff barriers among its members. The World Trade Organization (WTO), which began operating in 1995, further strengthened the enforcement of GATT rules. Several crisis-affected countries removed trade and investment barriers to comply with the IMF's conditions for relief. In addition, many financially troubled companies were sold to foreign multinationals. For instance, in Korea, Japanese automobile and electronics manufacturers can now sell their products. Volvo and Renault acquired Samsung's heavy equipment business and automobile ventures, and General Motors (GM) acquired Daewoo Motors. Such acquisitions will spur competition, as business groups will feel pressure to focus on their core business and to refrain from diversifying into unrelated businesses.

1.5. CHANGES IN BUSINESS GROUPS IN EAST ASIAN COUNTRIES: INTRODUCTION TO CHAPTERS

Part I of this book includes chapters that describe business groups in Japan and three newly industrialized countries (NICs)—Korea, Taiwan, and Singapore. Among these four countries, only Korea was directly affected by the crisis. Although the economies of Japan, Taiwan, and Singapore were strong enough to weather the worst of the financial crisis, the massive bankruptcies of banks and industrial corporations in this region during the crisis induced substantial changes in these countries' business environments.

Ahmadjian (Chapter 2) describes the recent changes in Japanese keiretsu. Japan has two types of business groups: (*a*) horizontal groups, which comprise large firms in diverse industries, and are centered on banks; and (*b*) vertical groups, which consist of buyers and affiliated suppliers and distributors, such as the Toyota group. Japan's homegrown banking crisis began in the early 1990s, even before the Asian Crisis, when the stock market and real estate markets declined dramatically after the burst of the asset bubble in the late 1980s. Due to questionable loans based on inflated real estate and share prices, several banks went bankrupt and some high-profile intergroup bank mergers occurred. In addition, accounting reforms, which forced firms to report the market value of their equity holdings, resulted in firms selling off both their shares in banks and their cross shareholdings in member firms. The tightening of requirements for consolidated accounting also made it harder for firms to manage their earnings by allocating gains and losses among group firms. Moreover, increased foreign ownership helped loosen interfirm ties between keiretsu firms. Ahmadjian examines the ownership and director ties of keiretsu firms to find out whether the keiretsu form was disrupted due to this series of events. She finds that although some peripheral relationships have been disrupted, the relationships among core firms have remained robust despite these changes.

Chang (Chapter 3) documents changes in business groups in Korea after the crisis. When the financial crisis hit Korea, thirteen of the top thirty chaebols went technically bankrupt. This chapter argues that although the Korean government did abolish intragroup debt guarantee practices, its heavy-handed approach to forcing chaebols to swap businesses so that each chaebol would focus on a few core businesses failed completely. The government's effort to force chaebols to reduce debt–equity ratios was hindered after chaebols merely revalued their assets and bought new equity issues by other affiliates. Chang argues that more fundamental restructuring of Korean business groups will occur only when corporate governance systems and accounting transparency are improved. Foreign investors and creditors, as well as banks that became larger and more powerful through several mergers, will induce chaebols to restructure further. In addition, intensified international competition, not government intervention, will force chaebols to reduce unrelated diversification.

Chung and Mahmood (Chapter 4) offer a description of Taiwanese business groups as an interesting contrast to the Japanese and Korean cases. Taiwanese groups are loosely coupled networks of firms, positioned in between chaebols and keiretsu in terms of hierarchical control. Because the Taiwan government policy uses tax incentives to favor new establishments, Taiwanese groups are more numerous and smaller than Korean chaebols are. These groups have grown consistently, particularly since the country liberalized its economy in the 1980s. This liberalization opened key industries previously monopolized by state enterprises, such as banking, telecommunications, and electricity to the private sector, creating opportunities for business groups to expand. The Asian Crisis did not deter Taiwanese business groups' growth. This chapter suggests that, at least in the short run, these groups will grow further and diversify more to exploit new business opportunities in the Taiwanese economy.

Tsui-Auch (Chapter 5) represents Singaporean business groups as a fine example of business groups run by the state. Although the Singaporean economy is one of the freest in the world, its development reflects the highly visible hand of the government. Emulating the keiretsu and chaebol models, the government created large government-linked corporate groups to spearhead development in sectors such as finance, air travel, and telecommunications. Unlike parastatals in many countries, government-linked corporations have generally been managed effectively and run like private businesses, with a focus on financial performance. The private businesses run by the ethnic Chinese were left alone, and have competed with the government-linked corporations in many areas. When the Asian Crisis occurred, the government realized it needed to restructure its financial sector and strengthen its corporate laws and accountancy practices. It pressured government-linked corporations and private banks to globalize, divest their noncore assets, and professionalize their governance. It also began monitoring banks' performance more vigorously. Yet, the pace of divestment by both government-linked groups and banking groups has been thus far gradual.

The chapters in Part II examine business groups in countries that were stars of emerging markets in the 1980s and 1990s, such as Malaysia, Thailand, and

Indonesia. The development of large business groups in these countries has been actively conditioned by the state, which has developed economic development policies that promote indigenous businesses at the expense of ethnic Chinese enterprises.

Gomez (Chapter 6) talks about Malaysian business groups and demonstrates how much the country was influenced by East Asian corporate models, specifically the chaebol and the keiretsu, in developing the national economy. In addition, affirmative action policies favoring indigenous Malay, known as *Bumiputeras*, contributed to the rise of several major business groups. Businesses run by the ethnic Chinese had to accommodate the state in order to survive and expand, which led to these entrepreneurs building connections with politicians. The Asian Crisis had a profound impact on domestic capitalists, especially well-connected ones. Some leading *Bumiputeras* capitalists lost control of their corporate assets since they were burdened with enormous debts and depended too much on state leaders. Their corporate activities were often influenced by politicians and affected by political crises. As a consequence, business groups with better political connection thrived. Others with the wrong connections lost their businesses.

Polsiri and Wiwattanakantang (Chapter 7) show Thai business groups as another case of deep state involvement and ethnic conflict. The Thai government also tried to restrict ethnic Chinese business and to promote indigenous capital. To encounter Chinese dominance, the government set up many state-owned enterprises and semigovernmental companies. Under the military regime, major profitable industries were monopolized by the state. In order to operate in this business environment, ethnic Chinese established close ties with the politicians, particularly the military leaders. These Sino-Thai businessmen provided top government officials capital and the entrepreneurial and managerial expertise that these officials lacked. Although the Asian Crisis affected Thailand severely, Thai business groups' ownership and governance structures did not change. Only banks and finance companies were closed down or taken over by the government and foreign financial institutions.

Hanani (Chapter 8) points out that the case of Indonesian business groups is similar to those of Chapters 6 and 7 in that the formation and fate of business groups were closely related to political connections. The Suharto government provided favors to close friends and families, who became owners of major business groups in the country. Other business groups run by ethnic Chinese also grew through close alliances with highly ranked government officials. Banks owned by business groups typically acted as 'cashiers' that provided credit to companies within the group. The financial crisis devastated the Indonesian economy. The restructuring of business groups deprived several founding families of their ownership in these groups. This chapter demonstrates that business groups that maintained close connections with the political regime that took power after Suharto survived and prospered. Others that lacked these generally failed.

Part III contains a chapter on Chinese business groups by Lee and Hahn (Chapter 9). The Chinese government attempted to industrialize the country in a short time by transforming traditional state-owned enterprises (SOEs) into modern joint-stock companies in the form of business groups, modeled after Korean chaebols. The government initially formed loose informal arrangements among companies, but quickly realized that more formal, equity-based arrangements were necessary for sharing resources among various companies. Measures such as spin-offs, mergers, and acquisitions of shares were used to create business groups. The state holding companies were supervised by the State Property Management Committee to maintain control of state property. Despite a series of reforms, many business groups in China have been losing money. Their viability in China is now being heatedly debated. Finally, Chapter 10 summarizes major findings from each individual chapter and draws conclusions about the future of business groups in East Asia.

This volume does not include chapters on several other East Asian countries. There is not a chapter on Hong Kong, one of the Four Tigers (NICs), because its business/political environment was in flux after China assumed control of it. Some Hong Kong business groups moved their headquarters to other countries, while others quickly became integrated with mainland China business. Several other East Asian countries, including Vietnam, Myanmar, and Cambodia, are still socialist regimes, and both their economies and private sectors remain comparatively underdeveloped. It may thus be premature to write about these nations' histories of business groups. Despite these omissions, the eight country chapters in this book cover most key nations of East Asia. They provide insight into how East Asian business groups' practices, as well as their past and future prospects, are influenced by specific institutional contexts. See Table 1.2.

Table 1.2. Comparative institutional factors

Countries Factors	Japan	Korea	Taiwan	Singapore	Malaysia	Thailand	Indonesia	China
Structure of capital	Strong indigenous capital	Dependence on foreign capital	Strong indigenous capital	State is the major provider of capital	Mixed interest between state and private sector	Mixed interest between state and private sector	Mixed interest between state and private sector	State is the major provider of capital but individual capitalists are on the rise
The role of the state	Laissez-faire	From developmental state to laissez-faire	From developmental state to laissez-faire	Developmental state	Mix between developmental state and predatory state	Mix between developmental state and predatory state	Mix between developmental state and predatory state	Developmental state
Ethnic divisions	Homogeneous	Homogeneous	Homogeneous	Diverse but dominated by ethnic Chinese	Conflict between indigenous and ethnic Chinese	Conflict between indigenous and ethnic Chinese	Conflict between indigenous and ethnic Chinese	Homogeneous

Appendix 1.1. Business groups listed in *Business Week's* Emerging Market 200 and Global 1000 in 1997 and 2003

Firm name	Market value 1997	Group name	Firm name	Market value 2003	Group name
Korea			**Korea**		
KOREA ELECTRIC POWER (KEPCO)	19361	State-owned	SAMSUNG ELECTRONICS	44188	Samsung
SAMSUNG ELECTRONICS	8801	Samsung	SK TELECOM	13343	SK
POSCO	6172	State owned	KT	11321	Independent (formerly state-owned)
DAEWOO HEAVY INDUSTRY	3125	Daewoo	KOREA ELECTRIC POWER (KEPCO)	10589	Independent (formerly state-owned)
SK TELECOM	2552	SK	KOOKMIN BANK	9309	Independent
HYUNDAI MOTOR	1998	Hyundai	POSCO	7303	Independent (formerly state owned)
			HYUNDAI MOTOR	5992	Hyundai Motor
Taiwan			LG ELECTRONICS	4971	LG
CATHAY LIFE INSURANCE	16020	Cathay	WOORI FINANCE HOLDINGS	3610	Independent
TAIWAN SEMICONDUCTOR MFG.	11381	TSMC	KT FREETEL	3548	Independent (formerly state-owned)
FIRST COMMERCIAL BANK	11194	State-owned	SAMSUNG SDI	3036	Samsung
HUA NAN BANK	10336	State-owned	KT&G	3001	Independent (formerly state-owned)
CHANG HWA COMMERCIAL BANK	10216	State-owned	SHINHAN FINANCIAL GROUP	2970	Independent
UNITED MICROELECTRONICS	7930	United Microelectronics	SAMSUNG FIRE & MARINE INSURANCE	2756	Samsung
CHINA STEEL	7855	Independent (formerly	KIA MOTORS	2722	Hyundai Motor

		state-owned)			
NAN YA PLASTIC	7214	Formosa	LG CHEM	2541	LG
CHINA DEVELOPMENT FINANCIAL HOLDING	6979	Independent	SHINSEGAE	2517	Shinsegae
FORMOSA PLASTIC	5681	Formosa	SAMSUNG ELECTRO–MECHANICS	2259	Samsung
SHIN KONG LIFE INSURANCE	5299	Shin Kong	CHOHUNG BANK	2174	Independent
TATUNG	4829	Tatung	S–OIL	1976	Independent
INTERNATIONAL COMMERCE BANK	4351	State-owned	HYUNDAI MOBIS	1967	Hyundai Motor
ACER	4099	Acer			
PRESIDENT ENTERPRISES	3246	President	**Taiwan**		
FORMOSA CHEMICALS & FIBRE	3236	Formosa	TAIWAN SEMICONDUCTOR MFG.	28713	TSMC
ADVANCED SEMICONDUCTOR ENGINEERING (ASE)	3032	Advanced	CHUNGHWA TELECOM	13846	Independent (formerly state-owned)
MOSEL VITELIC	2992	Mosel Vitelic	UNITED MICROELECTRONICS	9722	United Microelectronics
FAR EASTERN TEXTILE	2963	Far Eastern	CATHAY FINANCIAL HOLDINGS	9696	Cathay
TAIWAN CEMENT	2553	Taiwan Cement	HON HAI PRECISION INDUSTRIES	6903	Hon Hai
EVERGREEN MARINE	2528	Evergreen	FUBON FINANCIAL HOLDING	6475	Fubon
TAIPEI BUSINESS BANK	2459	State-owned	NAN YA PLASTIC	6465	Formosa
WINBOND ELECTRONICS	2396	Walsin	FORMOSA PLASTICS	5946	Formosa
ASIA CEMENT	2369	Far Eastern	CHINA STEEL	5431	Independent (formerly state-owned)

(*Continued*)

Appendix 1.1. (*Continued*)

Firm name	Market value 1997	Group name	Firm name	Market value 2003	Group name
HUALON TEIJRAN	2343	Hualon	MEGA FINANCIAL HOLDING	5126	Independent
CATHAY CONSTRUCTION	2196	Cathay	QUANTA COMPUTER	4931	Quanta
FUBON INSURANCE	2111	Fubon	ASUSTEK COMPUTER	4666	Asustek
PACIFIC ELECTRIC WIRE & CABLE	2080	Pacific Electric Wire & Cable	FORMOSA CHEMICALS & FIBRE	4494	Formosa
TAICHUNG BUSINESS BANK	2010	Independent	CHINA DEVELOPMENT FINANCIAL HOLDING	3911	Independent
CHINA AIRLINES	2004	Independent (formerly state-owned)	CHINATRUST FINANCIAL HOLDINGS	3869	China Trust
Singapore			TAIWAN CELLULAR	3231	Pacific Electric Wire & Cable
SINGAPORE TELECOMMUNICATIONS	27524	SingTel	COMPAL ELECTRONICS	2922	Kinpo
OCBC OVERSEAS CHINESE BANK	12526	OCBC	HUA NAN FINANCIAL HOLDINGS	2736	Independent
SINGAPORE AIRLINES	10946	SIA	AU OPTRONICS	2504	Benq
UNITED OVERSEAS BANK	9842	UOB	FIRST FINANCIAL HOLDING	2269	Independent
DEVELOPMENT BANK OF SINGAPORE	8655	DBS Group Holdings	CHINA MOTOR (CMC)	2243	Yulon
CITY DEVELOPMENTS	7381	Hong Leong	ACER	2127	Acer
HONGKONG LAND HOLDINGS	7267	Jardine Matheson	WINBOND ELECTRONICS	2117	Walsin
SINGAPORE PRESS HOLDINGS	6748	SPH	YULON MOTOR	2114	Yulon
JARDINE MATHESON	5018	Jardine Matheson	NANYA TECHNOLOGY	2090	Formosa

OVERSEAS UNION BANK	4662	UOB (merged)	BENQ	1981	Benq
JARDINE STRATEGIC HOLDINGS	3886	Jardine Matheson	LITE-ON TECHNOLOGY	1942	Liteon
Malaysia			**Singapore**		
TELEKOM MALAYSIA	14798	State-owned	SINGAPORE TELECOMMUNICATIONS	15209	SingTel
TENAGA NASIONAL	14135	State-owned	UNITED OVERSEAS BANK	10057	UOB
MALAYAN BANKING	12059	State-owned	DBS GROUP HOLDINGS	8298	DBS Group Holdings
SIME DARBY	7587	State-owned	OCBC BANK	6843	OCBC
PETRONAS GAS	6526	State-owned	SINGAPORE AIRLINES	6742	SIA
UNITED ENGINEERS (MALAYSIA)	6393	State-owned	SINGAPORE PRESS HOLDINGS	3526	SPH
GENTING	3661	Lim Goh Tong			
RESORTS WORLD	3650	Lim Gog Tong	**Malaysia**		
RENONG	3129	State owned	MALAYAN BANKING	8047	State-owned
ROTHMANS OF PALL MALL (MALAYSIA)	3011	Foreign	TENAGA NASIONAL	7288	State-owned
PERUSAHAAN OTOMOBIL NASIONAL	2824	State-owned	TELEKOM MALAYSIA	6459	State-owned
YTL	2792	Yeoh family	MALAYSIAN INTERNATIONAL SHIPPING	3744	State-owned
BERJAYA SPORTS TOTO	2645	Vincent Tan	MAXIS COMMUNICATIONS	3709	T. Ananda Krishnan
DCB HOLDINGS	2611	Rashid Hussain	PETRONAS GAS	3645	State-owned
AMMB HOLDINGS	2522	Azman Hashim	PLUS EXPRESSWAYS	3197	State-owned
MAGNUM	2496	Lim family	PUBLIC BANK	3127	Teh Hong Piow
MALAYSIAN INTERNATIONAL SHIPPING	2428	State-owned	SIME DARBY	3122	State-owned

(*Continued*)

Appendix 1.1. (*Continued*)

Firm name	Market value 1997	Group name	Firm name	Market value 2003	Group name
PUBLIC BANK	2354	The Hiong Piow	BRITISH AMERICAN TOBACCO (MALAYSIA)	2949	Foreign
RASHID HUSSAIN	2239	Rashid Hussain	RESORTS WORLD	2528	Lim Goh Tong
COMMERCE ASSET-HOLDING	1989	State-owned	GENTING	2484	Lim Goh Tong
EDARAN OTOMOBIL NASIONAL	1976	State-owned	COMMERCE ASSET–HOLDING	2248	State-owned
			CELCOM (MALAYSIA)	1889	State-owned
INDOCEMENT TUNGGAL PRAKARSA	2978	Salim Group	**Thailand**		
BANK NEGARA INDONESIA	2855	State-owned	PTT	3552	State-owned
BANK INTERNASIONAL INDONESIA	2651	Eka Tjipta Group	ADVANCED INFO SERVICE	3551	Shinnawatra
			SIAM CEMENT	3507	Crown Property Bureau
			SIAM COMMERCIAL BANK	2652	Crown Property Bureau
BANGKOK BANK	6068	Sophonpanich	PTT EXPLORATION & PRODUCTION	2218	State-owned
PTT EXPLORATION & PRODUCTION	3981	State-owned	KRUNG THAI BANK	2129	State-owned
THAI FARMERS BANK	3274	Lamsam	BANGKOK BANK	2003	Sophonpanich
TELECOMASIA	2565	CP	KASIKORNBANK	1902	Lamsam
SIAM CEMENT	2475	Crown Property Bureau			
Indonesia			**Indonesia**		
PT TELEKOMUNIKASI INDONESIA	15731	State-owned	TELEKOMUNIKASI INDONESIA	5671	State-owned
GUDANG GARAM	8305	Gudang Garam	BANK NEGARA INDONESIA	3237	State-owned

INDOFOOD SUKSES MAKMUR	4122	Salim Group	GUDANG GARAM	2315	Gudang Garam
HM SAMPOERNA	3635	Sampoerna	PT UNILIVER INDONESIA	2250	Multinational subsidiary
ASTRA INTERNATIONAL	3178	Astra Group	HM SAMPOERNA	2085	Sampoerna
INDOSAT	3086	State-owned			
THAI AIRWAYS INTERNATIONAL	2149	State-owned	**China**		
			CHINA MOBILE (HONG KONG)	44899	State-owned
			PETROCHINA	43512	State-owned
			CHINA PETROLEUM & CHEMICAL (SINOPEC)	35696	State-owned
			CHINA TELECOM	16386	State-owned
			CNOOC	11481	State-owned
			HUANENG POWER INTERNATIONAL	10252	State-owned
			CHINA UNICOM	7444	State-owned
			JIANGSU EXPRESSWAY	6049	State-owned
			CITIC PACIFIC	4015	State-owned
			GUANGDONG ELECTRIC POWER DEVELOPMENT	3240	State-owned
			SINOPEC SHANGHAI PETROCHEMICAL	3066	State-owned
			SHANGHAI LUJIAZUI FINANCE & TRADE ZONE DEVELOPMENT	2800	State-owned
			YANZHOU COAL MINING	2587	State-owned

(*Continued*)

Appendix 1.1. (*Continued*)

Firm name	Market value 1997	Group name	Firm name	Market value 2003	Group name
			MAANSHAN IRON & STEEL (MA STEEL)	2459	State-owned
			LEGEND GROUP	2333	State-owned
			BEIJING DATANG POWER GENERATION	2251	State-owned
			ALUMINUM CORP. OF CHINA (CHALCO)	2248	State-owned
			COSCO PACIFIC	2147	State-owned
			CHINA EASTERN AIRLINES	2061	State-owned
			CHINA SHIPPING DEVELOPMENT	1896	State-owned

Notes: Korean, Taiwanese, Malaysian, Indonesian, Thai, and Chinese firms (2003 only) are from the *Emerging Market 200 Listings* in 1997 and in 2003. Singaporean firms are from the *Global 1000 Listings* in 1997 and in 2003. Japanese firms in the Global 1000 Listings are not shown in this table because they are so numerous. 182 and 129 Japanese firms made the Global 1000 Listings in 1997 and 2003, respectively. Listings are in the decreasing order of market valuation in billion US$.

NOTES

1. See Granovetter (1995) for a review. Ghemawat and Khanna (1998) provide a table that summarizes the evidence that business groups are prevalent in developing countries. See McVey (1992) and Orru, Biggart, and Hamilton (1997) for examples of business groups in Southeast Asia, Strachan (1976) for Nicaragua, and Ghemawat and Khanna (1998) for India, Chang (2003b) for Korea, and Khanna and Wu (1998) for Chile. Business groups emerged in former socialist countries during the privatization process. During the rapid privatization in Czechoslovakia, various forms of cross-ownership among banks and investment trust funds were formed, and many of those investment trust companies turned themselves into holding companies (Coffee 1999). Similarly, Stark (1996) showed how previously state-owned firms in Hungary purchased small firms and formed groups.
2. Orru, Biggart and Hamilton (1997) compared the institutional environments and business groups in three Asian countries, Japan, Korea, and Taiwan, and three European countries—Germany, France, and Italy. Evans (1995) compared Brazil, Korea, and India to show various types of developmental states. Guillen (2001) demonstrated how import-substitution industrial policies pursued by Latin American countries and export-promotion policies by East Asian countries induced the formation of business groups in those regions.
3. Evans (1995) argues that a successful development state needs to have an internally coherent group of elite bureaucrats to bring state autonomy, and embedded social networks to enable the government to carry out policies more effectively. The extent to which these two building blocks exist differs greatly among East Asian countries. In some countries, the state is more akin to a predatory state, which Evans (1995) used to denote a state that preyed on its citizens, despoiling their common patrimony, and providing few services in return.
4. Campbell (2004) reviewed three main paradigms for institutional change, rational choice institutionalism, organizational institutionalism, and historical institutionalism, and argued for the 'second movement in institutional analysis', which blends insights from all three paradigms.
5. See Corsetti, Pesenti, and Roubini (1998) for a survey on the causes of the crisis.
6. World Bank, *East Asia: Road to Recovery*, 1998.
7. Notable economists, including Joseph Stiglitz, the Vice President of International Bank for Reconstruction and Development (IBRD), and Jeffrey Sachs, publicly denounced these policies. Sachs, J. 'The Wrong Medicine for Asia', *New York Times*, November 3, 1997; Sachs J., 'IMF Is a Power unto Itself', *Financial Times*, December 11, 1997; Stiglitz, J., 'Must Financial Crises Be This Frequent and This Painful?', Manuscript 1998; 'World Bank, IMF at Odds Over Asian Austerity—Some Economists Contend That Harsh Measures Could Worsen the Crisis', *Wall Street Journal*, January 8, 1998.

8. See the following for more information on the structural weaknesses of East Asian countries: IMF, *IMF-Supported Programs in Indonesia, Korea and Thailand: A Preliminary Assessment*, IMF, 1999; World Bank, *East Asia: Road to Recovery*, 1998; World Bank, *East Asia: Recovery and Beyond*, 2000.
9. See World Bank, *Recovery and Beyond*, 2000.

Part I

Japan and Former NICs (Newly Industrialized Countries)

2

Japanese Business Groups: Continuity in the Face of Change

Christina L. Ahmadjian

Business groups have been seen as both the powerhouses behind Japanese industrialization and the culprits behind Japan's decade-long inertia. Some have argued that Japanese business groups demonstrate how networks of organizations can achieve impressive economic returns that Anglo-Saxon models of capitalism fail to predict by pooling risk, sharing returns, and spreading knowledge (Gerlach 1992; Dore 2000). More recently, others have criticized business groups as a drag on the Japanese economy, claiming the tendency of affiliate firms towards mutual aid and 'closed' business relations has hindered the aggressive restructuring and reorientation needed to shock Japan out of its economic doldrums, which began when Japan's bubble economy burst in the early 1990s (Porter, Takeuchi, and Sakakibara 2000).

Observers have disagreed on whether the effect of business groups on the Japanese economy has been positive or negative, but most would agree that business groups are a critical feature of the Japanese business landscape. There has been relatively little research, however, on how these groups have changed since 1990. The business media have suggested that Japanese business groups are becoming obsolete as firms find more effective means of doing business. This *Financial Times* (Abrahams and Tett 1999) headline is typical: 'The circle is broken: Japan's keiretsu face collapse as traditional corporate relationships are undermined by bank mergers and a search for higher return on capital.' Implicit in such statements is the prediction that the ties binding Japanese firms into corporate groups are breaking, and that Japanese business relationships will look more like the arm's-length, short-term ties that characterize the USA (at least a stylized version of the USA).

On the other hand, theories of institutions and economic systems cast doubt on such facile pronouncements of change. Business practices interact with a complex and complementary system of institutions (Aoki 2001) and are embedded in ongoing social relations (Granovetter 1985). This feature makes dramatic change difficult, and even improbable; changes usually occur within the context of existing institutions and evolve in a path-dependent trajectory (Bebchuk and Roe 1999; Hall and Soskice 2001). Even as change occurs, existing patterns of social relationships may be recombined and reused for new purposes (Stark 1996). Researchers in this tradition suggest that Japanese firms are unlikely to completely give up their distinctive business practices and organizational forms even in the face of economic crisis and changing institutions. Therefore, claims about the demise of business groups should be treated skeptically.

This chapter begins with a survey of the literature concerning the origin of Japanese business groups and their function in Japan's economic development. This overview puts Japanese business groups in a comparative perspective and provides a reference point for understanding change. I then use the comparative institutional framework laid out in the introduction to this book to assess change in these groups from the early 1990s to the present. I argue that while changes in financial markets and patterns of corporate ownership were forces for change, normative pressures to preserve long-term relationships, except in the event of dire crisis, remained strong. I analyze two sets of primary data, including ties of ownership, banking, and directors for the 200 largest companies (by assets) in 1990 and 2000, and data on parts transactions between Japanese auto manufacturers and assemblers between 1990 and 1996. I also reference secondary data, including other research on changes in business groups and cases of change discussed in the mass media.

2.1. BUSINESS GROUPS IN JAPAN

Japanese business groups are best defined as clusters of firms, linked through overlapping ties of shareholding, debt, interlocking directors, and dispatch of personnel at other levels, shared history, membership in groupwide clubs and councils, and often, shared brands. Although there are many claims about Japanese business groups, there is a wide divergence between groups as portrayed by the mass media and casual observers of Japan, and the actual reality of these groups.[1]

Descriptions of Japanese business groups often begin with statements that Japan has two types of business groups: (*a*) horizontal groups, consisting of large firms in diverse industries, centered around banks (the so-called Big Six groups of Mitsui, Mitsubishi, Sumitomo, Fuyo, Sanwa, and DKB); and (*b*) vertical groups, of buyers and affiliated suppliers and distributors, such as the Toyota group. Figure 2.1 shows a stylized diagram of the horizontal and

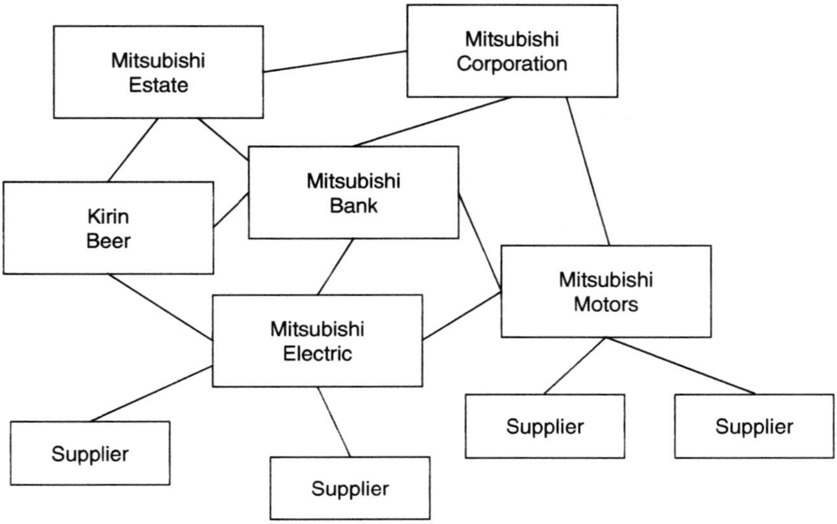

Figure 2.1. Stylized depiction of horizontal and vertical groups

vertical group configurations. The constellation of Mitsubishi Bank (now Tokyo Mitsubishi Bank as the result of a merger), Mitsubishi Corporation, Mitsubishi Electric, and the other firms represent an image of a horizontal group (although the Mitsubishi group and other horizontal groups are larger than this). These firms and banks are tied through cross-shareholding, directors, and trading relationships. Figure 2.1 shows how Mitsubishi Electric and Mitsubishi Motors have their own vertical groups of suppliers. Other members of the Mitsubishi group also have their own vertical groups.

Although this categorization describes many Japanese business groups, it is slightly misleading. These two categories do not exhaust all existing configurations. For example, there are clusters of affiliated firms such as railways, department stores, and travel agencies, and large manufacturers such as Hitachi or Nippon Electric Company (NEC) and their satellites of spin-offs in diverse businesses. Also, firms often have multiple group affiliations: members of horizontal bank-centered groups usually have their own groups of suppliers and affiliates.

Firms also cannot be categorized neatly as members of groups or as independents, although much research has done just that. First, purportedly independent firms are often embedded in their own networks of affiliations even if they are not associated with one of the big banks or large manufacturing firms that are known to have groups. Although there are numerous directories of Japanese business groups, such as *Dodwell's Industrial Groupings in Japan*, *Kigyo Keiretsu Soran*, and *Keiretsu no Kenkyu*, these directories do not exhaust the entire universe of business groups, and criteria for including firms within these groups vary across these volumes due to different definitions of group membership (Miwa and Ramseyer 2001).[2] Second, there are different degrees of affiliation among firms in a business group. Firms are tied through varying strengths of ownership, trading, banking, personnel ties, and shared histories and sense of group identification. A dichotomous measure cannot fully capture these nuances.

Japanese business groups have diverse histories. The webs of ownership and other ties that link firms arose at different periods in the history of Japan's development, and under different circumstances. Some of the best-known business groups—the Mitsui, Sumitomo, and Mitsubishi groups—are postwar reconfigurations of prewar conglomerates, the zaibatsu. The prewar zaibatsu were, in form and substance, similar to Korea's chaebols (their names share the same Chinese characters), and were controlled by powerful families.

One of the first actions of the US occupation government was to break up these zaibatsu, which it did by banning the holding company form, purging senior leaders, and selling off ownership stakes to the general public. Sales of zaibatsu assets accounted for about 40 percent of the Japanese economy prior to World War II (Morck and Nakamura 2003), attesting to the power of these groups. Because of these sales, individual shareholding soared to approximately 70 percent of all shares of Japanese firms by 1950 (Morck and Nakamura 2003).

After the complete dissolution of the zaibatsu, members of some groups began to regroup in the early 1950s. A club consisting of presidents of former Mitsubishi zaibatsu firms began to meet in 1952 (Hoshi and Kashyap 2001). Group members began to buy each other's shares from individual investors as mutual protection from the threat of hostile takeovers, which at that time were proliferating (Morck and Nakamura 2003).

Other business groups evolved along different trajectories. In the early postwar period, manufacturing firms, such as the automakers, grew their own groups by taking equity positions in suppliers, or by spinning off parts-making divisions into independent, but closely linked, group firms (Odaka, Ono, and Adachi 1988). Firms grew this way rather than through vertical integration for several reasons. Antagonistic labor relations encouraged manufacturers to externalize as much labor as possible. Firms lacked the capital to grow through vertical integration. Furthermore, small firms received significant tax benefits, leading firms to hive off operations into smaller units.

Japanese financial reporting requirements also supported the web of shareholding ties that linked firms into groups. Firms needed to report equity stakes only at historical prices, meaning they did not need to report losses on their portfolios of shares in affiliates and could hold unrealized gains indefinitely. Furthermore, because consolidated returns were not required, profits and losses could be allocated between affiliates and subsidiaries to avoid showing losses or avoid paying taxes on gains, depending upon which was more pressing.

Postwar Japanese business groups have no central, controlling headquarters or headquarters equivalent. Although many groups, most famously the Big Six bank-centered groups, sponsor regular meetings of presidents of group firms, these councils are best seen as organizations for exchanging information, rather than mechanisms of control (Gerlach 1992). In the Big Six horizontal groups, banks and trading companies have traditionally been central due to their financial and business relationships with other group members. Yet these firms should not be seen as having any special power. Although equity stakes link group members, these stakes are seldom sufficient for control. In fact, banks were permitted to hold no more than 5 percent of a firm's shares after the 1976 Anti-Monopoly Act gave banks ten years to reduce their shareholdings in a given firm from 10 to 5 percent (Hoshi and Kashyap 2001). Other group firms may cumulatively hold a substantial percentage of a firm's shares, but they rarely hold the majority of these shares. According to a report by the Japan Fair Trade Commission (JFTC) in 2001, members of the six major horizontal groups, on average, held 20 percent of shares of their group members, down from a peak of 25 percent in 1981 (Japan Fair Trade Commission 2001). The shareholding ratio was higher for the three groups that traced their origin to prewar zaibatsu (Mitsui, Mitsubishi, and Sumitomo). For these groups the ratio was about 25 percent, down from 32 percent in 1981. Business transactions were much lower, according to the same FTC study. In 2001, only about 6 percent of group members' total purchases came from other group members.

Because the Japanese economy comprises webs of interconnected firms and financial institutions, rather than being dominated by a set of distinct business groups, figures showing the percentage of economic activity that business groups account for are not very useful. Such numbers exist nevertheless, usually for the Big Six horizontal bank-centered groups. According to Toyo Keizai's *Kigyo Keiretsu Soran* (2000), Big Six companies (not including their member banks and insurance companies) employed 3.2 percent of Japan's total workforce in 1998 (as compared to 4 percent in 1988) and had 11.5 percent of Japan's total sales as compared to 13.6 percent in 1988. The percentage of total sales is particularly high because the Big Six include the giant trading companies (Ostrom 2000). Yet it is not clear what these numbers mean about the dominance of business groups in Japan, since there are more Japanese business groups than just these Big Six.

2.2. CROSS-SUBSIDIZATION IN BUSINESS GROUPS

There is extensive literature on the function of Japanese business groups, but there is still considerable disagreement on what these groups actually do, and whether their effects on the Japanese economy have been beneficial, harmful, or negligible. To some extent, this debate on business groups has varied with the times, specifically with the fortunes of the Japanese economy.

As the Japanese economy boomed, and Japanese firms began to dominate global markets, Japanese business groups were often portrayed as having oligopolistic tendencies, offering preferential terms of trade within the group, keeping away outsiders, and keeping Japanese markets closed to foreigners (Lawrence 1993). Yet subsequent empirical research did not support this argument. Caves and Uekusa (1976) found that members of the horizontal business groups were less profitable than were more independent firms, inconsistent with the oligopoly argument. Weinstein and Yafeh (1995) argue that foreigners were discouraged from entering group-dominated industries not because groups colluded to keep them out, but because of severe competition among affiliate firms that flooded the market.

Other research focuses specifically on the relationship between main banks and group members, arguing that business groups provided corporate governance. It proposes that main banks monitored firms and intervened to discipline and restructure firms that performed poorly. Kaplan and Minton (1994), for example, found banks were more likely to dispatch directors to boards of poorly performing firms, while Morck and Nakamura (1999) found this result particularly true for group-affiliated firms. Hoshi, Kashyap, and Scharfstein (1990) argue that main banks, because of their close relationships and information sharing with affiliate firms, can provide these firms with greater liquidity in times of crisis. They found these affiliates showed greater levels of investment. Several case studies have also documented how business groups intervene and restructure poor-performing members, as demonstrated by the Sumitomo group's bailout of Mazda in 1974 (Hoshi and Kashyap 2001).

Another stream of research examines various types of risk-sharing, redistribution of profits, and group benefits for poor-performing firms. In his widely cited study of performance of group and independent firms (again, note my earlier caveat about these simple distinctions), Nakatani (1984) found that members of groups showed lower rates of profits, but lower rates of variability of profits. Lincoln, Gerlach, and Ahmadjian (1996) found that within horizontal business groups, high performers subsidized low performers.

Some argue that group organization, particularly in vertical groups, lowers transaction costs. Gilson and Roe (1993) argue that minority ownership stakes are important safeguards for contracting in an economy that lacks thorough legal safeguards. Research by Flath (1993) and Lincoln, Gerlach, and Takahashi (1992) showed that equity ties between firms and industries overlaid patterns of transactions, consistent with a transaction cost explanation. Other research on vertical groups proposes that groups of closely linked, yet independent, firms promote learning, innovation, and flexibility (Nishiguchi 1994; Clark and Fujimoto 1991).

As the Japanese economy stagnated during the 1990s, researchers began arguing that business groups were either contributing to Japan's stagnation or were insignificant. Morck and Nakamura (2003) argue that business groups had become entrenched in mechanisms to lobby for government favors and preserve employment for their managers. Porter, Takeuchi, and Sakakibara (2000) blame business groups for inertia and for hindering Japanese competitiveness. Yafeh (2002) argues that business groups were politically inconsequential, and had mattered little to the Japanese economy. At the extreme, Miwa and Ramseyer (2001) assert that business groups were only figments of academics' collective imaginations that provide neat, convenient variables for analysis and fuel a publishing industry of guides to business group affiliation.

Miwa and Ramseyer's argument is provocative, but decades of empirical research has found that affiliation with business groups is related to various elements of firm performance and behavior. Webs of ownership and other ties link Japanese firms, and these firms cluster together into recognizable groups based on these ties, which overlap patterns of business transactions, although they are not exclusive to such patterns. Horizontal, bank-centered groups show lower levels of performance and greater risk-sharing, while case-based evidence further supports the observation that groups often help ailing members. Moreover, in groups such as Toyota, close relationships between key manufacturers and their suppliers have supported learning and innovation.

2.3. INSTITUTIONAL CHANGES IN THE 1990S

In the late 1980s and throughout the 1990s, Japanese economic institutions and markets underwent several significant changes. In this section, I examine some of these changes and how they affected business groups. As I will demonstrate in this and the next section, claims about changes to, or the end of, business groups are incorrect; change in some aspects of business group relations is balanced by remarkable continuity in others.

In the introduction to this book, Chang provided a comparative institutional framework for understanding how institutional changes are likely to lead to change in business groups. He highlighted the interaction of the state, markets, especially financial markets, and social and cultural norms with business groups. In other countries examined in this book, the Asian financial crisis provided a strong impetus for change by altering the structure of capital, forcing (or encouraging) the state to alter the institutional framework in which groups operated, and forcing (or encouraging) group entrepreneurs to alter their own practices. The effects of the Asian financial crisis, however, were not felt strongly in Japan. Rather, Japan's financial crisis was homegrown, the aftermath of the burst of the asset bubble in the early 1990s.

The institutional changes that most acutely affected Japanese business groups were in financial markets. They began in the later part of the 1980s, and picked up momentum in the mid-1990s, before the Asian financial crisis. I highlight four of the most important factors: (*a*) Japanese financial crisis, (*b*) disintermediation, or the increasing propensity for large firms to move from relationship banking to capital markets, (*c*) the 'Big Bang' and changes in accounting regulations, and (*d*) an increase in foreign investment. In comparison to other Asian countries, the state played a lesser role. Although regulatory changes, in particular, changes of accounting regulations, influenced groups' structure and behavior, the Japanese government did not seriously attempt to break up or weaken business groups as it did not regard business groups as relevant to its reform agenda. Norms around long-term

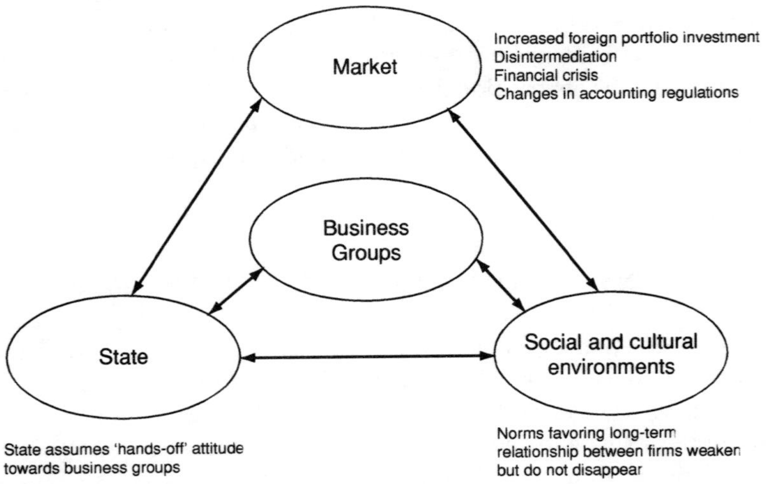

Figure 2.2. Japanese institutional environments

relationships were both a force for change in some cases, but a source of inertia in many others, as there was still considerable normative pressure for group members to maintain long-term financial and trading relationships, except for in cases of crisis (see Figure 2.2).

2.3.1. Financial Crisis

A crisis in both financial institutions' and firms' performance weakened the ties that bind groups. In 1990 and 1991, the Japanese stock market and real estate markets declined dramatically. A banking crisis, largely due to questionable loans based on inflated real estate and share prices, began to spread. In 1997, Hokkaido Takushoku Bank became the first major bank to fail in the postwar period. The government began to inject public funds into banks, and two banks, Long-Term Credit Bank (LTCB) and Nippon Credit Bank, were nationalized. The banking crisis persisted into the 2000s. In 2003, Resona Bank was nationalized, and Ashikaga Bank received an injection of public funds.

One result of this banking crisis was high-profile mergers across banks and across groups. For example, Sumitomo and Sakura Bank, itself a product of a merger between Mitsui Bank and Taiyo Kobe Bank, merged. Other influential mergers crossed group borders as well. For example, Fuji and DKB and IBJ (and Yasuda Trust) merged to make the Mizuho group, linking the Fuyo and DKB groups along with IBJ's network of ties. These cross-group bank mergers were also reflected in mergers between other group firms. Sompo Japan was created from insurance companies in the DKB and Fuyo groups, reflecting the Mizuho affiliations, while insurance companies in the Sumitomo and Mitsui groups merged to form Mitsui Sumitomo Insurance. Yet mass mergers between group firms had not, at least when this chapter was written, materialized; for example, a proposed merger between Sumitomo Chemical and Mitsui Chemicals fell apart at the last minute.

Another major change due to the financial crisis was that banks sold a large portion of the stock they held in publicly traded firms. In 1990, financial institutions held 43 percent of the market value of publicly traded shares, while in 2000 their share had declined to 30.1 percent (Tokyo Stock Exchange 2002). This sell-off was reflected in a decrease in cross-shareholding among members of groups, which declined from 26 to 17 percent (for the main six bank-centered groups, as measured by share value) during this period according to calculations by the NLI Institute (Kuroki 2001: 28).

In his survey of cross-shareholdings in Japan, Okabe (2002) notes that banks had several reasons to sell off their cross-held shares. They sold stock to raise funds to write off nonperforming loans. They also became sensitive about the value of their shareholdings, as the decline of stock market prices put banks in danger of going below required levels of capital adequacy (Okabe 2002: 32).

Banks also appeared to retreat from their role in bailing out firms. According to Hoshi and Kashyap (2001: 183), bank-led bailouts declined between 1977 and 1992. Corporate failures proliferated as banks did not play their usual role in restructuring. For example, Yamaichi Securities failed after Fuji Bank, its main bank, refused to support it. Sumitomo Bank, well-known for its rescue of Mazda in the early 1970s, refused to play the same role twice, allowing Ford to take a controlling stake in the troubled automaker (Hoshi and Kashyap 2001).

The financial crisis also spread to industrial firms, as major firms went bankrupt and other leading firms had historically low levels of performance. Particularly hard hit were trading companies, or sogo shosha, which were central players in groups as they were connected to many firms in groups through their business relationships. In their study of changes in business groups during the 1990s, Lincoln and Gerlach (2004) found that groups of poorly performing firms were more likely to weaken than were those of high performers; the stronger Sumitomo and Mitsubishi groups, as well as the Toyota and Matsushita groups, remained more cohesive than others did. This finding is consistent with the general picture of change: poor performance led firms to sell off their group holdings, caused bankruptcies and mergers and reconfigurations of group ties, and made firms less able to restructure other group members.

2.3.2. Disintermediation

Although changes in Japanese intercorporate relationships are often attributed to the burst of the asset bubble in the early 1990s, pressure for these changes actually began in the mid-1980s. Thus, seeds of the breakdown of business groups were sown during boom times—not during bad times. Reliance on bank debt decreased, loosening the tie between a firm and its main bank, one of the fundamental ties in the business group. Total borrowed funds from private lenders decreased from 78 percent of firms' financing in 1975 to 65 percent in 1995, while funding from the securities markets increased from 14 percent in 1975 to 22 percent in 1995 (Hoshi and Kashyap 2001). This trend was particularly true for large firms: Hoshi and Kashyap (2001: 246) note that for large manufacturing firms, bank dependence decreased by about two-thirds between 1970 and 1990. At the same time, a heated 'bubble economy' led banks to move away from their stable and risk-averse relationships with client firms, and to invest huge sums of money in real estate. Firms increasingly turned to extremely speculative (as it turned out) financial manipulations that seemed to provide a better return than business as usual did. In their structural analysis of business groups, Lincoln and Gerlach (2004) found evidence that groups actually moved apart during the bubble economy and showed signs of pulling together again after the bubble burst.

2.3.3. Changes in Accounting Regulations

Another critical change affecting groups was the revision of accounting regulations that had once facilitated high levels of cross-shareholding. In 1996, the Japanese government announced the 'Big Bang', a set of financial reforms designed to enhance Tokyo's status as a financial capital. Part of these reforms involved an overhaul of Japanese accounting regulations to make Japanese accounting standards consistent with international standards.

As part of these reforms, firms were required to report the value of their equity holdings at market value. This law went into effect in 2000 for securities held for investment and in 2001 for 'stable shareholdings' in firms' various affiliates and business partners. Another reform was tightened requirements for consolidation, which made it harder for firms to manage their earnings by allocating gains and losses among group firms.

Accounting reforms introduced a factor of risk into cross-shareholding: these stakes could no longer be held solely as a means to cement relationships, but were now a source of nonbusiness risk (Okabe 2002). Banks were especially eager to sell shares that had appreciated in order to reap one-time gains (Okabe 2002). By early 2004, most sell-offs of cross-held shares were by banks selling shares in firms and vice versa, as bank shares were devalued and still falling, although cross-shareholding among firms tended to remain stable (Okabe 2002).

These changes in accounting regulations and the resulting sales of cross-held shares reflect the state's crucial role in creating a framework of business law and accounting standards to maintain the fundamental basis of groups. It is important to note, however, that in contrast to Korea, where business groups themselves were a target of state policy, the Japanese government did not initiate these reforms to undermine business groups or to eradicate cross-shareholding; rather, it did so to make Japanese financial conditions consistent with international standards and to help revitalize the crisis-stricken Japanese economy. Although the 1990s was a time of heated rhetoric regarding corporate governance and reform, business groups were hardly mentioned as a problem that needed fixing. Notably, Japanese business groups were not implicated in any of the numerous corporate scandals in the 1990s; these incidents usually occurred at the firm level. Nor was there any criticism of powerful founding families and of financial manipulations among group members similar to that occurring in South Korea at the same time.

2.3.4. Foreign Investment

An increase in foreign investment brought more attention to interfirm ties. From 1990 to 2002, foreign investment in Japanese shares increased from approximately 4 percent of all publicly listed shares to over 16 percent (see Figure 2.3 for trends in shareholding among foreigners and domestic Japanese investors). Foreign investors were less likely than Japanese firms to see the sense in holding shares, exchanging directors, and carrying out preferential trading with familiar companies, and they were likely to encourage firms to unload these 'old' ties in favor of more profitable, new ties. There were also several high-profile cases of foreign firms taking controlling stakes in Japanese firms, and dramatically restructuring their group relationships. The best-known case was Renault's acquisition of Nissan, and the latter's subsequent reorganization (or, perhaps more precisely, gutting) of its group of suppliers. As Carlos Ghosn, Nissan's Renault-dispatched CEO, said: 'The keiretsu system ... is not working for Nissan. It may be working for someone else but not for us' (Kyodo News Service 2000). Another well-known case was

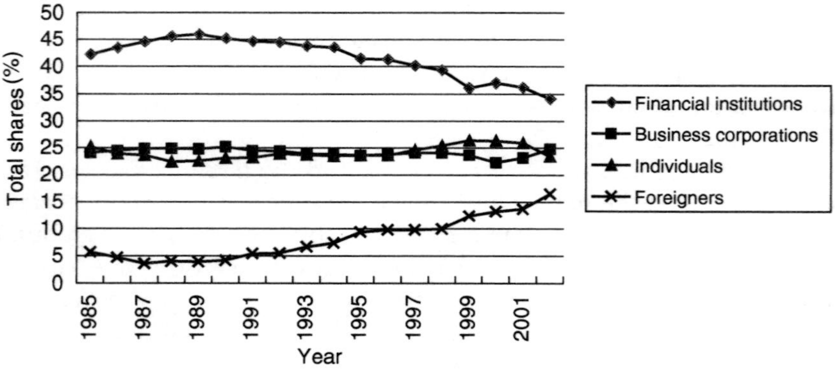

Figure 2.3. Trends in ownership of Japanese shares (unit share base)
Source: Tokyo Stock Exchange Fact Book 2003.

the purchase of the former LTCB by an American private equity firm, Ripplewood, and its subsequent rebirth as Shinsei Bank. In 2000, Shinsei became infamous for refusing to forgive debts of the retailer Sogo, sending a very public signal that it would not adhere to the long-standing norms of propping up client firms.

Nonetheless, the effect of foreigners on unraveling of group relationships should not be overestimated. Companies in which foreigners had controlling stakes were more likely to unravel group ties, but such situations were relatively rare. Moreover, even in industries where the foreign influence was most obvious, such as banking and autos, there was little diffusion of these new practices from foreign-owned firms to the other business groups. Toyota and Honda did not take Nissan's example and demolish their groups, while Shinsei was considered an outlier bank.

2.4. STABILITY OF BUSINESS GROUPS

In the previous section, I highlighted how changes in the institutional environment, such as changes in financing, changes in regulations for accounting, an increase in foreign investment coupled with a financial crisis, removed some of the support for business groups. Evidence of change included bankruptcies of major financial institutions, mergers across groups, and sales of cross-held shares. Yet, in the face of pressure for change, business groups appeared to remain quite stable.

According to a survey by the Japan Fair Trade Commission (2001: 9) of 180 firms belonging to Big Six groups, 38 percent of the respondents said that they believed that current business groups would be maintained, and 18 percent said that these ties would be strengthened. Only 18 percent said they would be weakened. Claims of group continuity were even stronger among members of the Mitsubishi group, with 91 percent of whose members surveyed thought the current group would be maintained (Japan Fair Trade Commission 2001: 9). These findings cast doubt on the claims by the mass media that Japanese groups are declining.

Data on cross-shareholding also suggest ongoing group stability. As Figure 2.3 indicates, the number of shares in corporate hands decreased only slightly from the 1990s to 2003. In his analysis of shareholding patterns, Okabe (2002) found little evidence that cross-shareholding among firms declined. In some cases, ties between group members may have become even tighter. In the mid-

1990s, Toyota began increasing equity stakes in several of its main suppliers (Shirouzu 1999) and remained committed to its core suppliers. Reporters for the *Financial Times* observed: 'Toyota's commitment to its supplier chain is underlined by the fact that no supplier [i.e. member of Toyota's supplier association] has closed in the past decade, even through the group's total production has dropped by 25 percent since its 1990 peak' (Burt and Ibison 2001).

There was also evidence that group members continued to cross-subsidize each other. For example, the Mizuho Bank raised US $9.2 billion of capital in 2003 by placing shares with some of its closest affiliates, including life insurance companies that already owned shares, and customers such as Tokyo Electric Power and Itochu (*Nikkei Weekly* 2003). According to press reports, the response of Mizuho's customers reflected a tension between loyalties to group and shareholders. The *Nikkei Weekly* wrote of Nippon Steel:

> Hit hard by the decline of Mizuho shares in its portfolio under a cross-shareholding arrangement, the steelmaker is bracing for a second straight year of group net loss in fiscal 2002. It initially intended to refuse Mizuho's request, but considering its ties with the bank, Nippon Steel felt it had to offer something. Consequently, the steelmaker concluded that it needed to demonstrate to its stockholders that Mizuho had a solid foundation upon which to rebuild its operations.

In 2004, Mitsubishi Motors sought to raise money from other Mitsubishi affiliates as its parent, DaimlerChrysler, struggled (Ibison 2004). Since the sale of Mitsubishi Motors shares by Mitsubishi group firms to DaimlerChrysler in the late 1990s suggested a weakening of business groups, so the willingness of Mitsubishi group members to again come to the assistance of a member was intriguing (and probably reflected desires both to protect the Mitsubishi brand and to render assistance to an old affiliate).

2.5. ANALYSES OF CHANGE AND STABILITY IN HORIZONTAL AND VERTICAL GROUPS

To further examine change and stability in business groups in the last decade, I analyzed two of the most important forms of linkage between members of business groups, ownership ties and purchase–supply transactions. Although both analyses indicated evidence that ties had broken over time, they showed strong evidence of continuity.

2.5.1. Changes in Horizontal Groups

To examine sources of stability in ownership ties, I investigated how the composition of ownership changed between 1990 and 2000 among 200 of Japan's largest firms. The data-set consisted of the largest 200 firms (by assets, measured in 2000). For these 200 firms, I collected data on their top 10 shareholders, their outside directors, and their top banks, as well as membership on the presidents' councils of the six most prominent horizontal business groups (Mitsui, Sumitomo, Mitsui, Fuyo, Sanwa, and DKB). For the analyses in this paper, I created a set of dyads consisting of all relationships (in equity, directors, and banking) between the 200 firms, as well as between these firms and the 50 largest banks, 10 largest life insurance companies, and 10 major casualty insurance companies. I collected the data for 1990 and 2000 from *Kaisha Nenkan*, an annual volume of corporate reports (Nihon Keizai Shimbunsha 1991, 2001).

I arranged the data into pairs of firms and each of their shareholders. I refer to a firm–shareholder pair as a dyad. For example, Mitsubishi Bank was one of the top ten shareholders of Mitsubishi Electric. The Mitsubishi Bank and Mitsubishi Electric pair was one dyad. There were 1,637 dyads (this number is less than 200 × 10 because dyads consisting of shareholders that were not on the list of 200 firms, banks, life insurance, casualty insurance, foreigners, or individuals were omitted).

I measured shareholding ties by whether firm or bank (B) in dyad firm (A,B) was one of the top ten shareholders for firm (A). A director tie was recorded when firm or bank (B) sent a director to firm (A). A banking tie was recorded when bank (B) was listed by firm (A) as one of its three top banks. A broken shareholding tie occurred when firm or bank (B) was one of firm (A)'s top ten shareholders in 1990, but was not on this list in 2000. This measure is rough, but was determined by data limitations: only data for the top ten shareholders were available. This measure probably overstates broken ties: if a shareholder went from shareholder 8 to shareholder 11 between the two periods, it would be recorded as a broken tie. That drop does, however, indicate a substantial decrease in relative shareholdings and is also an important signal of a break between firms. The top ten shareholders of a firm are easily available in guides to companies, and if a shareholder drops below this level, its ownership relationship with a firm disappears from the public record and entails a very significant drop in publicity.

Table 2.1 shows the ownership patterns of the sample of large firms in 1990 and 2000. Each column shows the percentage of dyads in which banks, life insurance, casualty insurance, individuals, and foreigners were among the top ten shareholders. Changes between 1990 and 2000 reflected the general trends

Table 2.1. Ownership patterns of 200 largest firms

Type of owner	Share of total dyads 1990	Share of total dyads 2000
Banks	0.54	0.47
Life Insurance	0.15	0.12
Casualty Insurance	0.04	0.06
Individuals	0.02	0.02
Foreigners	0.02	0.09

in cross-shareholding—banks generally disappeared from the top ten, and foreigners occupied the top ten more frequently.

Table 2.2 shows broken equity ties among the firms in the sample. A broken tie was defined as a case in which a shareholder was one of the top ten shareholders in 1990 but not in 2000. Column 1 shows that 29 percent of all dyads were broken during this period. Column 2 looks only at bank dyads, and finds that of 882 dyads that involved the 200 firms and 50 banks, 36 percent were broken. Thus, banks broke their shareholding ties at a higher rate than the sample as a whole did. Column 3 presents results for firm–bank dyad in which there was a strong banking relationship. I defined 'main bank' relationship as cases in which the shareholder was listed by the firm as number one, two, or three on its list of banks in 1990. The rate of broken ties here was far lower: only 10 percent of the dyads with a main bank relationship were broken during this period. Column 4 presents results for 244 dyads in which the firm and its shareholder had a directorship interlock, specifically when a director from the shareholder sat on the board of the firm in 1990. Of these dyads only 9 percent were broken. In the last column I examine dyads that involve firms and shareholders that are members of the same horizontal business group (here, I define horizontal business as a member of either the Mitsubishi, Mitsui, Sumitomo, Fuyo, Sanwa, or DKB group). Again, the rate of broken ties was lower than it was for the same period: only 17 percent of ties were broken.

Table 2.2. Broken equity ties among top 200 firms, 1990 & 2000

	All dyads	Bank dyads	Dyads with main bank relationship	Dyads with dispatched director	Dyads in same Big Six group
Broken ties	0.29	0.36	0.10	0.09	0.17
Total dyads	1637	882	315	244	184

These tables are simple, and lack the controls of a multivariate analysis. They suggest, however, that when examining the dissolution of shareholding ties it is important to look not only at the rate of broken ties across all firms but also at how the rate differs by firm category, and by firms themselves. Consistent with the prediction more peripheral ties were usually broken, while firms retained shareholding ties with their main banks, firms with which they had directorship interlocks, and members of the same group.

2.5.2. Changes in Vertical Groups

Another important tie linking members of business groups is trading ties (i.e. purchases and sales of parts and materials). Because it was impossible to obtain detailed lists of buyers and suppliers for the largest firms, I examined broken trading ties in a sample of parts transactions between Japanese auto manufacturers and their suppliers between 1990 and 1996. These data predate some of the major shocks in the industry, including Renault's equity participation in Nissan and Ford's and GM's increasing control of Mazda and Isuzu, respectively. These data do, however, track a period of declining performance and greater questioning about the validity of group relationships (e.g. Ahmadjian and Lincoln 2001).

The data-set includes transactions across most major parts categories among the eleven automobile manufacturers and approximately 500 suppliers. It is based on reports by IRC (1987, 1996), a business information company that publishes information on business groups. I obtained information on banking ties and ownership ties between the auto manufacturers and these suppliers from Nihon Keizai Shimbunsha (1989), and for unlisted firms (1987).

The data source reports transactions for 1984, 1987, 1990, 1993, and 1996. A broken tie occurred when an auto manufacturer and a supplier that had one or more transactions in period 1 ceased all transactions in period 2. Table 2.3 shows that broken ties (as measured by the ratio of broken ties) increased over time. The rate of broken ties increased from 0.002 between 1984 and 1987 to 0.048 between 1993 and 1996. Auto manufacturers during this period were increasingly likely to break ties, although the rate of broken ties remained low.

Table 2.3. Broken supply ties in the automobile industry, by year

Year	1987	1990	1993	1996
Broken ties	0.002	0.005	0.0008	0.048

Table 2.4 suggests that this propensity towards broken ties varied considerably by firm. Toyota was the least likely to break ties, while Isuzu, one of the more troubled firms, and one with a large foreign ownership stake, was more likely than others to break ties. Table 2.5 examines how the propensity to break ties varied depending on the nature of the tie. Column 2 shows that auto manufacturers were less likely to break a tie or cease transactions with a supplier if the auto manufacturer had an equity stake in the supplier. Column 3 shows that an auto manufacturer was less likely to break a tie with a supplier if it shared a main bank. Column 4 is perhaps the most interesting. It shows that no ties were broken between 1993 and 1996 among auto manufacturers and suppliers that had a more extensive than average relationship. On average, in this sample, an auto manufacturer procured 1.6 different part types from a given supplier. Broken ties occurred exclusively among suppliers that sold an auto manufacturer fewer than two types of part. The more extensive relationships, in which suppliers sold a range of parts, were not broken.

These results for transactions in the auto industry are consistent with those for shareholding ties among large firms. The rate of broken ties increased,

Table 2.4. Broken ties by firm

Firm	Broken ties	Dyads
Nissan	0.02	293
Isuzu	0.06	269
Toyota	0.01	343
Hino	0.05	164
Nissan Diesel	0.05	169
Mazda	0.03	288
Daihatsu	0.02	234
Honda	0.02	262
Suzuki	0.02	268
Fuji	0.04	247
Mitsubishi	0.01	359

Table 2.5. Broken ties with various relationships, 1993–1996

	All	Equity tie	Same main bank	Multiple transactions*
Broken	0.048	0.019	0.008	0
Total dyads	1220	204	133	204

*Buyer and supplier transact more than 2 parts

although the majority of linkages remained intact. Firms and financial institutions usually broke ties when the linkages were less close.

2.5.3. Conclusions from the Analyses

The two analyses indicate how transaction ties and ownership ties have been unwinding. Both suggest, however, that the pressures for change did not affect all ties uniformly, but were instead most likely to disrupt the more peripheral relationships. Shareholders that had other business relationships (e.g. banking relationships) and/or linkages (e.g. directors) were more likely to maintain ownership ties.

2.6. UNDERSTANDING CHANGE AND STABILITY IN BUSINESS GROUPS

One way to account for the coexistence of change and stability in Japanese business groups is to argue that even in the face of inevitable change some firms are slow to cast off long-standing practices in favor of new ones. Institutional theorists have observed similar instances when inertia and transformation have coexisted; they argue that over time, certain practices become taken-for-granted and seen as legitimate, and consequently persist beyond their economic usefulness (DiMaggio and Powell 1983; Zucker 1983). Although an economic crisis or changing dynamics of power and politics may render these practices less beneficial (Oliver 1992), firms are often unwilling to risk criticism by quickly abandoning highly legitimized practices (Ahmadjian and Robinson 2001).

Applied to business groups, this logic suggests that remaining stability in business groups is a sign of inertia, as firms remain unwilling to appear illegitimate by severing long-term ties to their group affiliates. A senior Japanese executive (a retired director from a major bank) whom I interviewed as part of a larger project on changes in Japanese corporate governance suggested how this logic operated in Japan. He said that for a bank or firm to sell all of its shares in another would be 'shocking'. Executives play golf together and drink together. The reaction to a firm's decision to sell off its shares in an associated firm would be, 'How can you be that cold?'

An alternative perspective is that although financial crisis, accounting changes, and foreign influence upset some groups, fundamental elements of groups remained because they had real economic benefits. Business groups in

Japan, it has been argued, have had a particularly important economic benefit in facilitating exchange relationships. For example, researchers often attribute the competitiveness of the Japanese auto industry to close ties between buyers and suppliers, which reduced transaction costs and maximized interorganizational learning (Clark and Fujimoto 1991; Nishiguchi 1994). Close relationships between members of horizontal groups encouraged the flow of information and assured effective reallocation of resources between stronger and weaker firms and industries (Gerlach 1992; Lincoln, Gerlach, and Ahmadjian 1996).

Because the closely linked clusters of firms that make up business groups are part of the fabric of the Japanese economy, any major disruptions of group relationships could have negative consequences. Aoki (1988) argues that in the Japanese economy, a set of distinctive elements: corporate groups; the banking system; the employment system; forms of interfirm transactions; the state; and the system of administrative guidance, are all complementary. The reliance on debt finance and long-term relations with a main bank, for example, provided firms with the long-term stability to support the permanent employment system, while the permanent employment system, with its development of firm-specific skills, supported distinctive patterns of interorganizational relationships. Removing any single part of this system would reduce the overall system's effectiveness.

It is very difficult to distinguish empirically between these two arguments and determine whether stability in groups, or any sort of economic practice, is evidence of either inertia or rational economic calculation. Yet the case studies and empirical analyses introduced earlier offer some hints. First, analyses of ties in both vertical and horizontal groups suggest that ties that were less closely related to ongoing business relationships were more likely to be broken. This result is consistent with the idea that ties of economic value are being preserved and those of lesser value are more likely to be severed. Firms' willingness to break ties when there is not a close economic interest was reflected in the failure of Nissan and Hitachi to bail out Nissan Mutual Life Insurance in 1997. Nissan's and Hitachi's ties to the insurance company were historical, as they were part of the prewar Nissan zaibatsu. Nissan Mutual sold policies to employees of Nissan and Hitachi, but Nissan and Hitachi had no important business relationship.

The fact that better-performing, stronger companies have been less likely to sever ties is also consistent with an economic rationale for business groups. Lincoln and Gerlach (2004) noted that among the horizontal groups the Mitsubishi and Sumitomo groups were more likely to remain intact, and Toyota and Matsushita also seemed to be maintaining many of their vertical ties. This result can be interpreted in various ways: that high performers have not encountered a crisis that could force them to break ties, that well-managed, high-performing firms continue to find value in group relationships, and that some firms might be better at finding and managing value in these relationships.

2.7. CONCLUSION

This chapter had two objectives. The first was to present an overview of Japanese business groups to facilitate comparison with other forms of business groups in East Asia. The second was to trace changes in Japanese business groups since the early 1990s, and to examine the degree to which economic crisis and institutional change led to the breakdown of groups.

Japanese business groups are best seen as networks of firms, related through a number of linkages, including equity, banking ties, interlocking directorates, and purchase–supply transactions. Groups are not distinct and bounded entities, and there are no clear distinctions between group and independent firms (although some firms are more closely intertwined with their banks and business partners than others are). Lists of business groups and simple categorizations of groups as horizontal or vertical are misleading, as they understate the extent of groups in the Japanese economy and oversimplify the complex webs of relationships in which Japanese firms are embedded.

Following the comparative institutional framework that is at the core of this volume, I identified the most important factors leading to change in Japanese business groups as changes in financial markets, including financial crisis, decreased reliance on bank loans, reform of accounting standards, and an increase in foreign portfolio investment. These pressures for change predated the Asian financial crisis, and the tendency of large firms to move from bank-based to capital-market-based financing even predated Japan's financial crisis in the early 1990s. The state exerted influence through a revision of accounting standards that led to increasing unwinding of cross-shareholding, but this reform was part of a wider-ranging program to align Japanese financial standards with global standards and did not target business groups. These pressures for change interacted with pressures for continuity. Although the more peripheral ties in business groups weakened, core ties were more likely to remain intact, reflecting continued normative pressures to retain financial and trading ties with fellow group members, unless crisis made them unsustainable. In contrast to the rhetoric about the unraveling of groups in the last decade, my analyses suggest that the decline of business groups was partial and varied across groups.

As weak groups spin apart and more peripheral ties are broken in stronger groups, a greater bifurcation between tightly linked members of surviving groups and more independent firms is possible. Some groups will survive and others will not. This split is already apparent in the contrast between Toyota and Nissan, which have now established two very different models: one of existing Japanese-style group management and the other with a far more arm's-length stance towards its suppliers. It is not clear which model will win. Nissan has overcome a near-death experience, while Toyota has been achieving record profits. One of the most interesting research questions in future years will concern the relative merits of these models.

My analyses in this chapter also suggest some changes even in surviving groups. In such groups, ties to members whose group affiliation is due solely to history or social relationships are more likely to be severed, and group interactions will be more closely tied to actual business concerns.[3] One reason for this trend is that banks and trading companies, which were linked heavily to group members and were a source of indirect ties, are becoming less central. Also, as noted earlier, with the new requirement to be valued to market, equity ties have become a source of risk. Firms are more likely to consider whether such linkages are in their best business interests (Okabe 2002).

In short, while some groups are weakening and some interfirm ties are being broken, there is little evidence that groups are disappearing completely from the Japanese economy. Rather, we cannot view the webs of ownership and other business relationships that tie Japanese firms into business groups as outdated and outmoded features of the Japanese economy. Business groups, and the ties within them, will exist so long as there are economic reasons for them.

NOTES

1. Foreigners generally use the term 'keiretsu' to describe Japanese business groups—so often that this term has entered the English language and is even defined in the *Oxford English Dictionary.* Curiously, Japanese are less likely to use this term to describe their own business groups; in Japanese usage, 'keiretsu' is used in more narrowly defined situations to describe firms linked through substantial ownership ties (although even in this case the term 'guruupu' or group is more common). The Japanese sometimes use the term 'keiretsu' to describe Toyota and the suppliers in which it holds substantial equity stakes, but they rarely refer to the Mitsubishi 'keiretsu', or the Sumitomo 'keiretsu' as non-Japanese journalists and academics are wont to do.

2. For example, the *Keiretsu no Kenkyu* directory lists Mitsui, Mitsubishi, Sumitomo, Fuji, Sanwa, Daiichi, Tokai, and Daiwa as groups, while *Dodwell* includes these groups plus Nippon Steel, Hitachi, Nissan, Toyota, Matsushita, Toshiba, and Tokyu (Miwa and Ramseyer 2001).
3. Lincoln and Gerlach's results (2004) support this argument.

3

Korean Business Groups: The Financial Crisis and the Restructuring of Chaebols

Sea-Jin Chang

Large business groups, known as chaebols, have been prominent in Korea for the last half-century. Chaebols encompass many affiliated firms under the same name. Some, such as Samsung, LG, Hyundai, and SK, are well known in the West. Chaebols play a critical role in Korean markets. In 1996, the top thirty chaebols accounted for 40 percent of Korea's output in the mining and manufacturing sectors. They enjoyed a dominant position in the Korean market. Several of these chaebols' affiliates are major competitors in global markets. As of 1997, ten affiliates of the top thirty chaebols made the Global Fortune 500 listing (see Table 3.1).

When the Asian financial crisis hit Korea in 1997, however, thirteen of the top thirty chaebols and Korea as a whole went technically bankrupt. Foreign and domestic observers were amazed by this collapse, as the Korean economy had been praised as an exemplar of economic development. The International Monetary Fund (IMF) provided relief funds, but required the Korean government to adopt draconian measures for restructuring. The Korean government rescued insolvent banks with an injection of public funds. It then sought to financially reorganize the chaebols by leveraging the banks to help chaebols lower their debt–equity ratios. In addition, it forced the chaebols to swap and reorganize their businesses so that each chaebol would focus on only a select few lines of business.

As of 2003, many questions about chaebols remain unresolved. Were they the real culprits of the crisis? How did they, along with the Korean economy, recover so quickly after the crisis even though they were not enthusiastic about restructuring? Are they now less susceptible to external shocks? Should the Korean government force them to restructure further? Can they once again grow and prosper?

This chapter examines chaebols' postcrisis restructuring efforts. It also assesses changes in chaebols' external environments and how these changes

Table 3.1. The listing of the top 30 groups in 1997 and their rankings in 2003 — Unit: billion won

		Top 30 groups in 1997						Rankings in 2003						
1997 ranking	Business groups	No. of affiliates	Assets	Sales	Debt/ equity %	Family ownership %	Affiliated ownership %	2003 ranking	No. of affiliates	Assets	Sales	Debt/ equity %	Family ownership %	Affiliated ownership %
1	Hyundai	57	52,821	67,990	436.7	13.8	41.6	15	12	7,667	23,768	361.5	1.6	26.0
2	Samsung	80	50,705	60,113	267.2	3.5	42.5	2	63	71,904	108,068	67.8	2.0	38.1
3	LG	49	37,068	46,674	346.5	5.4	34.0	3	50	55,200	78,237	152.1	7.3	34.1
4	Daewoo*	32	34,197	38,243	337.5	6.1	31.2	—			Bankrupt and group dissolved			
5	SK	46	22,723	26,640	383.2	14.1	30.1	4	60	46,315	51,801	179.1	2.1	52.9
6	Ssangyong	25	15,804	19,445	409.5	3.6	37.5	—	11	5,300	4,474	651.6	—	—
7	Hanjin	24	13,907	8,708	556.6	18.7	20.3	8	23	20,764	13,778	229.2	11.1	29.3
8	Kia*	28	14,121	12,001	516.9	20.8	9.6	—			Bankrupt and Merged with Hyundai Motors			
9	Hanwha*	31	10,592	9,657	751.4	5.9	26.7	13	33	10,318	7,560	206.5	1.5	37.8
10	Lotte	30	7,753	7,192	192.1	3.4	19.4	9	35	20,289	18,632	74.0	4.4	44.5
11	Kumho	25	7,399	4,443	477.6	2.0	37.8	17	15	9,340	6,848	369.6	3.4	50.4
12	Halla*	18	6,627	5,293	2065.7	18.8	30.5	—			Bankrupt and group dissolved			
13	Dong-ah*	19	6,289	3,885	354.7	12.0	42.2	—			Bankrupt and group dissolved			
14	Doosan	25	6,369	4,042	688.2	13.4	35.9	19	22	8,434	6,891	190.4	6.8	44.6
15	Daelim	20	5,849	4,832	423.2	8.8	25.1	23	15	4,593	5,362	107.4	7.8	44.7
16	Hansol	23	4,214	2,513	292.0	3.7	33.2	32	13	3,605	2,618	188.1	5.1	48.8
17	Hyosung	18	2,131	5,477	142.4	13.5	30.7	21	15	4,915	4,512	158.5	20.1	22.2
18	Dongkuk	17	3,698	3,075	218.5	15.6	32.5	30	7	4,079	3,026	138.7	19.1	17.9
19	Jinro*	24	3,826	1,391	3764.6	16.6	28.3	—			Bankrupt and group dissolved			
20	Kolon	24	3,840	4,134	317.8	7.6	36.5	26	32	4,334	3,891	143.4	4.5	52.3
21	Kohap*	13	3,653	2,521	590.5	8.5	30.8	—			Bankrupt and group dissolved			
22	Dongbu	32	3,423	3,154	261.8	12.8	33.2	20	23	6,676	3,991	147.1	7.5	36.8
23	Dongyang	24	2,631	1,847	307.3	4.8	44.0	25	15	3,283	1,501	357.8	3.9	48.3
24	Haitai*	15	3,398	2,715	658.5	3.9	24.9	—			Bankrupt and group dissolved			

25	Newcore*	18	2,797	2,279	1225.6	36.4	62.3	—			Bankrupt and group dissolved			
26	Anam	21	2,638	1,984	478.5	9.8	32.0	—	8	1,687	743	52.5	—	—
27	Hannil*	7	2,599	1,277	576.8	11.2	25.2	—			Bankrupt and group dissolved			
28	Keopyung*	22	2,296	1,058	347.6	17.4	41.5	—			Bankrupt and group dissolved			
29	Miwon	25	2,233	2,114	416.9	15.7	36.2	48	9	2,003	1,973	188.2	19.7	43.4
30	Shinho*	25	1,139	1,210	214.6	9.9	23.3	—			Bankrupt and group dissolved			

Source: Fair Trade Commission.

Notes:

1. *Denotes that firms were either bankrupt or under the bank-sponsored workout program as of December 1999.
2. The group-level sales, assets, and debt to equity ratio include nonfinancial services companies only.
3. The average family ownership and cross-ownership figures are the weighted average of the top 30 chaebols with the equity capital of individual chaebols as the weighting factor, following the FTC convention.
4. Hyundai Group spun off two small groups, each of which is headed by Hyundai Motors and Hyundai Heavy Industries, respectively.
5. The Fair Trade Commission has published the listing of top 30 groups since 1983 until 2002. Since 2003, however, the Fair Trade Commission announces the listing of large business groups of assets more than 2 trillion won, which are subject to restrictions in cross-shareholdings. The FTC added state-owned companies to this listing of large business groups of more than 2 trillion won in assets. As a consequence, the largest business group in 2003 was Korea Electric Power, a state-owned enterprise.

will affect their future. It considers how chaebols might be further restructured, and what they can do to become more competitive again in world markets.

3.1. CHAEBOLS IN THE KOREAN ECONOMY

As noted in Chapter 1, sociocultural environments, government policies, and underdeveloped markets help foster the rise of business groups. Chaebols are no exception (Amsden 1989; Kim 1997; Chang 2003). Figure 3.1 summarizes how the state, markets, and sociocultural environments shaped business groups in Korea. After Korea was liberated from the Japanese occupation, the Korean government during the Syngman Rhee regime sold reverted property to a small number of firms. Sales were based not on auctions but on the personal preference of high-ranking government officials. Friends and relatives of these officials thus had the best chance to buy such items (Kang 1996), and reaped huge windfall profits by doing so since sale prices were based on assets' book values. Because inflation at this time was very high, buyers bought assets for only a fraction of their fair market value. Such preferential treatment provided a foundation for the chaebols to grow. Chaebols such as Hanwha, Doosan, Samsung, SK, and Hyundai picked up those

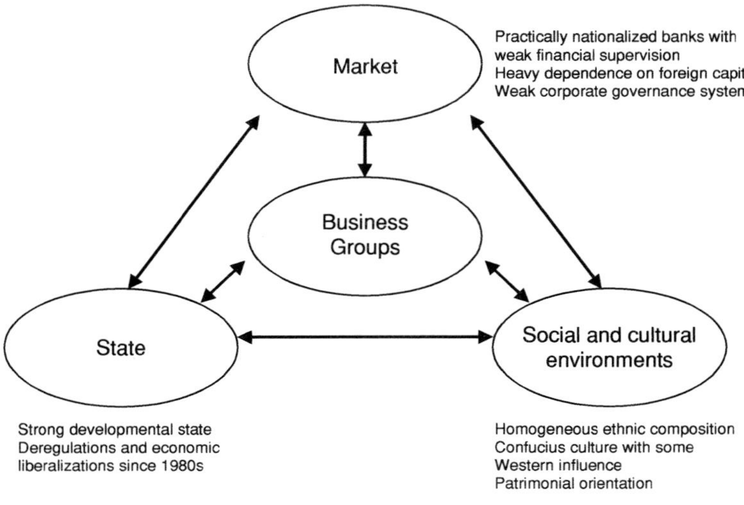

Figure 3.1. Korean institutional environments

assets and used them as the foothold for further growth. Widespread corruption, however, led to the collapse of the Rhee government in 1960, and the subsequent military coup.

After the *coup d'etat* in 1961, the new Korean president, Jung-Hee Park, launched an ambitious plan to industrialize Korea. Under the plan, the government subsidized chaebols' expansion, often through low-interest loans, into heavy equipment, chemicals, and export-oriented industries. It also absorbed and mediated the risk faced by new firms in the industries it supported. In many cases, it pledged payment guarantees to secure foreign loans for industrialization. When companies that enjoyed preferential credit from the government went bankrupt or faced similar difficulties, it interfered by freezing the debts, arranging for relief funds at lower interest rates from banks, converting debt to equity, and forcing healthy companies to acquire these troubled firms.[1] In the government's eyes, private companies' financial crises could lead to a national crisis, and thus merited governmental intervention. This assumption was particularly relevant for chaebols, and created the belief that chaebols were 'too big to fail'.

In addition, the government's actions significantly undermined the development of Korea's financial markets. Park nationalized all private banks and made them support government policies.[2] A bank could not deny a loan based on a borrower's creditworthiness when the government favored that borrower. Further, because they had to make loans according to the government's dictates, banks' available funds to other borrowers were relatively scarce. Interest rates for such loans were thus significantly higher than they would have been otherwise. Even after commercial banks were privatized in 1981, the Ministry of Finance intervened extensively in their lending practices and in setting interest rates. Bank managers had very little latitude in their asset management and therefore had little accountability for their banks' performance (Fields 1995; Park 1994).

Since banks lacked the ability to function properly, they began to require high levels of collateral as well as debt guarantees in order to protect their assets. Chaebols responded by extending debt guarantees among group affiliates. These guarantees nominally insured that a firm's affiliates would pay debts that the firm could not. Chaebols with more affiliates that could extend collateral and debt guarantees received better financial treatment and more opportunities for further expansion than smaller companies did.

This constellation of practices created a house of cards. First, government policies, such as subsidized loans, induced chaebols to prefer debt to finance their growth. Second, chaebols diversified extensively with the government's encouragement and used more debt to do so. Eventually, they had to rely on external sources of capital, which flowed into Korea as debt. Their debt to equity ratios increased from 100 percent in 1960 to over 500 percent in 1997. Some chaebols had ratios approaching 4,000 percent. Even slight downturns in their cash flow thus rendered them vulnerable.

Second, the widespread use of debt guarantees created situations where no affiliate firm could really guarantee repayment. If one affiliate firm involved in this practice became insolvent, its bankruptcy had a domino effect on its fellow affiliates. For example, when Daewoo Group collapsed in 1999, all of Daewoo's affiliates went bankrupt simultaneously due to these debt guarantees.

Thus, chaebols shifted their business risks to the government, and ultimately the public, while hoarding all the benefits if they succeeded. Since the government would support them if they failed, chaebols had a huge incentive to disregard risk and to diversify into unrelated business areas. Samsung's entry into the automobile industry even as this industry was consolidating worldwide is but one example of misguided diversification. Other chaebols that went bankrupt in the financial crisis pursued diversification strategies that lacked an economic rationale. 'Moral hazard' became prevalent in Korea,[3] and according to Krugman (1998b) was common to all Asian countries affected by the Crisis.

3.2. THE FINANCIAL CRISIS AND THE RESTRUCTURING OF CHAEBOLS

As the Asian crisis spread from Thailand to other Asian countries, foreign investors reexamined the Korean economy's fundamentals. They then started withdrawing their funds from Korea en masse. Foreign financial institutions also sharply reduced advances to Korean companies and began calling in their loans to Korean financial institutions. In turn, these actions created larger contractions in the stock and foreign exchange markets and induced the bankruptcies of larger Korean firms. During the crisis, the Korean won's value dropped 50 percent, the Korean stock exchange index dropped 40 percent, and thirteen of the top thirty chaebols either went bankrupt or were under bank-sponsored workout programs.

When Korea applied for emergency funds from the IMF, it was nearly bankrupt and had little bargaining power. Since the IMF perceived that chaebols were pivotal to Korea's crisis, it demanded that the Korean government force chaebols to reorganize. In early 1998, the government announced that it would require chaebols to reduce debt, abolish debt guarantees, sell unprofitable affiliate firms and concentrate on core businesses, and improve their financial transparency and corporate governance. As Chapter 1 of this book implies, however, it is not easy to implement drastic change quickly; these initiatives have either failed or been only partially successful.

3.2.1. Financial Restructuring

Attempts to restructure Korean chaebols' finances have focused on three main reforms: (*a*) significantly reducing debt–equity ratios, (*b*) abolishing debt guarantees, and (*c*) corporate workouts for weaker chaebols. Efforts to reduce debt have been modestly successful, as the government effectively nationalized the banking system after the Asian crisis and used this control to force banks to reduce their debt–equity ratios considerably by the end of 1999. Yet chaebols' debt in 1998 increased slightly (see Table 3.2); the decrease in chaebols' debt–equity ratio during this period was almost exclusively attributable to chaebols revaluing securities and real estate and their affiliate firms issuing new equity to each other. For example, their shareholders' equity rose from 46.9 trillion won in 1997 to 69.9 trillion won in 1998. Of this amount, 12.2 trillion won came from new equity issues, most of which went to affiliates. The remaining portion of this equity increase is attributable to massive asset revaluation. Chaebols got serious about reducing their debts only after the Daewoo Group went bankrupt in 1999.

The true degree of chaebols' indebtedness was revealed only when their combined financial statements became available for the 1999 financial year. The government required that chaebols present the combined statements of all domestic and foreign affiliates after subtracting all internal transactions. Table 3.2 shows the equities and debts of the four largest chaebols as listed in the combined financial statements of 1999, and highlights the substantial differences between their debt and equity levels for the aggregated and combined accounting data. In the combined statements, debts incurred by foreign subsidiaries were added and cross-shareholdings were crossed out. As a consequence, the average debt to equity ratio was 230.8 percent, which was much higher than was the average from the aggregated statements.

The initiative to eliminate mutual debt guarantees was more successful. As noted, such practices created ripple effects of bankruptcies among chaebol affiliates.[4] In 1997, the top thirty chaebols' total cross-debt guarantees, excluding payment guarantees related to industry rationalization, overseas construction, and technology development, which qualified for exemption, amounted to 63.5 trillion won. These chaebols reduced this amount to approximately 22.4 trillion won in 1998 and to only 1.3 trillion won by

Table 3.2. Changes in the debt and equity of the top 5 chaebols, 1997–9

1997 Aggregated financial statements

	Hyundai	Samsung	LG	Daewoo	SK	Sum/Average
Debt	61.7	50.0	42.9	42.7	23.9	221.2
Equity	10.7	13.5	8.5	9.1	5.1	46.9
Debt-to-equity ratio	576.6	370.4	504.7	469.2	468.6	477.9
Number of affiliates	62	61	52	37	45	

1998 Aggregated Financial Statements

	Hyundai	Samsung	LG	Daewoo	SK	Sum/Average
Debt	72.6	43.2	36.4	59.8	22.6	234.6 (174.6)
Equity	15.0	17.1	11.5	16.9	9.4	69.9 (53.1)
Debt-to-equity ratio	484.0	252.6	316.5	353.8	240.4	329.5
Number of affiliates	57	62	48	36	41	244

1999 Aggregated Financial Statements

	Hyundai	Samsung	LG	Daewoo	SK	Sum/Average
Debt	52.6	38.4	27.5	—	22.6	141.1
Equity	34.6	26.3	18.6	—	16.9	96.4
Debt-to-equity ratio	152.0	146.0	147.8	—	133.7	144.9
Number of affiliates	35	45	43		39	162

1999 Combined financial statements

	Hyundai	Samsung	LG	Daewoo	SK	Sum/Average
Debt	60.2	41.5	30.6	—	23.1	155.4
Equity	26.2	21.4	11.2	—	10.2	69.0
Debt-to-equity ratio	229.8	193.9	273.2	—	226.5	230.8
Number of affiliates	103 (30)	159 (39)	118 (35)		57 (33)	437(137)

Sources: The aggregated financial statements are from the Korea Fair Trade Commission, and the combined financial statements are from the Korea Financial Supervisory Board.

Notes:

1. The aggregated financial statements simply add the accounting items from the financial statements of individual affiliates without any consolidation. The combined financial statements consolidate all the affiliates that are effectively controlled by the chaebol chairmen.
2. Both aggregated and consolidated statements in the above exclude financial services affiliates.
3. Sum/Average denotes sum of debts, equities, and number of affiliates of five (four excluding Daewoo) and average for debt to equity ratios.
4. Number of affiliates in parentheses denotes domestic affiliates.
5. Daewoo Group went bankrupt. Figures in parentheses in 1998 statements are the sum of the other four chaebols.

2000. Most notably, the top four chaebols eliminated all such guarantees by the end of 2000.

The financial restructuring program comprised an effort to facilitate the smooth exit of nonviable companies and to transform financially weak, yet promising companies, into financially sound ones. This effort was generally unsuccessful. The major tools utilized in these workout programs were interest rate reductions, interest expense write-offs, and debt-to-equity swaps. New credit extension was minimal. Companies were required to sell or merge assets and business units that were either outside their core business lines or had little chance of recovering. Creditor banks required equity write-offs before they made debt-to-equity swaps. Both creditors and existing shareholders lost money on these swaps. Before initiating the corporate workout program, the Financial Supervisory Board announced the liquidation of fifty-five bankrupt companies in June 1998. By 1999, fifty-four companies belonging to seventeen business groups and thirty-nine medium-sized and large independent companies operated under the workout program. Many of these companies were not performing well, however, and twenty-nine of them were liquidated in November 2000.[5] The Korea Development Institute, a government-sponsored agency, contended the workout program merely extended financially troubled companies' lives rather than helping turn them around.[6]

3.2.2. Business Restructuring

The Korean government also attempted to consolidate industries and induce chaebols to focus only on their core competencies by implementing the so-called 'Big Deal' plan. This plan involved nine industries: semiconductors; petrochemicals; aerospace; railroad vehicles; power generation machinery; ship engines; oil refining; automobiles; and electronics. Highly capital-intensive with huge fixed assets, these industries faced serious overcapacity and inefficiency as a result of the Korean government's prior economic development policies in the late 1970s, which induced chaebols to enter these businesses. Essentially, the government wanted to undo its past efforts by forcing chaebols with weak competitive positions to leave these industries or sell their affiliate firms to other chaebols with strong competitive positions.

The 'Big Deal' is now regarded as a big failure. Few of the attempts to consolidate firms across chaebols worked. In a sense, this 'Big Deal' policy resembles past methods of dealing with prior economic crises and bankruptcies. After the second oil crisis, many Korean firms, particularly those in the heavy equipment and chemical industries, were in deep financial trouble.

The government also bailed out many failed firms by letting healthier firms take them over or merge with each other. Large subsidies were provided to firms involved in restructuring (Amsden 1989; Woo 1991). It is worth noting that the same industries that were subject to the 1981 restructuring were again reorganized after the 1997 crisis.

The biggest problem with the program was that the rationale for it was based on political rather than economic motives. Many argued that this idea was an attempt to demonstrate visible results rather than a real restructuring.[7] For instance, studies suggested that a merger between LG Semiconductor and Hyundai Electronics was not feasible and would create few synergies due to these firms' technological and production incompatibilities. Nonetheless, the Korean government pushed the two companies to merge.

3.3. CHANGES IN CHAEBOLS' FINANCIAL TRANSPARENCY AND CORPORATE GOVERNANCE

3.3.1. Corporate Governance Reforms

The Korean government initially seemed determined to reform chaebols' corporate governance structure and enhance their transparency and accountability. As a first step to do so, it required the top thirty chaebols to prepare combined financial statements that were consistent with international standards as of 1999.[8] The roles of outside directors and independent auditors were strengthened. In addition, the government punished independent auditors that failed to produce accurate information about the companies they audited. Moreover, an electronic reporting system was adopted and regulations on inadequate reporting for contingent liabilities, including cross-debt guarantees among affiliates, were strengthened.

As an adjunct effort, the government has exposed many common chaebol practices and helped curtail some of them. For instance, the Korea Fair Trade Commission demonstrated that chaebols had not reduced their cross-subsidies and transfers of wealth to their family members, even after they paid huge fines ensuing from the first three investigations.[9] The government's regulation of cross-shareholding has blocked chaebols from controlling affiliates without real infusions of capital. Continued enforcement of such regulations might help reduce such practices.

Second, the commercial laws were amended to simplify mergers and acquisition (M&A) procedures for both friendly and hostile M&As. In late 1998, the ceilings on combined and individual foreign ownership in a Korean firm were

Table 3.3. Big deals among chaebols

Industry	Government's plan	Implemented as of December 1999	Results as of December 2000
Semiconductors	LG Semiconductor and Hyundai Electronics merge into one company	Acquisition of LG Semiconductor by Hyundai Electronics was completed in July 1999	Due to the lost synergies and the plunge in DRAM prices, Hyundai Electronics is technically bankrupt. The government asked banks to buy bonds issued by Hyundai Electronics.
Petrochemicals, aerospace	Affiliates of Hyundai, Daewoo, and Samsung merge into one company	Aerospace businesses were combined into one in October 1999	The merged company kept losing money. The government provided 530 billion won in aid in 2000. Petrochemical deal did not go through.
Railroad vehicle	Hyundai, Daewoo, and Hanjin merge their operations	Hyundai, Daewoo, and Hanjin merged their operations in October 1999	Labor unions of three companies opposed the postmerger integration process. Overcapacity problem did not ease. The government is seeking a buyer.
Power generation machinery	Samsung and Hyundai sell their businesses to Korea Heavy Industries	Korea Heavy Industries acquired Samsung's and Hyundai's business	Doosan, the 12th largest chaebol, acquired Korea Heavy Industries.
Ship engines	Samsung sells its business to Korea Heavy Industries	Merged as planned	Profitable.
Petroleum refining	Hyundai acquires Hanwha Refinery	Hyundai acquired Hanwha Refinery in June 1999	Postacquisition integration has not yet taken place.
Automobiles	Daewoo acquires Samsung Motors	Deal did not go through	
Electronics	Samsung acquires Daewoo Electronics	Deal did not go through	

relaxed, as were the rules on tender offers. Moreover, the government streamlined regulations on corporate spin-offs and small-scale mergers. These steps to ease regulations on foreign ownership facilitated a rapid growth in foreign investment in Korean companies, although hostile M&As in Korea remain unlikely due to high cross-ownership among affiliates of the chaebols.

Third, the Korean government also required chaebols to abolish their group-level staff organizations. Chaebols, however, resisted this demand, and simply shifted this function to their flagship companies. Since chaebols continued to need to coordinate activities of group affiliates, the government's demand was naïve. Along with these measures, in an attempt to increase accountability, the government persuaded the chaebol 'chairmen' to assume the chief executive officer (CEO) positions in individual affiliates and thus made them liable for all wrongdoing.

Furthermore, to improve monitoring of top management, listed companies were first required to appoint at least one outside director. Starting in 1999, these firms had to ensure that outside investors represented at least 25 percent of their Boards of Directors.[10] Nonetheless, most of these directors were simply appointed by the dominant shareholders and had close relationships with the latter.[11] Thus, this measure has brought limited change. It will likely take some time before Korea has a sophisticated outside director system that helps institutional investors exert significant influence.

In tandem with the above measures, the rights of minority shareholders have been slightly improved. The representation requirements for filing class action lawsuits against the 'listed' and seeing a firm's accounting data were significantly reduced. Yet the government remained reluctant to further ease the requirement for filing class action lawsuits.[12] In addition, it has not yet acceded to minority shareholders' demand to be allowed to elect directors by accumulating votes among themselves.[13] Foreign and domestic fund managers continue to believe, however, that Korean companies fail to serve the interests of shareholders,[14] suggesting these reforms may not be fully effective. The Korean government will have to work harder to build on these reforms. It also needs to support the efforts of domestic and foreign shareholder activists and creditors, who have been the most vigorous and successful advocates for corporate reform in Korea. Their efforts have, for instance, influenced the SK Group to adopt substantive changes in governance.

3.3.2. Minority Shareholder Activism

Since 1998, the People's Solidarity for Participatory Democracy, a nongovernment organization, has coordinated minority shareholders and foreign institutional investors. It filed a lawsuit against explicit cases of expropriation such as those in Samsung Electronics and SK Telecom and exercised rights of minority shareholders at annual general shareholders' meetings.[15] Such efforts pressure the government to make changes in the legal framework that hold chaebols accountable for their behavior. In the case of SK Telecom, foreign investors such as the Tiger Fund collaborated with domestic minority shareholders to wage a proxy fight in the general shareholder's meeting. They obtained the right to appoint two outside directors. SK's founding family agreed to give these directors the authority to approve internal transactions above a certain amount. The People's Solidarity for Participatory Democracy also caused a stir at the general shareholders' meeting of Samsung Electronics over the company's unfair internal transactions. The People's Solidarity for Participatory Democracy is but one example of homegrown activists who will spur changes in governance mechanisms.

3.3.3. Foreign Investors and Creditors

Foreign investors and creditors will be an important force that will compel chaebols to restructure further. For instance, in Korea, foreign ownership increased to 40 percent of the total market capitalization in 2003. This increase has led to greater shareholder activism. Foreign investors have both actively monitored performance and worked with domestic shareholder activists such as the People's Solidarity for Participatory Democracy to file lawsuits against chaebols. A recent case of such an active participation of foreign investors in raising voices against chaebols is the bankruptcy of SK Global. SK Global, a general trading company of the third largest SK Group, was indicted for overstating profits by US$1.2 billion in 2003. Both its domestic and foreign creditors demanded that other affiliates of SK Group should bail out the firm by writing off any debts and by injecting fresh equity capital. The Sovereign Asset Management, a Monaco-based fund that owns nearly 15 percent of SK Corporation, a large firm in SK Group in the oil refining business, fiercely objected to any bailout and threatened to raise a lawsuit if SK Corporation supported SK Global at the expense of its shareholders.[16] In a press conference, the fund stated its goal as 'to turn SK Corporation into a role model for corporate governance and shareholder value for Korean business'.[17]

Although foreign investors and creditors will likely drive the further restructuring of chaebols, Korea's banking system, which was modeled after those of Germany and Japan, will probably not vanish overnight. Most Koreans still deposit their savings in banks, and Korean corporations rely mainly on bank loans to conduct business. These relationships will last for a while. Further, Rajan and Zingales (1998) argue that an arm's-length, market-based financial system is not necessarily superior to the relation-based financial system, especially when there is a shortage of capital.

Because the Korean government infused massive public funds into many banks to keep them solvent, it is increasing the relative power of the financial sector by forcing banks to merge with each other. For instance, it was able to compel Kookmin Bank, a leading bank with a relatively sound balance sheet, to merge with the Long-Term Credit Bank in 1999 and with the Housing & Commercial Bank, another bank with a sound balance sheet, in 2001 because of its large stakes in all three banks. The rationale for these mergers was to create a strong, large bank that could effect operational economies of scale and improve the quality of its credit analysis. The government also expected this merger to provoke voluntary mergers by the remaining commercial banks. Indeed, Hana Bank and Seoul Bank merged in 2002, creating the second largest bank in Korea. If such consolidations continue to take place, there will be only a few large banks left in Korea. These remaining banks may have a stronger position when bargaining with the chaebols, which will let them better monitor chaebols' investment activities.

Furthermore, foreign banks operating in Korea will diffuse Western banking practices to the banking industry in Korea. Cheil Bank, which was sold to Newbridge Capital, is independent from government pressure to provide extra loans to Hynix Semiconductor. Citibank and Hong Kong Shanghai Bank are expanding their retail bank practices in Korea. The intensified competition between foreign banks and large local banks will further develop the local capital markets.

3.3.4. Increased International Competition in Local Markets

Chaebols are also facing tougher competition both domestically and internationally. In the past, chaebols had a practical monopoly in many markets in Korea because of government policies that limited foreign entrants. Recently, however, the Korea Fair Trade Commission has actively policed chaebols' predatory behavior against domestic competitors and it has investigated chaebols' cross-subsidization practices. At the same time, Korea is removing trade and investment barriers to comply with the IMF's conditions for relief. Furthermore, chaebols' aggressive price cutting in international markets is increasingly difficult to practice due to the World Trade Organization's (WTO) rules.

Also, many financially troubled affiliate firms were sold to foreign multinationals during the crisis. For instance, Renault and General Motors (GM) acquired Samsung Motors and Daewoo Motors, respectively. Such acquisitions will spur intensified competition in Korea. As a consequence companies (like Hyundai, which acquired Kia, has to focus on its car business and refrain from diversifying into unrelated businesses) have to focus on core businesses in which they are competitive.

3.4. THE FUTURE OF CHAEBOLS

In a sense, the restructuring of chaebols shows some interesting parallels to the dissolution of zaibatsu after World War II.[18] In order to avoid resurrection of Japanese imperialism, General McArthur formally dissolved the zaibatsu into many independent firms (Hadley 1970). After the occupation ended, however, the firms rebuilt their network linkages, though in a less centralized fashion, into keiretsu. Although the zaibatsu reform resulted in removing the founding family entirely, the ex-zaibatsu firms simply regrouped voluntarily by exchanging shares and pooling resources. As a consequence, the internal operations of keiretsu remain a closed system, although direct control over individual affiliates has been weakened in comparison with the prewar zaibatsu. The chaebol reforms in Korea were triggered by the collapse of the Korean economy and forced by the IMF and World Bank The Korean government followed their guidelines rather closely in order to escape the default risk. The Korean experience, however, illustrates the limitation of corporate restructuring initiated by external forces.

We will now draw implications for Korean business groups in the light of globalization. Because we believe chaebols are creatures of market imperfections and government intervention, we argue that as these forces diminish, chaebols' influence will decline. The Korean financial market has undergone big changes. Institutional investors, especially foreign ones, have assumed bigger roles in the Korean capital market. Korean companies increasingly list their shares in the foreign stock market. More activity by securities analysts, convergence of international accounting standards, and international waves of M&As will induce Korean firms to adopt international accounting standards, thereby increasing transparency (Jang 2001). Shareholder activism and stricter enforcement of the Fair Trade Act will also make practices such as cross-subsidization more difficult. At the same time, increased market competition will force chaebols to focus upon their core businesses.

Chaebols and business groups in other countries will not, however, disband overnight. It takes time to build institutions and for the effects of competition to be felt. As institutional and market forces diffuse, business groups can survive or even prosper by focusing on sharing resources for which markets are still imperfect, such as human resources, brands, and technology. If business groups evolve in that direction, chaebols in the medium term may be more or less like the Japanese keiretsu, loosely coupled and voluntarily cooperating on a few investment projects when there is mutual strategic advantage in doing so.

In the meantime, the revamping of the corporate governance systems in Korea will unleash the power of professional managers. Korea's dramatic economic growth was based on not only founding families and government policies but also the efforts of countless Korean workers and managers. Although there were many competent managers in chaebol affiliates, they could not fully utilize their managerial expertise since they had only operational responsibility in business divisions. The improved corporate governance system will limit the power of chaebol chairmen and enable these professional managers to use their strategic acumen.

For instance, professional managers can introduce market discipline into the groups' internal markets. Although business groups in other countries actively share resources and trade among their divisions, their interdivisional transfer prices reflect market prices. Professional managers whose performance incentives are tied to their divisional performance cannot favor their affiliates against their outside customers. The introduction of market-based internal transfer pricing will instill discipline into the internal markets, thereby ending the perennial cross-subsidization within the chaebols. The key challenge to avoiding another crisis and ensuring chaebols' further success will be maintaining discipline when attempting to create synergies from internal markets. It has been easy to lose discipline and let cross-subsidization proliferate without control. In addition, allowing greater freedom to professional managers will further encourage Korean workers to exercise their creativity.

Some chaebol families have already initiated changes. Doosan Group undertook a major restructuring before the Asian crisis hit Korea. It hired a foreign consulting company and turned the group around by selling assets in underperforming businesses to foreign investors. Had it not been proactive, Doosan Group could have been the first casualty of the crisis. LG Group also transformed its ownership structure to a holding company structure, thereby discouraging the tunneling of profits across affiliates and providing clear performance-based incentives to professional managers in charge of operating companies.

Another mechanism for proactive change may stem from chaebols' efforts to access capital from foreign markets. Several Korean companies, including Korea Telecom, Hyundai Motors, and Samsung Electronics, have listed their stocks in foreign markets, especially by issuing American Depository Receipts (ADRs).[19] This voluntary listing means that these firms have adopted governance and contractual reforms that require them to make more transparent accounting information available to the general public.

The Korean government can further aid the economy by continuing to build institutional infrastructures upon which markets can develop and stabilize. Massive privatization efforts in former communist countries, such as Czechoslovakia and Russia, showed that markets do not automatically develop by privatization alone (Stark 1996; Kogut and Spicer 2001). Property rights, governance structures, conceptions of control, and rules of exchange help level the playing field by giving economic actors the freedom and confidence to organize, compete, cooperate, and exchange.

However, the economic restructuring in Korea after the Asian crisis also suggests that it is not easy for a government to induce lasting changes. Economic actors find new ways to continue old practices when these practices are outlawed. In Korea, chaebols have responded to the government's efforts to eliminate cross-subsidies and wealth transfers by becoming much more sophisticated in how they maintain these activities. For instance, rather than using their own financial services affiliates, chaebols deposited funds into unaffiliated financial institutions and let them lend money to the financially weak affiliates at favorable terms while using these deposits as collateral.

The Korean government is not, however, unique in its need to remain vigilant. Other countries, including the USA, have seen corporations find new ways to circumvent laws that address past malfeasance. Indeed, the Korean experience before and after the Asian crisis suggests that sociocultural environments are sticky; even the most major actors cannot fully control or anticipate the consequences of their initiatives.

NOTES

1. The most notable case was the massive government bailouts of the troubled firms in the heavy equipment and chemical industries in 1980 (Woo 1991).
2. See Nam (1994), Park (1994), Fields (1995), and Woo (1991) for more discussion of the government interventions in Korea's financial services industry.
3. Moral hazard refers to the tendency to take more risks if one knows it will be rescued in cases of failure.
4. Lieberman, I. and Mako, W. (1998). 'Korea's Corporate Crisis: Its Origins and a Strategy for Financial Restructuring', in M. Yun (ed.), *Korean Economic Restructuring: Evaluation and Prospects.* Seoul: Korea Institute for International Policy, p. 63.

5. *The Chosun Ilbo*, '29 Companies Were Liquidated', November 4, 2000.
6. *The Donga Ilbo*, 'KDI Severely Criticizes the Government's Restructuring Policies', December 9, 2000.
7. *The Chosun Ilbo*, 'Big Deal Became Empty Deal after Two Years', December 20, 2000.
8. In December 1998, the Corporate Accounting Standards were amended to conform to international standards and a new rule for accounting of financial institutions has been enacted. In September 1999, the Korea Accounting Research Institute was founded to propose accounting standards that are in line with international practices.
9. The Fair Trade Commission press releases, dated July 30, 1998, November 13, 1998, October 1, 1999, and December 14, 2000.
10. The proportion of outside directors on the boards of US firms was 78 percent in 2000 (*The Economist*, 'Outside Directors', February 10, 2001).
11. *The Economist*, 'The Chaebols Spurn Change', July 22, 2000.
12. Giving in to the demands of the People's Solidarity for Participatory Democracy, a non-governmental organization, the government planned to allow anyone with one share in a listed firm with more than 2 trillion in assets to initiate a class action lawsuit from the year 2002 onward.
13. However, no director has been appointed through such procedures at this time.
14. This survey was conducted by the Hangil Research Center at the request of the People's Solidarity of Participatory Democracy. Eighty-seven domestic fund managers and Sixty-six foreign fund managers took the survey during December 2000. The detailed survey results are available at http:\peoplepower21.org.
15. *The Economist*, 'Scourge of the Chaebol', March 27, 2000; *Business Week*, 'This Time Around, Goliath May Strike Back', March 29, 1999.
16. *The Economist*, 'A Successful Failure', May 31, 2003.
17. *Business Week*, 'Crackdown on Korea Inc.', May 19, 2003.
18. The main elements of the zaibatsu dissolution program included (*a*) the dissolution of zaibatsu holding companies, (*b*) barring old zaibatsu family members from resuming positions as company officers in the ex-zaibatsu enterprises, as well as (*c*) prohibiting the use of the traditional zaibatsu trade names and insignia.
19. As of June 2000, there were twenty-nine Korean companies issuing ADRs.

4

Taiwanese Business Groups: Steady Growth in Institutional Transition

Chi-Nien Chung and Ishtiaq P. Mahmood

Business groups are defined as 'sets of legally separate firms bound together in persistent formal and/or informal ways' (Granovetter 1995, 2005). They dominate most emerging economies, including Taiwan (Hamilton 1997; Chung 2001). There are, however, important differences among groups across countries. Some group forms, such as chaebols, have dense interorganizational relationships that are centered on a single person/family (see Chapter 3). Others, such as keiretsu, have looser ties that are maintained only by common identity (see Chapter 2). Hamilton and his associates (Hamilton and Kao 1990; Orrù, Biggart, and Hamilton 1991; Hamilton 1997) locate Taiwanese groups, known as jituanqiye, in the middle of the continuum between chaebols and keiretsu. Taiwanese groups 'are loosely coupled networks of firms owned by the same individual or related persons who join together in multiple enterprises' (Orrù, Biggart, and Hamilton 1991: 384). This chapter explores this 'neither market nor hierarchy' organizational form (Powell 1990; Powell and Smith-Doerr 1994) in Taiwan. Specifically, it assesses how the wave of economic liberalization in Taiwan in the late 1980s affected the strategy, structure, and performance of these large groups.

Both the recent economic shocks and increased deregulation across emerging economies have inspired scholars from different disciplines to discern how institutional transitions influence firms' activities (Ghemawat and Khanna 1998; Clark and Soulsby 1999; Khanna and Palepu 1999; Peng 2003). In theory, firms in emerging economies diversify in response to market imperfections and institutional vacuums. Over time, as these imperfections decline and new market institutions emerge, firms are expected to reduce their diversification. Some recent studies have observed, however, that although deregulation eventually reduces the benefits from diversification in the long run, the uneven pace of liberalization can create opportunities for diversification in the period immediately after deregulation. Since Taiwan has gone through a deregulation/liberalization process, we first examine whether groups in Taiwan became less or more diversified.

Second, as scholars of latecomer industrialization (Amsden 1989) note, business groups in emerging economies often diversify because they lack proprietary technologies and they can access overseas linkages that allow them to diversify by entering technologically unrelated industries. These linkages are neither homogenous nor static. For example, Hobday (1995) argues that as market environments and groups' resources, such as their technological sophistication and production costs, changes so do the importance of specific types of overseas linkages. We hence want to explore how the types of overseas linkages used by Taiwanese groups have evolved. Specifically, (*a*) have there been more or fewer overseas linkages over time, and (*b*) have there been any changes in the dominant type of linkage and the geographical sources of those linkages?

Third, as aspects of strategy, such as product diversification and types of external linkages evolve, we assess how groups align their structures with their strategies. As Chandler (1962, 1990) notes, this alignment is key for firm survival and performance. The mismatch between expansion and control constrains groups' organizational capability to process and coordinate increasing volumes of business and managerial decisions that accompany product and geographical diversification. As scholars of Chinese management (Wong 1985; Redding 1990; Fukuyama 1995) argue, Chinese owners' inclination to keep their groups' ownership and management in the hands of family members may constrain their businesses' prospects for growth. Considering how Taiwanese groups dealt with the tension between growth and control, especially after the institutional transition, is our third agenda. We will examine two dimensions of family control: (*a*) families' share of ownership, and (*b*) participation in key executive positions.

Fourth, we analyze how group performance has evolved during the institutional transition. In particular, we focus on both profitability and innovation. Profitability reflects static efficiency, and innovation is a measure of dynamic efficiency (Ghemawat and Costa 1993). The rise of competition that accompanies market liberalization is likely to reduce overall profitability and increase variance among individual groups. Similarly, faced with stiffer competition, groups' ability to sustain their competitive advantage might depend on their ability to innovate. Taiwan's institutional transition in the late 1980s allows us to examine if these two patterns are borne out by data.

This is the first large-scale empirical study that investigates the evolution of strategy, structure, and performance of Taiwan's top 100 groups in the past three decades. Distinct from previous studies, which examined a single or several groups (Takao 1989; Numazaki 1993) or the top 100 groups in a single year (Hamilton 1997), this paper examines the largest 100 groups over eight time periods. The scope of our analysis not only contributes to the understanding of Taiwanese groups in the last thirty years but also sheds light on how business groups respond to institutional changes in general.

The rest of the paper is organized as follows: In Section 4.1, we discuss Taiwan's early industrialization in the 1960s and 1970s, the institutional transition in the late 1980s, and recent developments in the 1990s. We consider the environmental factors that have affected the formation and transformation of Taiwan's business groups by the comparative institutional framework depicted in Figure 1.1. In Section 4.2, we describe our data sources and coding procedures. We describe the evolution of strategy, structure, and performance of the top 100 groups in Section 4.3. We present the evolution in product diversification, overseas linkages, ownership composition, family executives, profitability, and patents in sequence, focusing on the effects of institutional transition in the late 1980s. In Section 4.4, we conclude by summarizing our major findings, discussing implications for current theories, and suggesting directions for future studies.

4.1. INDUSTRIALIZATION, INSTITUTIONAL TRANSITIONS AND BUSINESS GROUPS IN TAIWAN, 1960s–2002

The Taiwanese state is less intrusive in the economy, as compared to that in Korea. The KMT (Kuomintang, the Nationalist Party) regimes led the markets

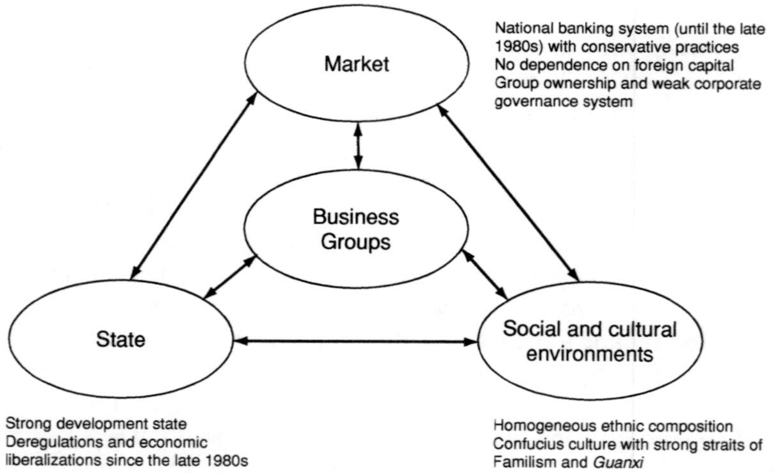

Figure 4.1. Taiwanese institutional environments

through industrial regulations, tax policies, and building-up of infrastructure. Rather than establishing symbiotic relationships with chaebols through direct financing, such as the Korean state, the KMT regime kept a certain distance from large business groups (Evans 1995). The distance between the state and business groups gives space to social and cultural institutions such as Chinese familism and *Guanxi* to shape the ownership and management of Taiwanese business groups (Hamilton and Biggart 1988). While lenient to social and cultural inheritance, the KMT regime was strict in financial and monetary policies and constrained foreign capital. The national banking system was conservative in corporate loans and requested substantial collateral. The administration was also reluctant to take foreign debts and had detailed regulations regarding foreign capital. Fields (1995) traces this conservative approach to the KMT's disastrous experience of financial breakdown in Shanghai in the 1940s. This approach not only affected the financing channels and ownership of business group but also contributed to Taiwan's survival of the Asian financial crisis in 1997–8. We summarize these arguments by the framework of Figure 4.1 and also provide historical details.

World War II destroyed most of Taiwan's existing infrastructure. With the assistance of US aid, the KMT government restored agricultural production and basic infrastructure to prewar levels within a decade. After a series of land reforms and stabilization of the currency, Taiwan's initial industrialization started in the late 1950s. The KMT government provided ample tax incentives to attract foreign investment to produce goods for export. This export-oriented strategy was spearheaded by licensing agreements, sometimes called OEMs (original equipment manufacturers) by scholars (Hobday 1995). Under OEM agreements, Taiwanese firms paid for the right to manufacture products, and foreign multinationals transferred the necessary manufacturing know-how. The government also set up research facilities such as the Industrial Technology Research Institute (ITRI) to conduct risky, expensive research and development (R&D) and transfer technological knowledge to domestic firms. The developmental model adopted by KMT is thus different from that of other East Asian countries such as Korea, which allocated bank credit and directed monetary policies (Cheng 2001). This model not only shaped Taiwan's economic structure but also affected Taiwan's business organizations.

Certain regulations and policies that accompanied this developmental model directly affected Taiwan's business groups. Chung (2001) suggests that regulatory institutions were central to the formation of Taiwan's large groups, especially the Statute for Encouragement of Investment, which was enacted in 1960. Its original intent, according to its designer, Li Kwoh-Ting, was to prompt Taiwan's initial industrialization. According to Li:

> In the early years of industrialization in Taiwan, private entrepreneurs and bankers with vision and a willingness to take risks were extremely rare... If private enterprises were not properly guided and assisted in their development the emergence of a vigorous private industry would be seriously retarded. (Li 1988, p. 47)
>
> The enactment of this statute is through tax relief, to promote savings and stimulate investment and exports, which in turn would invigorate business and industry, increase income, and raise tax revenue. As a result, despite large amounts of tax allowances, revenues actually increased considerably. (Li 1988, pp. 16–17)

For the policy planner, this statute influenced business groups' activities in unintended ways. In the 1960 ordinance, new investments (new firms) had income tax relief for five years. For firms with increased production capacity, this tax holiday applied only when the capacity was 30 percent greater than the original firm's (Statute for Encouragement of Investment, 1960 and 1970). Under this regulation, it was more attractive to establish new firms to capitalize on the tax holiday afforded to them and establish a group than it was to expand the original firm and form a multiunit enterprise. When the KMT removed restrictions on new establishments in most industries in 1964, Taiwanese entrepreneurs responded by setting up many business groups. Chung (2001) found that more than half of the 150 groups in his sample established their second firms between 1964 and 1968. Between 1950 and 1963, 36 percent of these groups established their second firms, while less than 5 percent of the groups set up their second firms after 1969.

By the early 1970s, Taiwanese society widely accepted and understood the group form as a way to organize business. Newspapers and business magazines began calling these groups jituanqiye. Getting a job in one of the big jituanqiye was seen as a wise career move in TV dramas, radio shows, and various novels. Reflecting the importance of business groups in Taiwan the first version of the directory *Business Groups in Taiwan* was published by China Credit Information Service in Taipei (see Section 4.2.1 for more details) during this period.

In the late 1980s, Taiwan experienced the largest wave of economic liberalization in its modern history. The market-centered transition opened up product, financial, and labor markets far more than they had been before. These changes were so significant that scholars labeled them the 'Great Transition' (Tien 1989).

Before the late 1980s, the Taiwanese state (i.e. the KMT) had dominated Taiwan's politics and economy (Amsden 1985; Gold 1985). Although it pushed economic growth through an export-oriented strategy and technological R&D, the state dominated most financial industries, public utilities, transportation, and other key manufacturing sectors (Wade 1990). The situation did not change until the mid-1980s when the KMT faced US pressure for fair trade practices, as well as internal challenges like political opposition, social movements, and dissatisfied capitalists. Economic liberalization was accompanied and accelerated by the political democratization that started in 1987, one year before the death of President Chiang Ching-Kuo (the son of Chiang Kai-Shek). Martial law was lifted, and labor protests and private mass media were allowed. Within a short period, not only were more open administrative policies initiated, but more liberal additions and amendments to the legal framework, such as the Securities and Exchange Law Amendments (1988), Banking Law Amendments (1989), the Statute for Upgrading Industries (1990), and the Statute for the Transfer of Public-Opened Enterprises to Private Operation (1991), were also inaugurated (Cornell 1993; Pistor and Wellons 1998).

With these changes, key industries previously monopolized by state enterprises such as banking, telecommunications, and electricity were opened to the private sector. Business groups had many opportunities to expand into new markets. Further, the equity and debt markets were deregulated (Semkow 1994), and the limits on foreign direct investment (FDI) and entry of foreign companies were also raised. Taiwan's experiences in the 1990s fit the definition of institutional transition, which is a set of 'fundamental and comprehensive changes introduced to the formal and informal rules of the game that affect organizations as players' (Peng 2003). Taiwan thus provides an ideal setting to test how such transitions affect strategy, structure, and performance.

The recent development of regulatory institutions from 2000 onward can be conceived as a continuation of the institutional transition started in the late 1980s. Unlike most of its counterparts in East Asia, Taiwan was largely unaffected by the Asian crisis. Many factors, such as the KMT's developmental strategy, a large trade surplus, heavy restrictions on currency trading, and relatively low ratios of corporate debt and nonperforming loans contributed to this exceptional case (*The Economist*, November 7, 1998). Thus, in contrast to other East Asian countries, which reformed their financial sectors because of the financial crisis, Taiwan's enactment of the Financial Institutions Consolidation Law (2000) and Financial Holding Company Law (2001) was triggered by the proliferation of banks and other financial service firms that followed the financial-sector liberalization in the early 1990s (*Far Eastern Economic Review*, May 17, 2001). The first law opened up the banking sector to mergers and acquisitions (M&As), permitted the government to force the merger of weak institutions, and allowed asset management companies to take over bad loans (*Far Eastern Economic Review*, December 21, 2000). The second law allowed affiliated firms of a financial holding company to consolidate their sales and marketing strategies and cross-promote their services and products to each other's customers. To a large extent, these two legal institutions broadened the financial-sector liberalization of the early 1990s and provided a new venue for business groups to diversify and grow. Many groups with financial arms consolidated and expanded their financial services. Some financial groups grew aggressively by merging with or buying other financial institutions.

Table 4.1 lists the top thirty groups in 1973 and 2002, respectively. The changes in the list clearly show that the development of Taiwan's business

Table 4.1. Top 30 groups in Taiwan

A. Top 30 groups in 1973

Rank	Group name	Year of establishment	Main industry	Sales (US$ million)
1	Formosa Plastics	1954	Plastic Products	397
2	Far Eastern	1954	Nonmetallic Products	146
3	Tainan Spinning	1953	Textiles	143
4	Cathay	1961	Plastic Products	128
5	Tatung	1918	Machinery	117
6	Yulon	1953	Transportation Equipment	112
7	Hsiao's Brothers	1956	Chemical Materials	102
8	Wei Chuan	1947	Food Products	91
9	Shin Kong	1952	Chemical Materials	85
10	Lai Ching Tien	1952	Chemical Materials	75
11	Pacific Electric Wire & Cable	1950	Electrical & Electronic Products	71
12	China General Plastics	1955	Plastic Products	64
13	Yuen Foong Yu	1950	Pulp & Paper Products	64
14	Sampo	1962	Electrical & Electronic Products	63
15	Tai Yu	1954	Food Products	55
16	Tuntex	1959	Textiles	55
17	Kao Hsing Chang	1951	Basic Metal	54
18	Cheng He Fa	1949	Food Products	49
19	All Sincere	1966	Food Products	49
20	Jang Dah Fiber	1962	Chemical Materials	48
21	Tai Ling Textile	1955	Chemical Materials	47
22	Kou Feng	1955	Textiles	46
23	Pao Tung	1958	Pulp & Paper Products	45
24	Lee Chang Yung	1959	Lumber & Wood Products	40
25	Jung Hsing	1951	Textiles	39
26	Taiwan Plywood	1959	Lumber & Wood Products	37
27	Chi Mei	1960	Chemical Materials	34
28	Hung Chow	1957	Textiles	32
29	Ve Wong	1951	Food Products	32
30	Kwang Yang	1963	Transportation Equipment	32

(*continued*)

Table 4.1. (*Continued*)

B. Top 30 groups in 2002

Rank	Group name	Year of establishment	Main industry	Sales (US$ million)
1	Formosa Plastics	1954	Plastic Products	20925
2	Lin Yuan Financial Holding	2001	Financing	15079
3	Shin Kong Financial Holding	2002	Financing	9561
4	Lien Hwa-Mitac	1955	Electrical & Electronic Products	9037
5	Kinpo	1973	Electrical & Electronic Products	8789
6	Hon Hai	1973	Electrical & Electronic Products	8358
7	Far Eastern	1954	Textiles	7305
8	President	1967	Food Products	7137
9	Liton Electronic	1989	Electrical & Electronic Products	6783
10	Yulon	1953	Transportation Equipment	5840
11	Evergreen	1968	Transport	5807
12	Quanta Computer	1988	Electrical & Electronic Products	5696
13	Tatung	1918	Electrical & Electronic Products	5200
14	China Trust Financial Holding	2002	Financing	5094
15	China Steel	1971	Basic Metal	5087
16	Benq	1984	Electrical & Electronic Products	4878
17	TSMC	1987	Electrical & Electronic Products	4704
18	United Microelectronics	1980	Electrical & Electronic Products	4667
19	Ho Tai	1947	Wholesale trade	4334
20	Acer	1979	Electrical & Electronic Products	4317
21	Fubon Financial Holding	2001	Financing	4159
22	Asustek	1990	Electrical & Electronic Products	3883
23	Walsin Lihwa	1966	Electrical & Electronic Products	3409
24	Chi Mei	1960	Chemical Materials	3263
25	Wistron	2001	Electrical & Electronic Products	3141
26	Hualon	1967	Chemical Materials	3037
27	Inventec	1975	Electrical & Electronic Products	2950
28	First International Computer	1980	Electrical & Electronic Products	2909
29	Advanced Semiconductor	1984	Electrical & Electronic Products	2650
30	Mega Financial Holding	2002	Financing	2528

groups is embedded in the institutional changes in the past thirty years, especially those involving financial groups that reorganized as financial holding companies after 2000.

Table 4.2 shows the aggregate economic significance of the top 100 groups. The size of the groups has grown steadily, but there is a clear jump after 1990. The average number of member firms per group was around 7.2 in the 1970s and 1980s, rose to 8.2 in 1990, 10.2 in 1994, 13.6 in 1998, and 24 in 2002. Over the same period, the contribution of the top 100 groups to national GDP rose from 30 to 85 percent. Although the gross domestic product (GDP) grew only

Table 4.2. Economic significance of the top 100 business groups in Taiwan, 1973–2002

	1973	1977	1981	1986	1990	1994	1998	2002
Group Sales (A)	3.5	6.3	13.4	23.7	62.3	102.1	150.6	240.9
National GDP (B)	10.8	21.8	46.9	80.5	158.9	246.3	277.4	282.2
Percentage (A/B)	32.4	28.8	28.6	29.4	39.2	41.5	54.3	85.4
Number of Group Firms Listed (C)	34	43	51	51	77	115	131	188
Total Number of Listed Firms (D)	64	82	107	130	199	313	437	639
Percentage (C/D)	53.1	52.4	47.7	39.2	38.7	36.7	30	29.4
Share of Market Capitalization	NA	NA	48	50.2	33.1	42	43.1	56.2
Number of Groups	100	100	100	97	100	100	100	100
Number of Member Firms	724	651	719	746	815	1021	1362	2419

Source: *Business Groups in Taiwan* (various years).

Notes: Group sales and GDP are in US billion dollars. The conversion rate for NT$ to US$ is 37.9 (1973), 37.95 (1977), 17.79 (1981), 35.45 (1986), 27.11 (1990), 26.24 (1994), 32.22 (1998), and 34.5 (2002). The value of GDP is quoted from *Taiwan Statistical Data Book*, 2003, and the market price and share of market capitalization of listed group firms are quoted and calculated from the *Taiwan Economic Journal* database.

slightly from US$277 to US$282 billion between 1998 and 2002, business groups' share of GDP increased from US$151 to US$241 billion. The number of group members listed on the Taiwan Stock Market jumped from 51 in 1986 to 77 in 1990, 121 in 1994, and 188 in 2002. These data indicate the growing importance of the 100 largest groups in Taiwan, especially since the institutional transition. In the following sections, we examine how this transition has affected these groups' diversification strategies and control structures.

4.2. EVOLUTION OF THE 100 LARGEST GROUPS, 1970s–1990s

4.2.1. Data

We used data for the 100 largest groups for eight periods, from 1973 to 2002. Our primary data source is the biennial directory *Business Groups in Taiwan* (BGT), which is compiled by the China Credit Information Service (CCIS) in Taipei, the oldest and most prestigious credit-checking agency in Taiwan and an affiliate of Standard & Poor of the USA. This directory collects sales information for the top 100 groups and is confined to groups whose core firms are registered in Taiwan. Consistent with our definition, the CCIS defines a business group as 'a coherent business organization including several independent enterprises'. The CCIS constructs database of business groups by examining interorganizational relationships such as shared identity, cross-shareholding, and interlocking directorates among these firms. In addition to self-identification, firms have to meet one of several objective criteria to be considered as member firms, including having overlaps of shareholders, directors, auditors, or decision-makers with the core firm and having a substantial proportion of their shares held by other group members. This directory is the most comprehensive and reliable source for business groups in Taiwan and has been used in previous studies (Hamilton and Biggart 1988; Hamilton 1997; Claessens, Djankov, and Lang 2000; Chung 2001; Khanna and Rivkin 2001; Amsden and Chu 2003).

We also supplemented the BGT directory with other sources. We adopted the Standard Industrial Classification (SIC) system published by the Taiwanese government (1996 version) to build our diversification measure. To figure out who the main shareholders and top executives of group firms are, we referred to both the family trees presented in the BGT and other biographical directories such as *Who is Who in Taiwan* and *Who is Who in Taiwan's Business*.

We used the top 100 groups reported in the directory from 1973 to 2002 at four-year intervals.[1] We believe the 30-year research period covers important stages of Taiwan's economic growth and allows for us to see the evolution of strategy, structure, and performance of Taiwan's conglomerates. We are especially interested in how the institutional transition in the late 1980s and early 1990s has affected business groups.

4.2.2. Product Diversification

Like their counterparts in other emerging economies (Amsden and Hikino 1994, Khanna and Palepu 2000), business groups in Taiwan entered new lines of business by establishing new firms (Hamilton and Kao 1990). Without an appropriate infrastructure for M & As, such as efficient markets for corporate control, most Taiwanese groups grew internally. To do so, they usually set up new firms rather than expanding existing units. As mentioned, Chung (2001) attributed this pattern to the tax incentives provided by the government. There is thus high diversification at the group level but little or no diversification at the firm level. Following Khanna and Palepu (2000), we constructed group level diversification according to the product information of each member firm.

We adopted the entropy measure of group diversification (Palepu 1985). Assuming a group operates in N industry segments, if P_i is the share of the ith segment in the total sales of the group, the entropy measure of total diversification DT is defined as follows:

$$DT = \sum_{i=1}^{N} P_i \log\left(\frac{1}{P_i}\right)$$

This measure takes into account two elements of diversification: (*a*) the number of segments in which a group operates, and (*b*) the relative importance of each segment. Due to the nature of product information provided by BGT, we used one-digit and three-digit SIC codes to calculate the entropy index.[2] The SIC system we adopted has 11 one-digit industries, 66 two-digit industries, and 229 three-digit industries. We calculated group level entropy by taking the weighted average of firm sales across industry codes.

Table 4.3 shows the descriptive statistics of product diversification of Taiwanese groups from 1973 to 2002. Diversification is increasing, as measured by both two-digit SIC counts and the entropy measure, suggesting that business groups participated in more industries over time. This trend is also reflected in the increasing number of member firms in Table 4.2. We observe a significant escalation of diversification between 1990 and 2002, the period after transition. The t-tests (one-tailed, 0.01 significance level) show that both the SIC count and entropy measure, as well as the firm number, were significantly higher after the transition than they were in the 1970s and 1980s. This difference indicates the positive impact of deregulation on diver-

Table 4.3. Strategies, structures and performance of the top 100 Taiwanese business groups, 1973–2002

	1973	1977	1981	1986	1990	1994	1998	2002
1. Total Diversification	NA	0.60	0.69	0.68	0.79	0.74	0.76	0.78
		(0.44)	(0.45)	(0.46)	(0.42)	(0.45)	(0.49)	(0.58)
2. 2-Digit SIC counts	3.96	4.07	4.25	4.76	5.11	5.91	6.53	9.03
	(2.37)	(2.44)	(2.68)	(3.38)	(2.84)	(3.53)	(3.93)	(6.29)
3. Overseas Linkages[2]	NA	NA	78	137	276	222	100	179
4. % of Family Directors	0.73	0.77	0.74	0.78	0.72	0.63	0.56	0.45
	(0.25)	(0.23)	(0.26)	(0.24)	(0.26)	(0.27)	(0.25)	(0.27)
5. % of Family Managers	0.40	0.42	0.36	0.38	0.33	0.25	0.22	0.17
	(0.29)	(0.31)	(0.33)	(0.32)	(0.29)	(0.25)	(0.23)	(0.20)
6. Return on Assets	NA	5.25	2.48	6.97	4.86	6.14	3.55	1.43
		(5.34)	(3.50)	(5.61)	(5.91)	(5.83)	(7.57)	(4.58)
Number of Groups	100	100	100	97	100	100	100	100

Notes:
1. Standard deviation (in parentheses).
2. The total number of overseas linkages of the top hundred groups.

sification. Our evidence is consistent with empirical evidence from other emerging economies undergoing similar transitions such as India and Argentina (Khanna and Palepu 1999; Carrera et al. 2003).

The rising of the SIC count is faster than that of the entropy measure during 1990 to 2002. One way to explain this divergence is to shed light on why groups diversify. In many emerging economies, including Taiwan, business groups—and the founding families whose wealth resided in them—often diversified into new industries to reduce risk without cannibalizing their current streams of rents. The divergence between SIC counts and the entropy index can be explained by the continuing importance of existing industries in which the groups operated vis-à-vis the new segments that they entered. Since SIC count does not take sales into account, the fast increase of this measure suggests that groups are willing to diversify and move into new areas, but with only limited resources. During initial periods of deregulation when market institutions have not been completely established, this strategy attempts to retain existing business lines while not losing new opportunities to grow.

Table 4.4 shows the list of industries in which the large groups participated. In the 1970s and 1980s, groups were involved in roughly similar industries. Except for trading and construction, manufacturing sectors constituted the most popular industries. Textiles, food, chemicals, and plastics were the major industries in both the 1970s and 1980s, reflecting the export-oriented, labor-intensive growth strategy of the KMT in the 1960s and 1970s. Foreign trade also topped the list in both 1973 and 1981. More than 44 percent of the groups set up trading companies to import intermediate goods for production and export their products. The trading business hence can be conceived as vertical integration to the manufacturing activities. Overall, industry participation by the top 100 groups maintained a consistent trend between 1970 and 1980.

The situation changed substantially after the transition in the late 1980s. Although groups remained oriented toward manufacturing, 36 percent of them established firms with financial functions. This move can be seen as resulting from the deregulation of financial services. Groups started establishing nonbank financial institutions such as investment companies. The top four manufacturing industries in the 1970s and 1980s were now ranked near the bottom. Fewer than ten groups remained in plastics. In contrast, the rise of the electrical and electronics sector to the third most important industry indicates that Taiwan's business groups started moving out of the labor-intensive and low-tech sectors and entering capital-intensive and high-tech areas (Amsden 2001).

By 1998, the changes were even more dramatic. Only two or three of the top ten industries were in the service sector during the 1970s to 1990s, while seven of the top ten industries were in the service sector in 1998. Also, 65

Table 4.4. Industry participation of the top 100 groups in 1973, 1981, 1990 and 1998

Top 10 industries in 1973	Percent	Top 10 industries in 1981	Percent	Top 10 industries in 1990	Percent	Top 10 industries in 1998	Percent
Foreign trade	44	Foreign trade	46	Foreign trade	52	Financing	65
Textile mill products	39	Textile mill products	28	Financing	36	Electrical & electronic machinery	49
Food manufacturing	27	Food manufacturing	27	Electrical & electronic machinery	31	Foreign trade	44
Chemical matter manufacturing	27	Chemical matter manufacturing	26	Food manufacturing	23	Wholesale trade	35
Fabricated metal products	23	Wholesale trade	24	Fabricated metal products	22	Infrastructure construction	29
Plastic products manufacturing	22	Plastic products manufacturing	24	Wholesale trade	22	Data processing & information	25
Transport	18	Fabricated metal products	23	Buildings construction	21	Rental & leasing	23
Nonmetallic products	16	Electrical & electronic machinery	21	Chemical matter manufacturing	18	Buildings construction	20
Chemical products manufacturing	15	Nonmetallic products	20	Textile mill products	16	Securities & futures	18
Electrical & electronic machinery	15	Buildings construction	18	Machinery & equipment	15	Real estate	18
Number of groups	100		97		100		100

Source: Compiled and calculated from *Business Groups in Taiwan*, 1974, 1982/83, 1992/93, and 2000.

percent of the groups had set up financial companies and thirteen groups had established their own commercial banks, reflecting the ongoing effects of institutional transition. At the same time, all labor-intensive industries, such as food and textiles, disappeared from the list. About half the top 100 groups had entered the electrical and electronics sector.

4.2.3. External Linkages

As shown earlier, Taiwanese groups participated in more product markets over time, especially in the 1990s. According to scholars of latecomer industrialization (Amsden 1989; Kock and Guillen 2001), groups in emerging economies often use overseas linkages with firms in developed economies as a way to diversify by entering technologically unrelated industries. For example, licensing agreements with foreign multinationals have often been an important starting point for groups in emerging economies that want to develop technological capabilities. Hobday (1995) notes, however, that as successful groups move up the technology ladder improving their capabilities from basic production to product design to product innovation and finally to advanced product/process innovation, their objectives also shift. Instead of focusing on acquiring generic technologies through licensing, these groups attempt to access specialized technologies through joint ventures or outright acquisition of technologically sophisticated firms in developed economies.

As Table 4.5 shows, the number of domestic patents granted to Taiwanese groups has steadily risen. In addition, these patents have shifted from incremental innovations done on shop floors ('new style patents') to actual new inventions ('new invention patents'), suggesting that Taiwanese firms have moved from being OEM manufacturers to being innovators in several technologies (Hobday 1995; Amsden and Chu 2003). At the same time, as groups have used outward FDI or licensing to maintain their cost competitiveness, they have begun to export technologies. Consequently, we explore how groups' patterns of overseas relationships and the geographic locations of their partners have changed.

We approached this issue by examining the three most common types of overseas linkages in Taiwan: licensing, joint ventures, and acquisitions. From the BGT yearbook, we identified the fifty-nine countries reached by these linkages. We then clustered these fifty-nine countries into four geographic clusters—USA, Japan, Europe, and developing countries.[3]

As Figure 4.2 shows, subcontracting and licensing agreements had been an important component of groups' overseas linkages. The importance of licensing agreements (indicated by its ratio to all types of external linkages)

Table 4.5. Patent types by year, 1950–2000

Year	New invention	New style
Before 1981	84	275
1982–1986	135	228
1987–1990	176	599
1991–1994	452	744
1995–1998	2172	756
1999–2001	4758	842
Total	7777	3444
Percentage	69	31

Note: The *Intellectual Property Office* of the Taiwanese government maintains the online patent database (http://www.patent.org.tw). In line with the German and the Japanese patenting system, patents granted in Taiwan differentiate between two types of patents: (*a*) New invention, designating a wholly new product, material, or manufacturing process; and (*b*) New style, representing a minor modification in the shape or color of a product.

declined over time, however, whereas the importance of joint ventures and acquisition has increased. As Hobday (1995: 112–13) notes, the Taiwanese business group Tatung provides a case in point. As Tatung moved up the technology ladder, access to generic technologies through licensing became relatively less important. At the same time, liberalization in the labor market led to a steady rise of labor costs and reduced Taiwan's appeal as a destination for OEM. In response to these dual pressures, Tatung and many other Taiwanese groups began to pursue FDI and joint ventures in other developing countries, such as Southeast Asia and China, with lower factor costs.

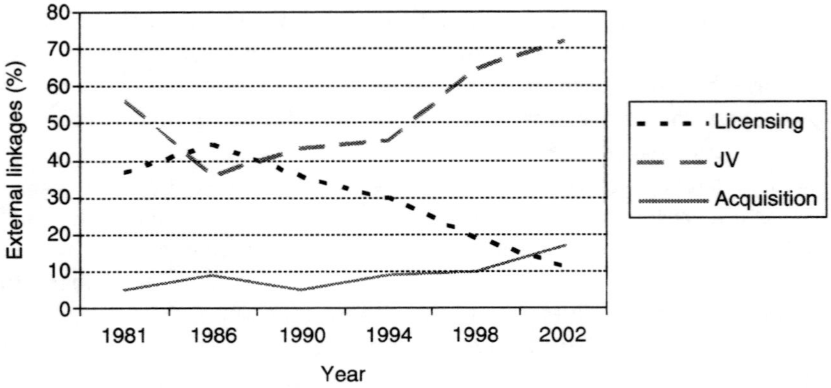

Figure 4.2. Distribution of external linkages 1981–2002

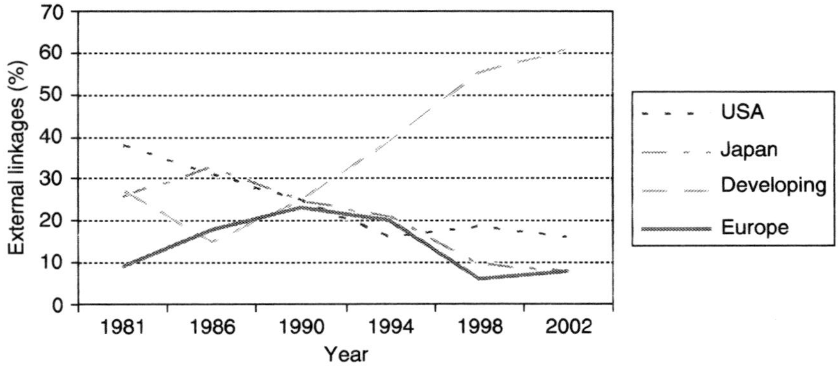

Figure 4.3. Distribution of external linkages across geographic regions 1981–2002

Figure 4.3 shows that the share of overseas linkages with the USA and Japan has declined since the mid-1980s, and the share with developing countries has increased sharply. Thus, like their counterparts in other emerging economies, Taiwanese groups also used overseas linkages to access new technologies, enter new markets, and reduce production costs. As Table 4.3 shows, the total number of linkages has decreased since the mid-1990s. This dip reflects a decline in the number of licensing agreements and joint ventures; acquisitions continue to rise.

4.2.4. Network Ownership and Family Control

This section focuses on the issue of capital sources and their impact on group ownership. In particular, it shows where groups acquired the necessary capital and managerial talent to grow, and considers how these resources have affected group structures. As Table 4.2 shows, the number of group affiliates listed on the Taiwanese stock market has increased in the last decade. Yet this listing entails that founding families' ownership is diluted. Some 'culturalist' scholars of Chinese management argue that these families' reluctance to sell shares to 'outsiders' has constrained business groups' ability to grow (Fukuyama 1995: 69–82). Our evidence shows a different scenario: groups have been growing for the past three decades, especially in the 1990s. This finding leaves us with two questions: Is the family still the controlling owner while groups grow? If it is, how does it maintain its control?

We collected and examined the ownership data of group firms between 1988 and 1998,[4] the period when groups expanded extensively. We first recorded the major shareholders and the percentage of their shareholding for each member firm. We then assigned one of five categories to each of the shareholders: family, affiliate, government, foreign, and institutional. *Family ownership* is the proportion of firm shares owned by family members. Family member is defined as an individual with the same last name as the group founder or individuals with different last names but who appear in the family tree. *Affiliate ownership* is the portion owned by other units in the same group, including nonprofit organizations such as schools, hospitals, and charity foundations. *Government ownership* is the proportion of shares owned by governmental units, such as the Ministry of Economic Affairs, and government-linked agencies, such as the development funds set up by the Taiwanese government's Executive Yuan. *Foreign ownership* is the percentage of shares owned by foreign companies and individuals that are not affiliated with the group. *Institutional ownership* is the part of firm shares owned by financial institutions such as commercial banks, insurance companies, investment companies, mutual funds, and venture capital. In total, we coded shareholder data for 9,841 cases of firm-year, with an average of 5.1 shareholders per firm.

Figure 4.4 shows the ownership composition of the group firms between 1988 and 1998 at two-year intervals. Since BGT listed only major shareholders, the aggregate percentage is around 76. At the surface, the culturalists seem to be incorrect since family ownership dropped from 23 to 4 percent in a decade. At the same time, affiliate ownership rose from 35 to 53 percent. Other categories maintained more or less the same proportions.[5] Hence, our study is consistent with previous research that indicates groups often use 'pyramidal structure' to handle the ambivalent needs of growth and control

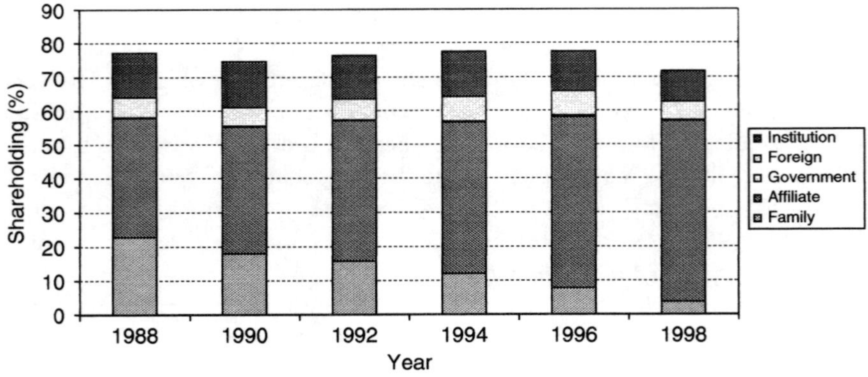

Figure 4.4. Ownership composition of group firms by year 1988–98

(Claessens, Djankov, and Lang 2000; Chang and Hong 2000; Chung 2004). The pyramid is a multiple-level ownership network constructed by chains of interorganizational shareholding. It is often structured with a control center at the top, a few intermediary firms in the middle, and many subordinate firms at the bottom.

Figure 4.5 demonstrates this pyramidal structure for Formosa Group, one of Taiwan's top conglomerates. The control center, which is composed of the group founder, Mr. Wang and his family, owned controlling shares in three major firms, Formosa Plastic, Nan Ya Plastic, and Formosa Chemical & Fiber. Through these three firms, Wang indirectly controls the rest of the group. Each of these three firms controls 33.3 percent of the shares in Formosa Heavy Industry, Tai Su Transportation, and Formosa Fairway. A similar pattern also appears in Formosa Petrochemical. Though Wang and his family hold only 17, 8, and 12.5 percent of the shares in the three major firms, their controlling power is enhanced by mutual shareholding among these three flagships. In short, the controlling family can control the whole group by maintaining sufficient equity in the controlling center. Studies by finance scholars (La Porta, Lopez-de-Silanes, and Shleifer 1999; Claessens, Djankov, and Lang 2000) indicate that the pyramidal structure allows the ultimate controller to own significant voting rights with minimal cash. At the same time, by creating separation between ownership and control, pyramids provide controlling families with opportunities to expropriate minority shareholders. Claessens, Djankov, and Lang (2000) did not find a significant relationship between ownership structure and corporate value in Taiwan, but more recent research by Yeh, Ko, and Su (2003) found evidence of expropriation. Taiwan's remaining unscathed by the Asian financial crisis has allowed groups to avoid tightened regulations and shareholder activists' aggressive scrutiny.

4.2.5. Two-tier Management and Professional Managers

Similar ambivalence about growth and control also appears in groups' managerial arrangements. As they became larger and more diversified, groups had to find managerial talent outside the founding families. How have these families maintained control over their executives?

To identify the backgrounds of group firms' key executives, we first coded the chairman of the board's (*Tung Shih Chang* in Mandarin pronunciation) and chief executive officer's names (*Tsung Ching Li* in Mandarin pronunciation) for each firm. The presiding director is the only legal representative of the corporation according to the Company Law of Taiwan (Ke 1995: 167–70).

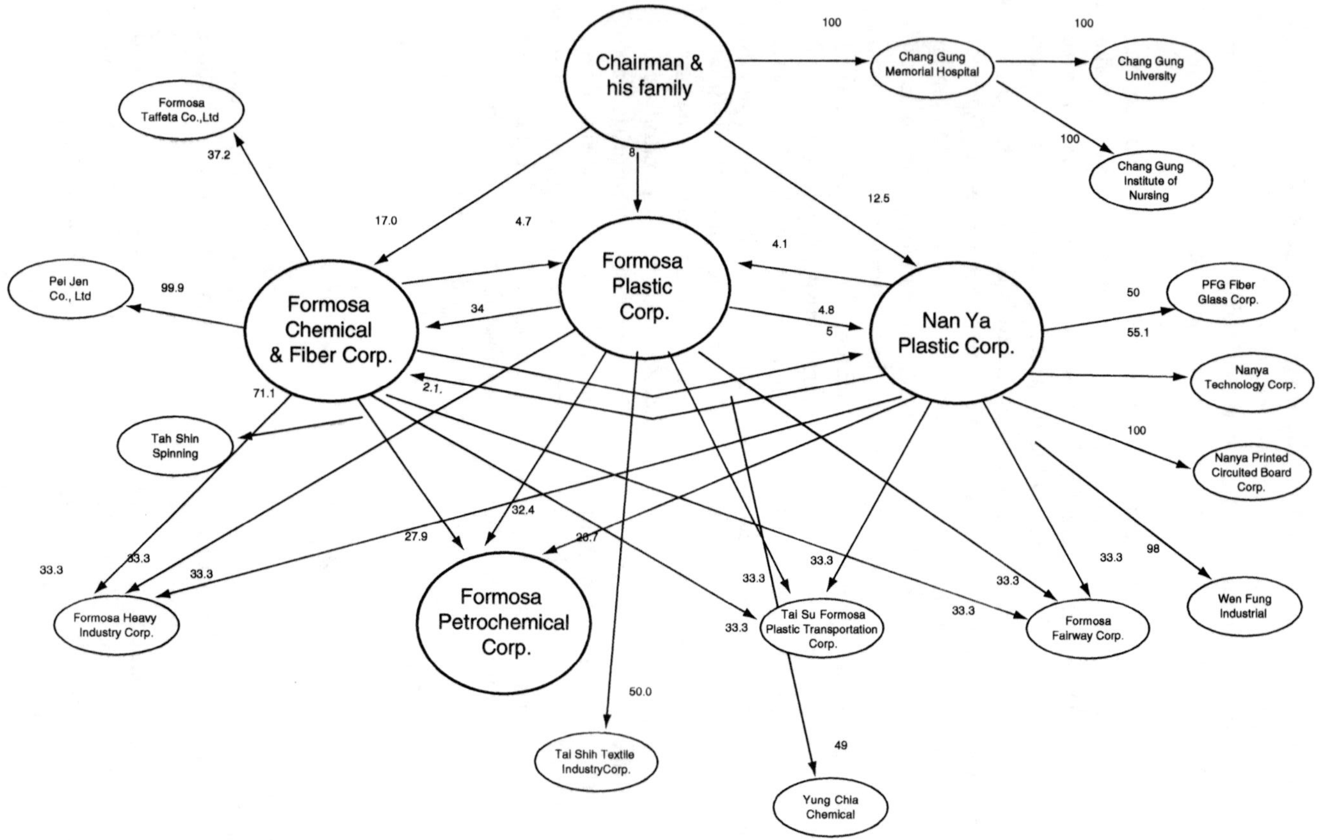

Figure 4.5. The equity ownership network of Formosa Group (1998)

Note: Dark circle for company of more than 10 billion Taiwanese dollar in assets.

Source: *Business Groups in Taiwan, 2000,* China Credit Information Service.

The board chairman oversees the business administration of the whole corporation, can sign contracts with external parties, sets firm goals, develops strategic plans, and coordinates resources. The chief executive officer (CEO), who is one level below the chairman in company charts, executes the chairman's decisions and supervises all the firm's divisions and personnel (Chen 1991). We then decided who the family executives are by using the same standard we used to decide family shareholding.

Table 4.3 shows family members about twice as likely to be the chairmen of the board than they are the CEOs. This observation is consistent with other field studies on overseas Chinese firms (Bruton, Ahlstrom, and Wan 2003). If family control is the goal, it is more efficient for the family to focus on strategic concerns and leave daily operations to 'outsiders' (e.g. professional managers).

Further, although the family ratios at the director and manager levels are quite stable from 1973 to 1986, they decline sharply after 1990. Again, this drop demonstrates the impact of transitional deregulation. As business groups grow, diversify, and have more external linkages, founding families have to include more 'outsiders' into the 'inner circle' to deal with this complexity (Thompson 1967). The 'outsider' is not, however, equivalent to the US professional manager, who is frequently recruited from the external market. Professional managers in Taiwan's business groups are often promoted from within. They have served in the group for a long time in different units. Most are confidants of the founding family, and many own equity in the company for which they work (Chung 2003).

4.2.6. Performance: Profitability and Technological Innovation

Table 4.2 shows no discernible pattern over time in average group profitability, although the profit rate is substantially lower in 2002 due to the worldwide recession. Table 4.2 also indicates an increase in the variance of group performance in the 1990s. With the institutional transition, this increase might be attributable to how individual groups adjust strategy and structure in an uncertain environment.

Just as profitability indicates a group's static efficiency in using its existing resources, innovation indicates a group's dynamic efficiency in enhancing its resources. As groups in Taiwan move up the technology ladder, innovation may become more important to competitive advantage than profitability is. As Table 4.5 shows, groups have become more innovative over the past decade. Most of these groups, such as Taiwan Semiconductors Manufacturing Corporation (TSMC), United Microelectronics, Mosel, and Walsin Lihua are either in electronics or computers. Table 4.6 lists the top ten innovative

Table 4.6. List of top 10 most innovative groups in 1998

Group name	Local patent application*
United Microelectronics	854
TSMC	572
Hon Hai	426
Mosel	169
Walsin Lihwa	159
Shinlee	138
Lien Hwa-Mitac	94
Umax	61
Kinpo	47
Quanta	45

Note: *Combining both new style and new invention patents together.

groups in Taiwan in 1998 in terms of domestic patents. All but Shinlee are electronics groups.

These numbers are consistent with those based on US patents by Mahmood and Singh (2003), who showed that Taiwan groups are important patentees, although the share of groups among the top twenty-five patentees was lower than it was in Korea. Taiwanese government institutes, such as Industrial Technology Research Institute (ITRI), and independent firms have been successful innovators, however, explaining this discrepancy. Nonetheless, 57 percent of the US patents granted to the top twenty-five assignees over 1970 to 99 went to group firms. This result is consistent with the argument that groups in emerging economies, including Taiwan, act as institutionalized entrepreneurs and are Schumpeterian agents for innovation and growth.

4.3. CONCLUSION

We discussed the evolution of strategy, structure, and performance of Taiwanese business groups in the past three decades. First, we found these groups became more diversified, especially after deregulation. This result contradicts existing theories of diversification, which suggest groups diversify to exploit institutional inefficiencies and market imperfection and become less diversified as the economy develops further. As noted by Khanna and Palepu (1999: 279), the intermediary capabilities of diversified groups 'are likely to become more, not less, valuable for exploiting new business opportunities in the economy' in the short run, even though diversification is unlikely to benefit these groups as new institutions emerge over the long run. Other studies

(Guillen 2000; Peng 2003) also recognize that large groups known for their political connections may be best positioned to tap into new opportunities opened up by deregulation, at least in the early stages of transition. Thus, our finding is consistent with institutional arguments about diversification.

Second, we found that Taiwanese groups have recently relied less on licensing and more on joint ventures and acquisitions. As the production costs in Taiwan rose after deregulation, Taiwan became less competitive in the global market for OEM licensing. In addition, Hobday (1995) notes that licensing has certain drawbacks. Taiwanese groups were often subordinate to the decisions of foreign licensors and depended on foreign companies for technology, components, and marketing channels. As Taiwanese groups became more technically sophisticated, they began to face the dual threat of being undersold by the emerging low-wage economies and being out-competed by their technology suppliers. Their success hence depended on the ability of groups not only to become innovative in capability but also to find cheaper sources of production. Consequently, Taiwanese groups began to rely more on joint ventures and acquisitions to access both innovative technologies from developed economies and low-cost production sites in Southeast Asia and China.

Third, as groups grew in size, scope, and international exposure, they needed to develop new control structures (Chandler 1990). We found that groups developed ways to handle the founding families' desire to retain ownership and management control. More ownership shares moved from the hands of family members to affiliated firms, creating multiple-layer pyramids of cross-shareholding. Founding families thus retain considerable voting power with limited amounts of capital. Families also created a two-tier management system, which delegated routine administration to general managers and held onto important decision-making power. These findings contradict the arguments of culturalists (Wong 1985; Redding 1990; Fukuyama 1995), who predicted that Taiwanese groups would not be able to grow due to their cultural recipes. Our evidence suggests that this argument precludes the possibility of cultural change and the innovative solutions devised by organizations to survive and evolve. Our study implies that a contingent view that gives more allowance for cultural permutation and organizational change will be more sensible.

Fourth, we did not find a clear pattern of change in profitability over time, but instead found that the variance of profitability increased between 1973 and 2002. This result suggests that factors at the individual group level, such as the alignment between strategy and structure, deserve more attention. However, neither Chandler's work nor the research that followed it (Rumelt 1974; Suzuki 1980; Hoskisson, Hill, and Kim 1993; Whittington and Mayer 2000) paid much attention to institutional transitions in emerging economies, which started to occur only in the late 1980s. Future research should examine how the combination of strategy and structure affects profitability in a transitional context (Chung, Mahmood, and Feng 2004).

Similarly, we found that the most innovative Taiwanese groups are relatively specialized in either electronics or computers. This result might indicate the complex trade-offs that business groups must make, especially in transitional economies; although such transitions make diversification more attractive in the short to medium run, rising competition and decreasing profit margins might force Taiwanese groups to become more focused in the long run in order to achieve dynamic competitive advantage through innovation. Also, as rising costs are forcing Taiwanese groups to move up the technology ladder, we expect them to continue pursuing more acquisitions and joint ventures and fewer licensing agreements.

Overall, we predict that Taiwanese groups will become less diversified and more innovative during the next ten to fifteen years. In line with this argument, groups will likely sell, close, or merge unprofitable units. Taiwanese groups might also use more joint ventures and alliances with each other to survive an increasingly competitive environment, resulting in more new establishments that are owned by multiple families and a transformation of family groups into 'groups of family' (Chung 2004). We also expect groups to rely less on family members to fill their top executive positions. Yet instead of recruiting professional managers from markets, groups are likely to promote long-term employees with proven loyalty and capability. The recent CEO succession of Acer, one of Taiwan's leading groups, is a case in point. Stan Shih, the founder and chairman of Acer, decided to hand over the executive power not to a family member but to one of Acer's long-term managers.

Finally, the fact that Taiwan came out of the Asian financial crisis relatively unscathed meant, unlike the chaebols in Korea or the groups in Indonesia, Taiwanese jituanqiye were spared the urgency for refocusing and professionalization along the line of Western model of corporate governance. Rather, significant changes in strategy and structure of Taiwanese groups that we observe have been driven primarily by the institutional transition that started in the late 1980s.

NOTES

1. As can be seen in Table 4.1, BGT did not collect data on the *exact* 100 largest groups. This discrepancy is due to various conditions for data collection in different periods. For 1986, some targeted groups refused to provide data, which resulted in a smaller sample.

2. Unlike most US data, there is no ready-to-use industry coding in the BGT directory. Also, the directory did not provide a digital format until 2000. We therefore examined the paper directory and manually assigned a SIC code to each member firm.
3. In counting overseas linkages, we ignored a small number of cases in which Taiwanese business groups established companies for third-party investments in places such as the Virgin Islands or the Cayman Islands. These cases amount to 3 percent of the 813 overseas linkages Taiwanese groups forged between 1981 and 1998.
4. We were not able to collect shareholder information before 1988 since the BGT did not report the percentage of shareholding until that time.
5. The percentage of government ownership is between 0.17 and 0.3 percent between 1988 and 1998. We hence cannot depict this component clearly in the bar chart.

5

Singaporean Business Groups: The Role of the State and Capital in Singapore Inc.

Lai Si Tsui-Auch

To analyze business groups in Singapore, one first needs to examine the government-linked corporations. Their creation and development reflects Singapore government's active role in the economy. Besides legislating all Singaporean firms, the government has founded corporations in which it owns a controlling share. These corporations are unusual hybrids of state and private enterprises. They compete with private firms, including multinational corporations, and sometimes with each other. They have generally been well managed and run like private businesses, with a focus on bottom-line performance (US Embassy in Singapore 2001; Singh and Ang 1998). In addition, they have not been used for social and employment purposes. Their performance is much debated, however, as some argue that it is comparable to their counterparts' in the private sector (Sun 2002), while others assert it is below that of their counterparts (Webb and Saywell 2002).

The ethnic Chinese enterprises enjoy much less economic power than the government-linked corporations. The aggregate contribution of their enterprises ranks third, behind that of multinational corporations and government-linked corporations (Chan and Ng 2001). Only few of them run large-scale businesses. They are concentrated primarily in banking and finance, real estate and property development, hotels and restaurants, and light manufacturing. Like their Chinese counterparts elsewhere in the region, they are largely family controlled (Gomez and Hsiao 2001).

On the surface, it appears that the Asian crisis caused an upheaval in Singaporean business practices. The government quickly restructured the financial sector and strengthened corporate laws and accountancy practices. It pressured both government-linked corporations and private banks to undertake economic globalization, divest their noncore assets, and professionalize their governance. Nevertheless, the business strategies and management structures of domestic enterprises in the state and private sectors also exhibit substantial stability.

In this chapter, I document the development and change in Singaporean business groups before and after the Asian crisis and outline these groups' future challenges. The chapter consists of five parts. In Section 5.1, I briefly summarize how I identify business groups. Section 5.2 presents the state–capital relations in multiethnic Singapore that have shaped the evolution of these groups. Section 5.3 describes the development of the groups' business strategy and management structures before the Asian currency crisis. Section 5.4 analyzes the extent of the changes in these groups after the crisis. I summarize changes and continuity in the business groups in Section 5.5 and consider these groups' future challenges in the Conclusion.

5.1. BUSINESS GROUPS IN SINGAPORE

In analyzing the Singaporean businesses, I focus on business groups. I avoid classifying single firms and conglomerates into a single category. It is important to compare the comparable, and hence I compare government-linked groups and ethnic Chinese business groups in the private sector. The existing databases (such as CBRD (Centre for Business Research and Development) and DP Info Network), however, show the rankings only for individual companies by total assets, net sales, and total equity; they do not rank business groups by these measures. Based on the ranking of total assets, I chose to analyze publicly listed enterprises. These enterprises publish annual reports that provide lists of subsidiaries and associated companies. For each sector (state versus private), I selected ten business groups (see Table 5.1).

According to the Singapore Ministry of Trade and Industry's Department of Statistics (2001), the government-linked corporations are entities in which a holding company wholly owned by the Singaporean government (through the Ministry of Finance, Inc.) has an equity interest of 20 percent or more. Temasek Holdings is the largest of these holding companies. It does not conduct trade or business but instead holds investments, thus deriving income from dividends, interest, and rentals. Its sole shareholder, the Ministry of Finance, Inc., can veto its decisions. Temasek Holdings owns more than 200 first-tier and second-tier subsidiaries that cover a wide spectrum of industries including transportation and logistics, ship repair and engineering, power and gas, telecommunications, media, financial services, manufacturing and properties (*Directory of Government-Linked Corporations 1994*, the most recent directory that has been released to public). As a private limited company, it is not required to publish detailed accounts, and hence data about its operations are scanty. Therefore, I study ten large publicly listed

Table 5.1. Basic data for selected business groups

Business Groups	Sectors G: GL P: private	Total Assets (S$ million)	Number of subsidiaries	Number of associated companies	Ranking of major companies by total assets in 1999*	% of total market capitalization as of Dec. 31 2002	Shareholdings by government/family (%)	Ownership by associated companies (%)
DBS Group Holdings	G	149,375	114	22	1	5.61	55.30	0
United Overseas Bank	P	107,469	121	20	2	6.43	26.05	0.35
Oversea-Chinese Banking Corp	P	84,051	117	18	3	4.32	20.09	15.64
Singapore Telecom	G	35,157	150	21	8	7.67	67.54	0
Hong Leong	P	18,770	99	40	9,14,27,100	1.16	CDL 13.73	CDL 0
City Developments Ltd. (CDL)						N.A.	HLA 66.94	HLA 0.41
Hong Leong Asia (HLA)						N.A.	HLF 30.77	HLF 0
Hong Leong Finance (HLF)						N.A.	TRL 47.38	TRL 0
Target Reality Ltd. (TRL)								
Singapore Airlines	G	18,580	23	29	7	4.31	56.86	0
Capital Land	G	16,326	529	63	–	0.97	62.94	0
Keppel Corporation	G	11,475	451	57	5	0.99	32.05	0
Neptune Orient Lines	G	8,110	151	46	12	0.38	32.60	0
Asia Food & Properties	P	6,280	176	19	11	N.A.	21.16	0
SembCorp Industries	G	6,037	199	92	15	0.50	50.90	0
Singapore Technologies Engineering	G	4,351	86	30	19	1.65	55.96	0
Wing Tai Asia	P	2,654	51	14	23	N.A.	42.42	0
SMRT Corporation	G	1,925	23	3	–	N.A.	62.89	0
Far East Organization	P	1,711	33	19	40,54	N.A.	OPHL 11.41	0
Orchard Parade Holdings Ltd. (OPHL)						0.41	YHS 45.53	
Yeo Hiap Seng Ltd. (YHS)								
G K Goh	P	512	21	10	28	N.A.	53.63	0
Lee Kim Tah Holdings	P	323	23	7	110	N.A.	52.85	0
SNP Corporation	G	257	41	4	164	N.A.	54.96	0
Tye Soon	P	95	15	3	206	N.A.	63.93	0
Khong Guan Flour Milling	P	35	4	3	234	N.A.	20.36	8.66

Sources: Annual reports (sectors, total assets, number of subsidiaries and associated companies, shareholdings by government/family and by associated companies); Business Research & Development and Faculty of Business Administration, NUS (the ranking of major companies of business groups); PULSES January 2003 (market capitalization).
Notes: G: government-linked corporation; P: Private corporation. Capital Land and SMRT Corporation are not ranked by total assets as Capital Land was formed only in 2000 through a merger of DBS Land and Pidemco, and SMRT Corporation was listed only in 2000.

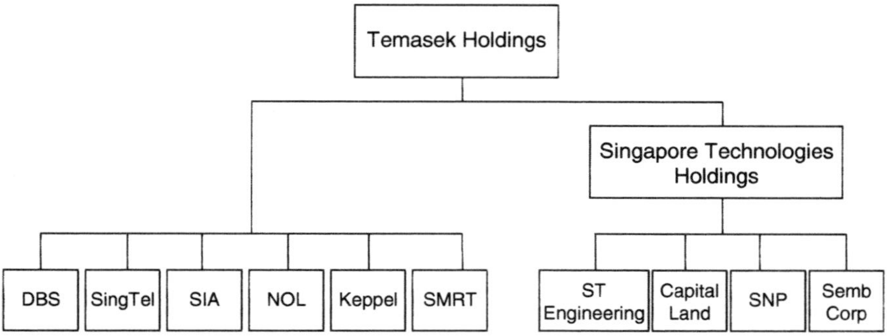

Figure 5.1. Relationships of selected companies and their group holdings

companies owned by the Temasek Group. Four are owned through Temasek's unlisted company, Singapore Technologies Holdings, which was founded in 1989 to manage the national defense-related entities (see Figure 5.1). The ten companies I selected for this study have each formed a group of associated companies and subsidiaries. Associated companies are entities in which the group generally has between 20 and 50 percent of the voting rights, and over which the group has significant influence, but does not control these companies' financial and operating policy decisions. A subsidiary is a company in which the group, directly or indirectly, holds more than half of the issued share capital, or controls more than half of the voting power, or controls the composition of the board of directors. The consolidated financial statements in the annual report incorporate the financial statements of the core company and its subsidiary companies only (excluding associated companies).

I do not select companies of the other three holdings for various reasons. Health Corporation of Singapore has equity holdings in seven government-linked hospitals only, according to the *Directory of Government-Linked Corporations* (1994). The Ministry of National Development Holding has mainly dormant company shares in government-linked corporations. The Government Investment Corporation has only three operations and ten offices worldwide, and most board members are unknown (US Embassy Report 2001).

My discussion of the private sector focuses on the ethnic Chinese family-controlled business groups. Family businesses are the most prevalent of indigenously owned enterprises. The ethnic Chinese business groups, like their counterparts elsewhere in the region, consist of independent firms that are loosely linked to a mother or core company, which often pursue unrelated diversification rather than vertical integration, and resemble a web structure rather than a unitary organization (Hamilton 1997). These groups have usually emerged from small, private companies that were founded by Chinese who emigrated from the maritime provinces of China (Guangdong and Fujian) or by their descendants. For this study, I identify well-known and widely reported business groups, six of which are comparable to the largest government-linked groups by total assets.

I obtained data for the business groups in the private sector from company annual reports, academic and media reports, oral history transcripts from the national archives, biographies of business owners, and personal interviews and informal conversations with business families and their employees. The data of the government-linked groups were sourced from company annual reports, academia and media reports, and personal conversations with their managers.

The general profiles of the selected business groups are presented in Table 5.1. These groups are arranged in descending order according to their total assets. Six out of the ten largest companies listed are government-linked. The top three (one government-linked and two ethnic Chinese) are banking groups. Twelve core companies—Development Bank of Singapore (DBS), United Overseas Bank (UOB), Overseas Chinese Banking Corporation (OCBC), Singapore Telecommunications (SingTel), City Development Ltd (CDL), Hong Leong Asia Ltd (HLA), Singapore International Airlines (SIA), Keppel, Neptune Orient Lives (NOL), Asia Food & Properties, SempCorp, and ST (Singapore Technologies) Engineering—of which seven are government-linked, are among the top twenty companies by total assets. Nine core companies—DBS, UOB, OCBC, SingTel, CDL, SIA, Capital Land, Keppel, and ST Engineering—of which six are government-linked, were among the top twenty Singapore Exchange's (SGX) mainland companies by market capitalization as of December 31, 2002, accounting for 33.11 percent of the SGX's total market capitalization. Of all these companies, SIA is the most well known internationally. It has been the 'only Asian company outside of Japan to make *Fortune*'s 50-company "All-Star" list' for the last three years. It has been voted, for the third straight year, 'the most admired company in Asia outside of Japan' in an annual poll of business executives conducted by *Fortune* magazine (*Straits Times*, February 25, 2004: A15).

In terms of ownership, the government owns substantial percentages in corporations linked to it (e.g. 32 percent of Keppel Corporation). As for the ten private business groups, two of them (Hong Leong and Far Eastern Organization) are represented by more than one core company. The controlling families own at least 20 percent of all the core companies listed here except CDL of Hong Leong and Orchard Parade Holdings Limited (OPHL) of Far East (mostly through subsidiaries of their respective groups). Only four of the fourteen core companies in the ten private groups have associated ownership. The only core company in which associated companies own more than 10 percent of the total shares is the OCBC.

Table 5.2 summarizes the identified groups' principal activities and levels of diversification. The government-linked groups compete directly with private business groups in all activities except food and beverages. They apparently monopolize activities in telecommunications and post as well as engineering. They also dominate activities in transportation, building, and construction. Three of the government-linked groups engage in four or more principal activities; two engage in three activities, and five engage in one to two activities. Among the private business groups, four engage in four or more activities, five engage in three activities, and only one is narrowly focused in one activity.

5.2. STATE–CAPITAL RELATIONS IN MULTIETHNIC SINGAPORE

To document the development and change of business groups in Singapore, it is important to analyze the state–capital relations in the multiethnic society, with a particular focus on the evolution of ethnic Chinese businesses (see Figure 5.2).

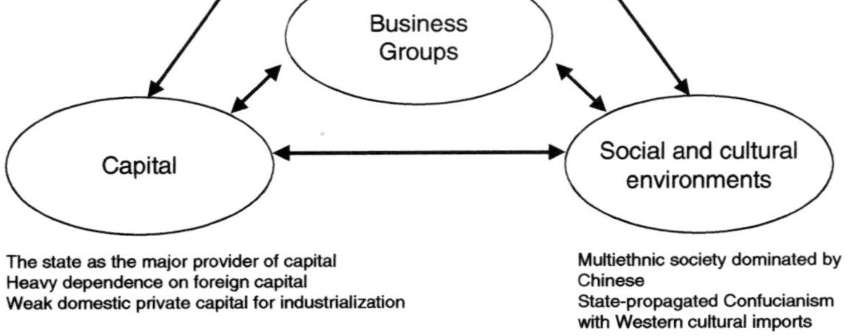

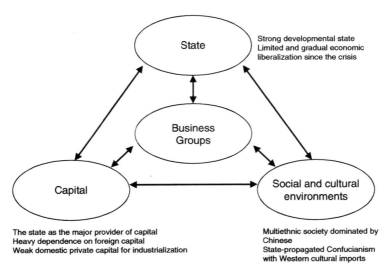

Figure 5.2. Singaporean institutional environments

Table 5.2. Principal activities of selected business groups

	Business Groups	Banking & Finance	Hotels & Restaurants	Investment & Stockbrokers	Property	Telecom & Post	Transportation	Retailing & Trading	Building & Construction	Engineering	Food & Beverage	Other*	Total no. of sectors involved
Government-linked	DBS Group Holdings	✓		✓									2
	Singapore Telecom					✓							1
	Singapore Airlines				✓		✓					✓	3
	Capital Land		✓		✓								2
	Keppel Corporation	✓			✓	✓			✓	✓			5
	Neptune Orient Lines						✓			✓			2
	SempCorp Industries			✓					✓	✓		✓	4
	Singapore Technologies Engineering					✓	✓		✓			✓	4
	SMRT Corporation						✓	✓		✓			3
	SNP Corporation			✓								✓	2
Private	United Overseas Bank	✓	✓		✓			✓				✓	5
	Oversea-Chinese Banking Corporation	✓	✓		✓								3
	Hong Leong	✓	✓		✓			✓					4
	Asia Food & Properties				✓						✓		3
	Wing Tai Asia		✓	✓	✓			✓			✓		5
	Far East Organization		✓	✓	✓						✓		4
	G K Goh Holdings			✓									1
	Lee Kim Tah Holdings			✓	✓				✓				3
	Tye Soon						✓	✓			✓		3
	Khong Guan Flour Milling			✓				✓			✓		3

Sources: Annual reports.

Notes: *SIA (insurance); SembCorp (utilities); ST Eng (machinery & equipment); SNP (printing & publishing); UOB (insurance); AFP (agri-business).

5.2.1. Ethnic Chinese Business till 1959

As early as the tenth century, the Southeast Asian region became the focus of multilateral trade that was dominated by Chinese and Indian traders (Brown 1994). From 1819, under British rule, the colonial government groomed Singapore to be a major import/export center that would absorb traders from China and British India and immigrants already settled in British Malaya. Most Chinese immigrants came from poor, rural families. Among those who came business or trading families, typically in treaty ports, some received Western education and adopted Christianity (Tsui-Auch 2004). In the latter half of the nineteenth and the early twentieth century, many migrated to urban areas in Singapore and became traders, subcontractors, or shopkeepers. When the British colonists departed, the Chinese entrepreneurs expanded their businesses and took over the dominant economic interests of Singapore, including the import/export trade (Chan and Chiang 1994). Over time, the successful Chinese became compradors to the European business firms. Some got together to establish banks to offer financial service to their fellow merchants, often on the basis of dialect group, and to help them send remittances to China (Lee 1990). These banks continue to be the largest ethnic Chinese businesses.

5.2.2. Developmental State-led Economic Development from 1959 onwards

Prior to the self-government of Singapore in 1959, the ethnic Chinese business community had become an important economic and political force. After the People's Action Party (PAP) came to power in 1959, however, it attempted to forge a multiethnic and multicultural society, de-emphasizing the 'Chineseness' of Singapore in response to the 'internal ethnic imperatives as well as the regional geographical compulsions' (Vasil 1995: 34). The ethnic Chinese business community came into conflict with the PAP and openly backed the opposition Socialist Front, which was sympathetic to the promotion of Chinese culture and education (Rodan 1989).

Following the separation of Singapore from Malaysia in 1963, the PAP government further alienated the ethnic Chinese business community by adopting a 'two-legged' policy that relied on multinational corporations and government-linked corporations for industrialization (Rodan 1989; Chan and Ng 2001). The government emphasized industrial development and steered the country away from its dependence on import/export trade. The Western-educated ruling elites were intellectuals, professionals, and labor leaders with socialist leanings who had few ties with ethnic Chinese capitalists. They were wary of the ethnic business community (Cotton 1995), regarding the Chinese traders as rentiers who did not engage in real production (Low, L. 2001a). Due to this distrust, the lack of indigenous capital for industrial development, and the small domestic economy, the state became dependent on foreign capital for economic development. Hence, it was not interested in assisting Chinese businesses in industrialization. Instead, it used tax incentives to entice multinational corporations to establish manufacturing operations and hire local personnel. Inspired by the Japanese keiretsu, and Korean chaebols, it created large government-linked corporate groups and statutory boards both for national security objectives and to spearhead development in other sectors such as finance, air travel, and telecommunications (Tsui-Auch and Lee 2003). The ethnic Chinese businesses had to compete with the government-linked corporations in many sectors (Rodan 1989; Low, L. 2000b).

Although the state was generally not attentive to the interests of Chinese firms, it did pay some heed to the family-controlled Chinese banks because these enterprises facilitated the import/export trade and their owners had close working and personal relationships with political leaders (Hamilton-Hart 2000; Low, L. 2000a). Several former and current ministers and top civil servants have served as chairmen and directors in local banks (Loh, Goh, and Tan 2000; *Straits Times*, July 7, 2002; Yeung 2003).

In contrast to many other countries, the state's intervention in the banking sector was particularly strong. The Monetary Authority of Singapore (MAS), the de facto central bank of the country, did not enjoy the substantial autonomy afforded to central banks in many Organisation for Economic Cooperation and Development (OECD) economies. The President of Singapore appoints its senior management. The Banking Act of 1970 stipulated that banks and insurance companies have to seek MAS' approval when they appointed their chief executive officers (CEOs), directors, and principal officers (Mak and Li 1999). This is illustrated by Wee Ee Cheong, Deputy Chairperson of the United Overseas Bank: 'A few years ago, the major shareholder of a small bank proposed to appoint two of his family members as Directors but this was rejected by the Authority [MAS] ...' (quoted in Tee 1995: 177).

5.2.3. State-engineered Sociocultural Continuity Amid Change

The state's commitment to economic growth and multiethnicity after independence led to the severing of ties with religions that might interfere with capitalist economic development and nation building (Tamney 1995). As in other rapidly modernizing, export-oriented economies, such as Taiwan and Hong Kong, Singapore emphasized Western education over classical or religious doctrines. The English-educated ruling elite designated English as the sole language of instruction in 1983 in light of the difficulties in achieving bilingualism (Borthwick 1988). The English-educated Chinese became embracing individuals with diverse cultural values and a high exposure to Western technology and management models.

Being alarmed at the persuasive influence of Western culture and rapid sociocultural change, the state sought to counteract it by initiating public campaigns. In 1979, it embarked on a language and cultural campaign that was aimed to foster Chinese to identify themselves with their cultural heritage and values. In 1984, the government attempted to revive religious commitment through a Religious Knowledge Program (in which Confucianism was a focus for the Chinese) but recognized it as ineffective and finally abandoned it. Yet, the metaphor of the family has remained in use as the means by which to mobilize the citizens to support the state imperative for economic development and to rally the multiethnic population to maintain social and political order in a disordered region (Tsui-Auch 2004). In fact, how the business groups have been run reflect much influence of the family values.

5.3. SINGAPOREAN BUSINESS GROUPS: EVOLUTION AND DEVELOPMENT

5.3.1. Government-linked Corporations and their Groups of Subsidiaries and Associated Companies

Although government-linked corporations are clearly vital to Singapore's economy, there is no precise measure of their centrality. The number of these firms increased from 361 in 1985 to 720 in 1994 (Low 1995; *Directory of Government-Linked Corporations* 1994). As reported in *Straits Times* on June 25, 1999, Temasek's listed companies amounted to S$88.2 billion or 25 percent of the SGX's total market capitalization. Along with its own share of S$46.5 billion, or 13.2 percent of SGX's market capitalization, Temasek commanded S$134.7 billion or 38.2 percent of the SGX as of May 1999 (Low 2002). The Ministry of Finance (1993) estimated that the public sector and government-linked corporations accounted for 60 percent of Singapore's gross domestic product (GDP). However, the Ministry of Trade and Industry's

Department of Statistics (2001) estimated that government-linked corporations contributed only 12.9 percent of GDP in 1998, and that the nongovernment-linked corporations (such as the statutory boards) accounted for another 8.9 percent, for a total public sector share of 21.8 percent. This estimate is low relative to the contribution of multinational corporations, (i.e. 42 percent) (Low, L. 2001b). Nevertheless, this latter estimate includes only government-linked corporations in which the government holds equity of at least 20 percent.

Temasek Holdings was founded in 1974 as a limited-investment holding company to manage the state's investments in government-linked corporations. It owns stakes in 'most of the country's biggest companies, including SIA, SingTel, and DBS Group Holdings' (*Streats,* February 13, 2004: 14). For sectoral or national security reasons, the Ministry of Finance holds special shares in some of these corporations, including SIA, SingTel, and ST Engineering. There are also cross-holdings between government-linked corporations, as in the case of the DBS group. Temasek Holdings owned 12.64 percent and the Ministry of National Development (MND) Holdings owned 13.89 percent of its shares in 2002.

The government-linked corporations and their groups of subsidiaries and associated companies prompted industrialization and economic development in Singapore. Temasek Holdings' role has combined economic and political concerns. In its first-tier corporations, it has not only proposed broad strategies but also preferred to appoint former politicians, civil servants, and high-ranking military officials to positions as chairmen, directors, and senior management (Low, L. 2001b). Nevertheless, it has appraised and compensated these individuals using the standards of the private sector.

Although government-linked corporations have catalyzed Singapore's economic success, critics have asserted that (*a*) these corporations tend to be risk-averse; (*b*) they receive special privileges because of their links to the government; (*c*) they use capital less efficiently than private firms do; (*d*) they have crowded out private investment and usurped entrepreneurial activity; and (*e*) their unrelated diversification makes them 'jacks of all trades, but masters of none' (summarized in the US Embassy of Singapore Report 2001; Webb and Saywell 2002; Worthington 2003). In particular, several of these groups have taken stakes in everything from video-game design to French-style bistros (US Embassy of Singapore Report, 2001). The government began pushing these groups to diversify their noncore holdings only after it became clear that highly diversified business groups provided less potential to long-term shareholder value than did the less diversified groups.

5.3.2. Ethnic Chinese Business Groups

Ethnic Chinese businesses duplicate the structure of the traditional Chinese family. The patriarch of the family is the head of the enterprise. He has unquestioned authority and runs the business with a small inner circle of family members and friends. Although he originally centralizes management in his own hands in the founding years, he often decentralizes it over time by assigning sons to different branches or business lines and forming business groups (Hamilton 1997; Wong 1985). In addition, companies within a group are interlocked in complex formal and informal relationships, including cross-holdings and interlocking directorates, and conduct intragroup trade, capital, technology, and personnel transfers (Loh, Goh, and Tan 2000).

Typically, the sons inherit the business. To maintain control and avoid disclosing financial information about the company, family members are not supposed to sell their shares to outsiders. When they need to raise outside equity, the founding family seeks to control the public-listed companies through an associated bank, financial company, or holding company (Fukuyama 1995). The layers of ownership obscure the family's control of the company. Because they lacked assistance from their government and faced anti-Chinese movements in Southeast Asian countries, these families wished to reduce risks. Geographically, they extended their businesses beyond Singapore to other countries in the region. They also diversified from trading to manufacturing, finance and insurance, hotels and restaurants, and/or property development (see Table 5.2). Nevertheless, some of these groups adapted to the state's industrialization policy because Singapore was economically and politically stable. Hence, some ethnic Chinese traders supported state-led economic change and industrialization (Tsui-Auch, 2005).

To finance their expansion, business groups began listing some of their companies on the SGX in the late 1960s. To meet the reporting and auditing requirements, business groups realized they needed to recruit outside managers with relevant professional training to handle auditing, reporting, and personnel management. Hiring such individuals also gave these groups legitimacy with a variety of domestic and international constituencies (Tsui-Auch 2004). Moreover, these business groups expanded faster than the supply of family members willing to manage the groups' enterprises did.

Nevertheless, the business families maintained family control through direct and indirect ownership, occupying top management positions, and grooming sons to succeed the founding patriarchs. This strategy of maintaining family control and corporate rule over generations while co-opting outside management talent resembles that of government-linked corporations.

Government-linked corporations also recruited outside management talent, but maintained corporate control and rule in the hands of the closely-knit political elite.

5.4. BUSINESS GROUPS AFTER THE ASIAN CRISIS

The Asian crisis affected Singapore, but less than it did other countries in the region. It hit the property sector and the banks especially hard, as many groups in these industries were involved in extensive regional networks. Business groups in Singapore were negatively affected by the devastated property sector, economic slowdown, and the political and economic changes in Southeast Asian countries, as many of them were involved in webs of regional networks. Although Singapore's growth rate returned to 10 percent in 2000, it has fluctuated since then (e.g. −2.5 percent in 2001 and 2.2 percent in 2002) because of the regional and global economic slowdown.

5.4.1. Policy Changes in the Singaporean State

Because of the ruling party's political dominance and popularity, the government forged a consensus for its financial and economic policies within the close-knit elite circle and enforced these policies in three respects. First, it urged domestic firms to undertake global rather than regional business strategies, thus moving beyond the crisis-ridden Southeast Asian region to China, the USA, and Europe for overseas investment (Yeung 2000). Second, it began to deregulate the telecommunications and financial sectors, and promised to liberalize electricity generation and retailing soon. Of particular importance is its liberalization of the financial sector, in which both government-linked and private business groups dominate. It removed the 40 percent foreign shareholding limit for local banks to allow foreign banks to compete freely with local banks (Low, L. 2001a) and announced plans to issue six full bank licenses to foreign banks. Third, to reduce the risk of a bubble economy built on speculation, and to avoid a bank-induced crisis, MAS began monitoring banks' performance, and demanded that banks divest nonfinancial activities by July 17, 2004 (*Streats*, July 4, 2003: 14). To discourage families' rule over local banks, the MAS required the banks to establish 'nominating committees' for board and top management positions and to obtain its approval for their personnel selection.

Finally, in light of the keiretsu and chaebols' debacles, as well as the growth (in both employment and economy) generated by small and medium-sized entrepreneurial firms in the USA, the Singaporean government attempted to divest the noncore assets of government-linked groups (Low, L. 2000b, 2001b, 2002). By so doing, it hoped to help these groups raise funds for further foreign acquisitions and create new investment opportunities for the domestic private sector (US Embassy Report 2001).

5.4.2. Change and Continuity in the Government-linked Groups

According to the Temasek Charter put forth in July 2002, the government would divest its holdings in government-linked corporations if these businesses were 'no longer strategic to Singapore or when viable market alternatives or regulatory frameworks are in place'. For example, Keppel Group, a huge conglomerate of 600 companies across many sectors, streamlined its businesses after it suffered a sizeable loss in 1998 (its first since the 1985 recession). It has closed down unrelated companies, enforced mergers of nine companies, and reduced cross-shareholding (*Business Times*, November 6, 1998). It now has 508 companies, including subsidiaries and associated firms (see Table 5.1). Although the overall policy is to divest noncore assets, the process has been gradual. For instance, the DBS group sold its stake in equity investments and some properties, notably the DBS Land. Nevertheless, the DBS Land was acquired by Pidemco, a Singapore Technologies group subsidiary and has since been renamed as Capital Land (US Embassy Report 2001).

In line with the government's policy to go global after the currency crisis, government-linked groups prompted the pace of foreign acquisitions and shareholding beyond Southeast Asia (see Table 5.3). Two groups (Capital Land and SingTel) have bought some foreign companies, and the other four have acquired only one or two ventures outside the region. These groups' status as 'government-linked' nature might hinder them from investing more aggressively, as other countries in the region have resisted the groups' attempts to acquire domestic firms. For instance, SingTel's failure to acquire Cable & Wireless of Hong Kong Telecom was attributed primarily to the People's Republic of China's (PRC) reluctance to permit a Singaporean government-owned entity to control their telecom assets (see Jayasankaran 2001; Mauzy and Milne 2002).

The state had attempted to reduce its role in government-linked corporations before the crisis began. The results of this effort have been mixed. On the one hand, out of the six companies for which ownership data is available,

Table 5.3. Government-linked groups' foreign ventures beyond Southeast Asia

GL Groups	Number of foreign ventures beyond Southeast Asia	Number of economy/(ies) in						No. of foreign ventures with shareholdings ≥ 50% held by the group
		East Asia	South Asia	Australia	Africa	Europe	America	
DBS Holdings	1					1		1
Singtel	7	3	2		1	1		2
NOL	2						2	2
SNP	2	2						0
SingTech	1						1	1
Capital Land	18	3		12		3		4

Sources: Annual reports.

the government's stake actually increased in three of the business groups between 1996 and 2002, decreased insignificantly in two, and significantly in only one (see Table 5.4). On the other hand, these groups have seen an infusion of professional managers into senior management positions. As the government-linked corporations are increasingly commercially driven and involved in joint ventures with private firms, they have increased their hiring of personnel from the private sector (see Table 5.5). Between 1996 and 2002, there was a decrease in personnel drawn from other government-linked corporations (from ten out of seventeen to six out of nineteen) and a significant increase of personnel drawn from the private sector (from one out of twenty-one in 1996 to seven out of nineteen positions) for the positions of chairpersons, CEOs, and managing directors in the ten corporations. For example in the DBS a former JP Morgan banker, John Olds, was recruited to be the CEO. He is believed to have led the DBS to make stunning profits and recover from the crisis, but he departed after serving only 3 years (*Straits Times*, December 19, 2000). In general, the pace of change in corporate rule remains gradual. In fact, twelve out of nineteen positions remained in the hands of the state sector in 1992 (see Table 5.5).

5.4.3. Change and Continuity in the Ethnic Chinese Business Groups

The ethnic Chinese business groups have also exhibited both stability and change since the Asian crisis. Despite yielding a better performance than the DBS in general, the overcapitalized UOB group and OCBC group have to untangle cross-shareholdings with affiliated nonbanking companies by July

Business groups	Shareholdings by group holdings (%) A		Shareholdings by subsidiaries (%) B		Shareholdings by associated companies (%) C		Shareholdings by other GLCs/group holdings (%) D		Change in government's stake (%) A+B+C+D
	1996	2002	1996	2002	1996	2002	1996	2002	
DBS Group Holdings	19.61	12.64	11.67	28.77	3.96	0.00	21.64	13.89	−1.58
Singapore Telecom	N.A.[a]	67.54	N.A.	0.00	N.A.	0.00	N.A.	0.00	N.A
Singapore Airlines	54.33	56.86	0.00	0.00	0.00	0.00	0.00	0.00	+2.53
Capital Land	N.A.	60.60	N.A.	0.00	N.A.	0.00	N.A.	2.34[b]	N.A
Keppel Corporation	31.21	32.05	0.00	0.00	0.00	0.00	0.00	0.00	+0.84
Neptune Orient Lines	33.35	32.60	0.00	0.00	0.00	0.00	0.00	0.00	−0.75
SembCorp Industries	N.A.	39.06	N.A.	0.00	N.A.	0.00	N.A.	11.84	N.A
Singapore Technologies Engineering	66.78 (1997)	55.45	0.00	0.00	0.00	0.00	0.75[c]	0.51[d]	−11.57
SMRT Corporation	N.A.	62.29	N.A.	0.60	N.A.	0.00	N.A.	0.00	N.A
SNP Corporation	49.00[e]	54.94	0.00	0.00	0.00	0.00	0.00	0.02[f]	+5.96

Sources: Annual reports.

Notes:

[a] Reasons for the unavailability of the 1996 information for the following GLCs:

Singapore Telecom: the list of the top 20 shareholders first appeared in the 2002 Annual Report but not in reports of preceding years.

Capital Land: formed only in 2000 through a merger of DBS Land and Pidemco.

SembCorp Industries: listed only in 1998.

SMRT Corporation: listed only in 2000.

[b] Deemed interest (indirect shareholdings) of Temasek Holdings Private Limited through Singapore Technologies Pte Ltd. (Under Section 7 of the Companies Act of Singapore, Temasek Holdings is, in general, considered to have deemed interest in a listed company if any of Temasek's subsidiaries or associates (as defined in that section) have any voting shares in that listed company.)

[c] Deemed interest of Temasek Holdings Private Limited (but information about through which company is not revealed in the annual report).

[d] Deemed interest of Temasek Holdings Private Limited through Singapore Telecommunications Group of Companies, Keppel Group of Companies and DBS Group of Companies

[e] In 2000, the Singapore Technologies Holdings acquired a 49 percent stake in the company from Temasek Holdings. Later in the year, it merged with Pan Pacific Public Co Ltd, a SGX Sesdaq-listed company.

[f] Deemed interest of Temasek Holdings Private Limited (but information about through which company is not revealed in the annual report).

Table 5.5. Professional backgrounds of chairpersons, CEOs and managing directors, 1996 and 2002

	Number of chairman, CEO and MD	
	1996	2002
GLCs	10	6
Statutory Boards	2	1
Civil Service	1	0
Multiple Government Sector	0	1
Military	1	1
MPs and Ministers	2	3
Private Sector	1	7
Total	17	19

Sources: Annual reports and media reports.

17, 2004, in line with government mandates (*Streats*, July 4, 2003: 14). For example, the OCBC group, which has the largest pool of noncore assets among the three largest banks, has unwound a large portion of its cross-shareholding with Fraser and Neave (a beverage, property, and publishing giant). Nonetheless, like the government-linked groups, the ethnic Chinese groups have made only limited forays outside Southeast Asia. The Hong Leong Group is the only group that has actively acquired foreign ventures. Two others (Asia Food and Properties Group and Wing Tai Holdings) have made limited acquisitions beyond Southeast Asia (see Table 5.6).

Between 1996 and 2002, family ownership decreased in seven groups, increased in one, and remained unchanged in one (see Table 5.7). As for the Hong Leong Group, family ownership has reduced only in one out of the four listed companies (Table 5.7). In general, these families are reluctant to cede control to outsiders. The infusion of professional managers into the ethnic Chinese groups has not always proceeded smoothly. At OCBC, the elderly board directors who voted with the founding family stepped down in 2000. Since then, more than 110 senior managers have been recruited from all over the world to manage the bank (*Far Eastern Economic Review*, 2001). OCBC also hired Alex Au, a former Hong Kong banker, as CEO in 1999. Yet Au appeared to lack the board of directors' support on strategic issues (*Dow Jones International News*, March 27, 2002) and resigned abruptly in April 2002. Several banking analysts suspected that Au resigned because Lee Seng Wee (the Chairperson and the largest shareholder) took a hands-on approach in strategic issues (*Dow Jones International News*, March 27, 2002; *Straits Times*, August 31, 2001).

Table 5.6. Ethnic Chinese business groups' foreign ventures beyond Southeast Asia

Business groups	Number of foreign ventures beyond S.E. Asia	Number of economy/(ies) in						No. of foreign ventures with shareholdings ≥ 50% held by the Group
		East Asia	South Asia	Australia	Africa	Europe	America	
Asia Food & Properties	1				1			0
Wing Tai	2	2						0
Hong Leong	23	8			1	5	9	9

Sources: Annual reports.

More generally, few business groups have hired outsiders to their most senior positions (see Table 5.8). Family members are the chairpersons in all the corporations, except Khong Guan Flour Milling. In this case, however, members of the controlling family hold the position of the CEO and several other senior management posts. In another case, the Ng family of the Far Eastern Organization employed two outside professionals to assume the position of CEO to ensure a smooth transition after acquiring the Yeo Hiap Seng Co. from the Yeo clan. Nevertheless, its second-generation heir, Philip Ng, took over the position since June 2002. Members of founding families assert that outsiders are more short-term oriented, while the family has a long-term commitment to the business group. Further, they contend that close family ties facilitate fast decision making, especially during corporate crises, because there is more trust among family members. Kwek Hong Png, who took over the Hong Leong Group from his father, argues:

> I have seen both the old man's style and Western-style management. The latter is bogged down by many tiers of the decision-making process. Consequently, you lose speed and as a result you also lose the deal. For example, it took us just 48 hours to tender for Grand Hyatt Taipei. You can say that I have incorporated in my management style and business approach the best of both worlds (*Asiamoney*, November, 1994: 47).

One point to note is that the local banking groups (both government-linked and private), which have long been protected by MAS, began to confront global competition on their home turf (Yeung 2000). The state set the example by merging the DBS and the state-owned Post Office of Singapore Bank (POSB). The DBS would then be able to tap into deposit-rich POSB and position itself to be a dominant force in the regional banking industry (*Straits Times*, July 25, 1998). The other large family-controlled banks swiftly modeled after DBS, engaging in merger and acquisition (M&A) to achieve economies of

Table 5.7. Ownership of major companies of ethnic Chinese business groups, 1996 and 2002

Business groups/major listed companies	Family ownership (%)		Shareholdings by associated companies (%)		Change in group ownership (%)
	1996	2002	1996	2002	
UNITED OVERSEAS BANK					
United Overseas Bank Limited	30.85	26.05	0	0.35	−4.45
OVERSEA-CHINESE BANKING CORPORATION					
OCBC Limited	28.18	20.09	1.87	15.64	+5.68
HONG LEONG					
City Developments Limited	17.27	13.73	0	0	+3.54
Hong Leong Asia Limited	51.80	66.94	0.46	0.41	+15.09
Hong Leong Finance Limited	69.44	30.77	0	0	−38.67
Target Realty Limited	17.40	47.38	0	0	+29.98
ASIA FOOD & PROPERTIES					
Asia Food & Properties Limited	72.01[1]	21.16	0	0	−50.85
WING TAI ASIA					
Wing Tai Holdings Limited	44.71	42.42	0	0	−2.29
FAR EAST ORGANISATION					
Orchard Parade Holdings Limited	11.83	11.41	0	0	−0.42
Yeo Hiap Seng Limited	50.39	45.53	0	0	−4.86
G K GOH					
G K Goh Holdings Limited	55.38	53.63	0	0	−1.75
LEE KIM TAH HOLDINGS					
Lee Kim Tah Holdings Limited	70.93	52.85	0	0	−18.08
TYE SOON					
Tye Soon Limited	64.94	63.93	0	0	−1.01
KHONG GUAN FLOUR MILLING[2]					
Khong Guan Flour Milling Limited	20.36	20.36	8.66	8.66	0.00

Note: Information is obtained from 1997 Annual Report as Asia Food & Properties Ltd is not listed in 1996.

scale for further growth and expansion. The OCBC acquired Keppel-TatLee Bank (previously owned by the government-linked Keppel Group; see *Straits Times*, February 26, 2002) and UOB made a friendly takeover of the Overseas Union Bank (OUB). After the M & A, the DBS was estimated to climb to twenty-third position among Asian banks in terms of total assets, with the UOB in the thirty-second position, and the OCBC in the forty-third position (*Straits Times*, July 7, 2002). Lee Hsien Loong signaled that Singapore's small domestic banking market should accommodate only two local banks, and one of which is, according to observers, beyond doubt the government-linked DBS (*Straits Times*, May 17, 1999; May 18, 1999; July 7, 2002). Although

Table 5.8. Relationships of chairmen, CEOs and managing directors to the controlling families of ethnic Chinese business groups, 1996 and 2002

Business groups (major listed companies)	Chairman		CEO/MD	
	1996	2002	1996	2002
UNITED OVERSEAS BANK				
UOB Limited	F	F	F	F
OVERSEA-CHINESE BANKING CORPORATION				
OCBC Limited	F	F	F	N
HONG LEONG				
City Developments Limited	F	F	F	F
Hong Leong Asia Limited	F	F	N	N
Hong Leong Finance Limited	F	F	F	F
Target Realty Limited	F	F	F	F
ASIA FOOD & PROPERTIES				
Asia Food & Properties Limited	F	F	F[1]	F
WING TAI ASIA				
Wing Tai Holdings Limited	F	F	F	F
FAR EAST ORGANISATION				
Orchard Parade Holdings Limited	F	F	N	N
Yeo Hiap Seng Limited	F	F	N	F
G K GOH				
G K Goh Holdings Limited	F	F	F	F
LEE KIM TAH HOLDINGS				
Lee Kim Tah Holdings Limited	F	F	F	F
TYE SOON				
Tye Soon Limited	F	F	F	F
KHONG GUAN FLOUR MILLING				
Khong Guan Flour Milling Limited	F	N	F	F

foreign banks may be interested in acquiring local banks, Lee announced that 'Singapore banks must still be controlled by Singaporeans' (*Straits Times*, July 3, 2002).

5.5. CONCLUSION

Although the Asian crisis did not affect Singapore as much as it did many other countries in the region, it nonetheless prompted the government to urge public and private business groups to divest lines of business, expand their presence beyond the region, and adopt professional management. Some business groups have followed such advice, but change has been very gradual.

This gradualist response to government advocacy should not, however, be surprising, as it reflects the embeddedness of firms within their sociocultural environment. Indeed, wholesale change by business groups, especially in the face of past success, would be more unlikely than the actual response has been.

In many ways, business groups in the state and private sectors share much in common. They expanded and diversified tremendously and adopted professional management before the Asian Crisis. Although different factions held corporate rule in government-linked and private business groups, neither faction ceded control to outsiders. Indeed, consistent with the comparative institutional perspective outlined in Chapter 1, the primary differences between public and private groups are attributable to the distinct constraints each faces. Yet at the same time, the resistance to change within each type of group makes the results of such change different from what they would otherwise be.

The increased hiring of outsiders into senior management positions indicates that government-linked business groups are subject to normative pressures that advocate professional managers. Nonetheless, trusted insiders still remain prominent in government-linked business groups. Further, fundamental belief that government-linked corporations are instruments for nation building and safeguards of national security is likely to inhibit their full divestment (Webb and Saywell 2002). This belief is reinforced and reproduced by the continued recruitment of ex-civil servants and military officials into senior management positions. These personnel are likely to resist divestment and greater competition from the private sector (US Embassy Report 2001; Saywell and Plott 2002). Further, the government has relative autonomy to ignore market pressures to divest its equity in these corporations.

In contrast, private business groups (banks, to a lesser extent) are freer to disregard government pressure to hire outsiders into top management positions; this freedom is demonstrated by continued prevalence of founding family members in these positions. At the same time, private business groups are somewhat more attentive to market pressures, and most of them have—albeit gradually—reduced family ownership. Moreover, to the extent that outside ownership increases in these business groups, it is less likely that they can claim that a line of businesses is essential and hence should not be sold.

Although the forces that ensure continuity in the midst of pressure for change are sizable, it bears emphasizing that my account of continuity is not functionalist. Indeed, these forces significantly constrain the growth and perhaps the long-term viability of Singapore's business groups. For instance, the status of many firms as government-linked reinforces persistent distrust in these corporations, hindering them from seizing full investment opportunities in the rapidly changing world economy. Further, the pressure within these groups to view all businesses as 'essential' might keep the government from raising funds by selling firms. Similarly, the ethnic Chinese business groups are challenged to take advantage of economic globalization. Like their government-linked counterparts, these groups have had trouble retaining outside talent. To expand, these groups will need fresh perspectives and resources beyond those offered by trusted insiders, regional network ties, and traditional business activities.

Essentially, both the government-linked groups and private business groups have been embedded in norms of trusting insiders and cultural preferences for control that are fundamental to the local institutional environment. Actions in tune with such norms might have enhanced not only legitimacy but also efficiency in past operations, as close, personal connections make for good collaboration (Biggart 1991), and tight control forges integration and economical use of resources (Mauzy and Milne 2002). With increasing integration into the world economy and generational changes in leadership, however, business groups will have few alternatives but to loosen their group/family control, although they will do so only slowly and with great internal resistance.

Part II

Emerging Market Countries

6

Malaysian Business Groups: The State and Capital Development in the Post-Currency Crisis Period

Edmund Terence Gomez

To study the development of corporate Malaysia, it is necessary to analyze how the Malaysian state has influenced its economy, especially in regard to the development of large firms. In particular, the state's control of the financial sector has helped it promote both the rise of big business groups and encourage more generally the development of domestic enterprises.[1] This pattern of enterprise development has been strongly influenced by East Asian corporate models, specifically the Korean chaebol and the Japanese keiretsu. The Malaysian government has used these models as templates because of its desire to promote the development of large, international conglomerates.

Applying the institutional framework adopted for this study (see Figure 6.1), this chapter indicates how, in response to the need to achieve equity in wealth distribution among the main ethnic communities in Malaysia, the state promoted the rise of ethnic Malay-owned business groups. In the late 1960s, among the three main ethnic groups—the Malays, the Chinese, and the Indians—the Chinese were the predominant domestic economic force, owning 22.8 percent of total corporate equity in the country; the Malays owned a mere 1.5 percent, and the Indians 0.9 percent. Foreign firms, then the largest owners of corporate equity in the Malaysian economy, owned 62.1 percent of share capital in private firms operating in the country. However, Chinese business ubiquity became the justification for the government's concerted attempt to redistribute wealth to achieve economic parity among the ethnic communities. In effect, this meant positive discrimination in favor of the Malays, implemented through the New Economic Policy (NEP) between 1971 and 1990.

The NEP entailed partial abandonment of laissez-faire economic management in favor of greater state intervention through public enterprises. This

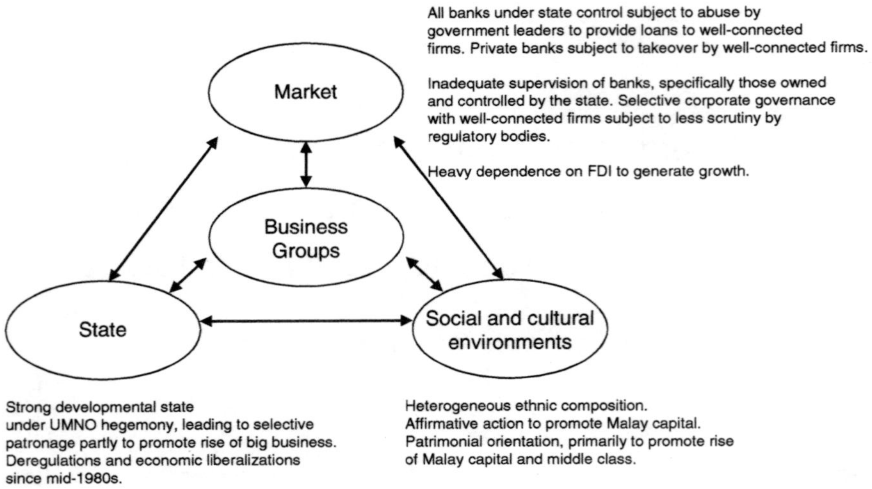

Figure 6.1. Malaysian institutional environments

intervention involved ethnic affirmative action, including the accelerated expansion of the Malay middle class and capital accumulation on behalf of the Malays. From the mid-1980s, the government began to selectively promote the interests of individual, usually well-connected, Malay businessmen, as a means to create a pool of new private capitalists. Politicians in power would selectively distribute state-created concessions, or rents, in the form of licenses, contracts, and privatized projects. Funds to acquire these rents were secured through favorable loans from banks owned or controlled by the state. Through this tripartite link between the state, private capital, and financial institutions, by the early 1990s a new group of well-connected business conglomerates had emerged in Malaysia.

Sustained government patronage has led, however, to large businesses depending on the state for support. Thus, despite phenomenal state support for big business, corporate Malaysia does not have dynamic, self-sustaining entrepreneurship, a point made obvious following the 1997 currency crisis.

Section 6.1 provides a brief history of corporate Malaysia, with a dual focus on the development of large business groups and of the role of the state in developing domestic enterprises and influencing ownership and control patterns. The Section 6.2 traces the impact of the currency crisis on corporate Malaysia. Section 6.3 reviews state policies introduced to deal with the crisis as well as their outcome, especially on property rights. The Conclusion discusses corporate Malaysia's future.

6.1. THE STATE, EQUITY DISTRIBUTION, AND ENTERPRISE DEVELOPMENT

Business groups have long been a part of corporate Malaysia. In the colonial and immediate postcolonial periods, foreign enterprises, especially British concerns, dominated the economy. Chinese capital was widespread, but the amount of it was small relative to the amount of foreign capital. By the 1970s, control of the economy was concentrated primarily in a few large British and Chinese corporations. Of the 100,000 shareholders in sixty-two large corporations, 797 owned 69 percent of the total RM1.4 billion of equity in these firms. The top 1 percent of these 797 shareholders owned 29 percent of this RM1.4 billion equity, while the top 50 percent owned 97 percent and the bottom 20 percent only 0.4 percent (Lim 1981: 114).

When the NEP was introduced in 1970, its stated objective was to achieve national unity by eradicating poverty, irrespective of race, and restructuring society so as to achieve interethnic economic parity between the predominantly Malay *bumiputera* 'sons of the soil' and the predominantly Chinese non-bumiputera.[2] The NEP goal was to be attained by increasing bumiputera corporate equity ownership to 30 percent and by reducing the poverty level to 15 percent by 1990. The measures used to achieve these goals included: (*a*) improving poor citizens' access to training, capital, and land; (*b*) changing the education and employment patterns among bumiputeras through ethnic quotas favoring their entry into tertiary institutions; (*c*) requiring companies to restructure their corporate holdings to ensure at least 30 percent Bumiputera ownership; and (*d*) by allotting publicly-listed shares at par value or with only nominal premiums to Bumiputeras.

Although the NEP sought to reduce ethnic inequality in wealth, income, and employment, the government declared that no particular group would experience loss or feel any sense of deprivation due to the policy. According to the government, 'restructuring' was to be achieved primarily through economic growth. Asset redistribution was to be undertaken through various forms: taxation, funding public enterprises, and the banking system, which would provide Bumiputeras with preferential credit access and funding for the acquisition of corporate equities.

These programs soon aroused non-Bumiputera dissatisfaction with the NEP, and such fears were exacerbated when public enterprises moved into sectors in which the Chinese had been prominent, particularly banking, property, and construction. The Urban Development Authority (UDA), established in 1971, ventured into construction and property development. By

1976, two Chinese-controlled banks, Malayan Banking and the United Malayan Banking Corporation (UMBC), had fallen under state control following runs on them. During the next decade, several other financial institutions established by the Chinese, along with one Indian-controlled bank, were taken over by the state or Bumiputeras (see Gomez and Jomo 1999: 60–6). The management of several of these banks was investigated by the authorities for alleged malpractices or violation of banking regulations, which contributed to their eventual takeover by the government before they were divested to state agencies or select Bumiputeras.

State control of these banking institutions facilitated the transfer of funds to well-connected businessmen, usually justified as positive discrimination in favor of Bumiputeras. Inevitably, NEP implementation fostered the emergence both of a large Bumiputera middle class and a well-connected Malay business elite, which owned large enterprises. Small and medium-sized firms were not neglected, but this elite had received the lion's share of state resources through the distribution of government concessions, including the privatization of government enterprises.

State policies like affirmative action and privatization have also profoundly affected enterprises held by non-Bumiputera, especially the Chinese. Privatization frequently involved the sale of government assets. Often, the government sold enterprises to well-connected businessmen without putting them up for public bidding. Chinese capitalists, especially those with equity in large business groups, continued to prosper despite the NEP, but they increasingly needed to accommodate the state (see Gomez 1999; Searle 1999). Most Chinese, however, were able to develop their enterprises because they were forced to compete more effectively in an environment in which they were discriminated against.[3]

Table 6.1 indicates that Chinese equity ownership increased from 27.2 to 45.5 percent from 1970–90, although it slipped throughout the 1990s. Equity held by Bumiputera individuals and government trust agencies increased from 2.4 percent in 1970 to 20.6 percent in 1995 before falling to 19.1 percent in 1999. It is questionable, however, whether the extent of equity ownership by Bumiputeras amounts to only 19.1 percent, since much of the equity held by nominee companies, which are used to shield owners' identities, likely belongs to well-connected businessmen and political parties.[4] The most significant change in corporate ownership patterns was the appreciable decline in foreign ownership of Malaysian corporate equity from 63.4 percent in 1970 to 25.4 percent in 1990, although this percentage increased during the 1990s.

Although these figures indicate profound changes in equity ownership patterns between 1970 and 1999, Table 6.1 does not reveal how much state control and influence over the corporate sector has increased as a result of the

Table 6.1. Ownership of share capital (at par value) of limited companies, 1969–99 (in percentages)

	1969	1970	1975	1980	1985	1990	1995	1999
Bumiputera Individuals and Trust Agencies	1.5	2.4	9.2	12.5	19.1	19.2	20.6	19.1
Chinese	22.8	27.2	n.a	n.a	33.4	45.5	40.9	37.9
Indians	0.9	1.1	n.a	n.a	1.2	1.0	1.5	1.5
Others	—	—	—	—	—	—	—	0.9
Nominee Companies	2.1	6.0	N/A	N/A	1.3	8.5	8.3	7.9
Locally-Controlled Firms*	10.1	—	—	—	7.2	0.3	1.0	—
Foreigners	62.1	63.4	53.3	42.9	26.0	25.4	27.7	32.7

Sources: *Seventh Malaysia Plan, 1996–2000*; *Eighth Malaysia Plan, 2001–2005.*
Notes:
N/A: Not available.
*Locally-controlled firms refer to companies whose ownership could not be disaggregated further and assigned to specific ethnic groups.

NEP's implementation over three decades, especially after Mahathir Mohammad became prime minister in 1981.[5] Mahathir's long tenure as prime minister, which ended in October 2003, was characterized by his consolidation of power. Mahathir was also criticized for concentrating power in the office of the presidency of the party he led, the United Malays' National Organization (UMNO), which has hegemony over the ruling multiparty *Barisan Nasional* (National Front) coalition. Mahathir justified this concentration of power as a means to help Malaysia become fully developed by 2020 as well as create a new class of dynamic, entrepreneurial Malay capitalists who could compete in an international business environment.

To aid his vision of Malay capitalists, Mahathir appointed his close ally, businessman Daim Zainuddin, as finance minister in 1984. Both men were captivated with business and developing the Kuala Lumpur Stock Exchange (KLSE) as an avenue to help create large conglomerates. Between 1989 and 1993, equity market capitalization as a percentage of gross domestic product (GDP) increased from 105 to 342 percent. By the mid-1990s, the KLSE's market capitalization relative to GDP was the highest among Southeast Asian countries. The KLSE had also emerged as the fourth largest bourse in Asia and the fifteenth largest in the world in terms of market capitalization.

Mahathir's autonomy allowed him to selectively distribute government-created rents to a select group of businessmen who, by the mid-1990s, controlled many large conglomerates (see Appendix 6.1).[6] By 1997, the leading corporations included many individuals who were connected to one of the then three most powerful politicians—Mahathir, then deputy prime minister and finance minister Anwar Ibrahim, and then government economic advisor Daim Zainuddin (see Appendix 6.1). Almost all Malay and non-Malay businessmen who were among Malaysia's leading corporate figures before the Asian Crisis had enjoyed state patronage, specifically awards of privatized contracts (see Gomez 2002).

6.2. ENTERPRISE DEVELOPMENT AND OWNERSHIP AND CONTROL PATTERNS

Diversified growth has been a popular business strategy in Malaysia ever since the colonial period. Chinese immigrants diversified into any field that held out the prospect of high returns, and Bumiputeras who controlled quoted companies began doing the same in the 1980s. Malays differed from the Chinese, however, in using loans to diversify. They continued to do so from the 1980s until the onset of the Asian Crisis.[7]

Prior to the Asian Crisis, many Malaysian conglomerates used a holding company structure to own firms and grow the business group.[8] These groups also often used cross-shareholding and pyramids. Cross-shareholding allowed one person to secure control over many quoted companies with little or no personal equity in these firms. Through this mechanism, the majority shareholders of the holding company could appoint directors of the listed firms they controlled, usually to help them ensure that vested corporate ventures were implemented, even when these deals were not in the interest of minority shareholders. Since this pattern of control allowed one person to control board appointments, minority shareholders had little recourse to removing errant or irresponsible company directors even when these directors grossly violated their fiduciary duties.

There is little evidence, however, that well-connected Malays or Chinese businessmen have used this mechanism, although it is widely believed that the latter collaborate to protect their economic interests. Chinese capitalists have long cooperated with each other, most notably during the colonial period. By 2003, however, the shareholding patterns among Chinese-owned firms indicated they tended to function independently. Case studies of the largest quoted Chinese enterprises revealed that these firms had established interethnic ties, especially with influential Bumiputeras, to help them protect and expand their interests (see Gomez 1999).

Malaysian business groups also use interlocking directorships (see Appendix 6.2). There are two major types of interlocking directorate ties: (*a*) ownership ties, in which two or more organizations are jointly controlled by a single board of directors, and (*b*) direct interlock ties, in which two companies share one or more persons as members of their respective boards (Burt 1983: 3). The latter is common in Malaysia. Theoretically, such ties should help reduce competition and enhance monopolization of economic sectors. The large voting rights of these common directors allow for greater internal corporate control, leading to more intercompany transactions that are not necessarily beneficial to all shareholders of a company, particularly minority shareholders.

The most important interlocking directorate ties involve owner–directors, who hold directorships in a number of firms under the control of a holding company. One example of an owner–director is T.K. Lim, a director of Kamunting Corp and its associated firm, Bandar Raya Developments, both of which are part of the Multi-Purpose Holdings Group. Lim also sits on the board of Land & General, controlled by Wan Azmi Wan Hamzah, in which he also had an interest. Through such common directorships, the owners of the holding firm can ensure that the boards of their subsidiaries and associate companies will not oppose any intergroup transactions that they propose.

6.3. DAIM AND THE RISE AND FALL OF WELL-CONNECTED CAPITALISTS

Although Daim had little grassroots support and owed all his political appointments, as UMNO treasurer, government economic advisor, and as finance minister, to Mahathir, he has influenced the corporate sector more than anyone else has. During his appointment as finance minister between 1984 and 1991, Daim was widely criticized for abusing his position to develop his corporate base. When he was appointed to the Treasury in 1984, Daim announced that he had divested his vast business interests, including shares in firms involved in virtually all key sectors of the economy (banking, plantations, manufacturing, wholesaling and retailing, property development, and the media). Despite this claim, in 1992, one year after he had stepped down as finance minister, the total value of Daim's assets was reportedly RM 1 billion,[9] including assets in Australia, Britain, Mauritius, and the USA (see *The Star*, May 19, 1992). While holding public office, although he denied his active interest in business, he was seen as the most powerful entity in the corporate scene because his closest business associates had quickly emerged as major corporate figures because they ran enterprises ultimately owned or controlled by Daim or UMNO.[10] Daim's close ally, Halim Saad, for example, who had publicly acknowledged his role as trustee of UMNO's vast corporate assets, would eventually secure control of the party's most important companies through an ailing quoted firm, Renong.

Nevertheless, since the rise of well-connected businessmen was linked to the patronage of influential politicians, their fortunes depended on whether their patrons remained in power. After Anwar was removed from office in September 1998, thus allowing Mahathir to concentrate even more power in his office, most businessmen associated with the ex-deputy prime minister have struggled to protect their corporate interests; many of them are no longer prominent. More generally, most businesses owned by well-connected individuals are no longer among the top 100 Malaysian firms (see Appendix 6.3). Similarly, when Daim fell out of favor with Mahathir in 2001, the corporate assets owned by his business allies and proxies were taken over by the government.[11]

Notably, the Chinese appeared to have fared better in the Asian Crisis, as did government-owned listed firms. Mahathir has argued vehemently that the Asian Crisis was the primary reason for his lack of success in developing domestic capitalists, an argument that had some justification (see Jomo 2001). It was, however, questionable whether the prime minister had helped nurture entrepreneurial companies that could weather crises.

6.4. CURRENCY CRISIS AND CORPORATE DECLINE

One reason why these large-scale enterprises declined so rapidly following the crisis was their pattern of development. Many well-connected firms had secured favorable loans from state-owned financial institutions to acquire rents, in the form of licenses, contracts, and privatized projects. Most of these rent recipients had used numerous corporate maneuvers like shares-for-assets swaps and reverse takeovers to capture control of quoted firms. These companies were, in turn, used for other types of corporate maneuvers, including mergers, acquisitions, and takeovers, to develop their business interests. As share prices escalated, stock was used as security to secure more loans from banks for further acquisitions. These corporate strategies contributed appreciably to the increase in the KLSE's market capitalization in the 1990s (see Gomez 2002).

Publicly listing a firm had emerged as an effective means for raising funds for corporate expansion. Between 1980 and 1990, the number of publicly listed companies increased only slightly, from 250 to 305. By 1995, however, 529 companies were quoted on the KLSE, and 708 were listed before the onset of the currency crisis. In 1990, the total market capitalization of quoted firms was RM132 billion; by 1996, this figure had increased to RM807 billion (Low, C.K. 2000a: 44).

Public-listing also enabled an owner of a quoted firm to buy other listed and private enterprises, thus letting him control a diversified corporate empire, yet not holding stock in his own name. In this way, control facilitated cross-shareholding, along with all the abuses of this practice that were noted previously. Further, an increase in a quoted firm's market capitalization enabled that firm to secure more loans from foreign and local banks with equity as collateral.

The enormous inflow of foreign funds as portfolio investments (FPI) and loans during the 1990s also contributed appreciably to the increase in market capitalization of quoted stock. Most of these funds were channeled to well-connected firms, which were increasingly laden with debts but were expanding rapidly through their access to numerous state-generated rents. The attraction of FPI by well-connected firms suggested foreign investors wanted to secure quick capital gains from their investments.

In Malaysia, the Asian Crisis first began with a fall in the ringgit's value, and continued with precipitous drops in the stock prices of listed firms. Between July 1997 and early 1998, the ringgit fell from around RM2.5 against the dollar to a record low of RM4.88. The Composite Index of the KLSE plunged from a high of 1,271 in February 1997 to 262 in August 1998. Between 1997 and 1998, private investment fell by 57.8 percent, private consumption by 12.4 percent, public consumption by 3.5 percent, and public investment by 10 percent. By the second quarter on 1998, the Malaysian economy was in a severe recession, registering an annualized GDP growth rate of –6.8 percent (Gomez and Jomo 1999: 188; Chin and Jomo 2001: 117–18). By contrast, in the decade before the crisis, the economy had registered almost double-digit growth rates, boosted to some extent by high savings and investment rates, factors which also helped offset an even more dire state of affairs following the crisis.

Foreign inflows of funds during the boom years also included heavy borrowing from abroad by some Malaysian banks and companies. The central bank, Bank Negara, noted that the net foreign liabilities of commercial banks had increased from RM10.3 billion at the end of 1995 to RM25.2 billion in June 1997, while their net external reserves position deteriorated from –RM5.3 billion to –RM17.7 billion over the same period.[12] Moreover, patronage involving the disbursement of loans to the well connected, including funds for the acquisition of shares rather than productive economic activities, was extremely rampant. Of the RM39 billion loaned by banks for share acquisition, almost 45 percent went to individuals. During the crisis, just fifteen corporate groups accounted for 20 percent of Malaysia's bank loans

(Chin and Jomo 2001: 113–15). One company, the highly diversified, publicly listed Renong, had accumulated debts totaling about 5 percent of all loans accumulated in the Malaysian banking sector. Inevitably, this situation meant that when stock prices plunged, defaults on bank loans increased significantly.

At the end of 1997, Malaysia's outstanding debt was equivalent to 160 percent of GDP. Fortunately for Malaysia, the bulk of this debt was in ringgit, not foreign currency. Most financial institutions in Thailand, Indonesia, and South Korea, the countries most badly affected by the crisis, had borrowed in foreign currencies, mainly US dollars, to re-lend in local currencies at higher interest rates. One International Monetary Fund (IMF) report comparing Malaysia and Thailand revealed that 'Malaysian financial institutions have not had as large a role in international intermediation as their Thai counterparts. Most of their international borrowing has taken place through head offices and branches or bilaterally with foreign institutions, and so Malaysian banks have accounted for only a small portion of international bond issues and syndicated borrowing. Although foreign liabilities or commercial banks expanded rapidly between 1989 and 1993, they fell subsequently' (Callen and Reynolds 1997: 169).

Between June 1997 and August 1998, nonperforming loans (NPLs) held by domestic banks rose from RM9.3 billion to RM42.2 billion. The banks with the most NPLs were all government owned: Sime Bank, Bank Bumiputra, and Malayan Banking. Bank Bumiputra needed a capital injection of RM1.1 billion and the government bought its NPLs. Sime Bank, then controlled by Mahathir's former political secretary, also declared huge losses and was subsequently taken over by the well-connected Rashid Hussain group.

The crisis also affected firms owned by many well-connected businessmen, who now owned corporate stock that was worth far less, leaving them severely overleveraged. The government bailed out several of these companies, sometimes for exorbitant prices, and took over two major privatization projects. The reasoning behind much of this assistance was questionable. For instance, Petronas acquired Proton, the group's car-manufacturing concern, ostensibly to sustain Malaysia's automobile industry. Yet it would have been possible to involve Chinese firms that were well established in both automotive component-parts manufacturing and motor vehicle assembly and distribution. This move would have also greatly promoted interethnic relations. Mahathir recognized the dynamism of Chinese entrepreneurs, but seemed reluctant to capitalize on it, probably because Chinese automobile firms are either independent or are aligned with enterprises that are not beholden to the Malaysian government.

6.5. ENTERPRISE REFORM IN THE POSTCRISIS PERIOD

The government did introduce new policies and corporate governance measures to deal with the problems exposed in the corporate sector. The most controversial postcrisis measure was enforced bank consolidation, which was implemented in spite of strong public protest (see *Far Eastern Economic Review*, July 22, 2001). In addition, many private firms attempted to adopt a more focused approach to business.

6.5.1. Bank Consolidation

In mid-1999, a government proposal associated with Daim sought to merge Malaysia's fifty-eight financial institutions into six anchor banks. Under the original consolidation plan, banks owned by prominent Malays who were not closely associated with Daim did not receive anchor bank status even though their owners had much banking expertise and had developed their enterprises with relatively little government assistance. In addition, it appeared that Malaysia's most dynamic banks were being brought under Daim's indirect control. Inevitably, the Chinese were upset with the proposed consolidation exercise, as the merger of some of their most enterprising banks would diminish their presence in this sector. With a general election then impending, and since Mahathir was aware that his party needed non-Malay, especially Chinese, support to secure a strong presence in parliament, the number of anchor banks was increased from six to ten and included several better-run and/or thriving institutions (see Table 6.2). This decision reportedly sparked a rift between Mahathir and Daim (see *Far Eastern Economic Review*, July 5, 2001).

Table 6.2 provides two key insights. First, it reveals how power became increasingly centered in the office of the prime minister. Other arms of the government and public institutions have become subservient to the executive. Second, it exposes the impact that concentration of political power can have on property rights. Majority ownership of a company means nothing when a strong state is determined to push through corporate restructuring. Those most susceptible to a takeover have generally benefited greatly from state patronage, but were aligned with a political patron who has fallen out with the prime minister.

Table 6.2. Bank consolidation anchor banks and their partners

Anchor bank	Merger partners	New owner
Original Six		
Malayan Banking	Pacific Bank, EON Bank, EON Finance	Malaysian government
Maybank Finance Aseambankers	Malaysia International Merchant Bank, Delta Finance, KBB, Sime Finance	
Multipurpose Bank Multipurpose Finance	RHB Bank, RHB Sakura Sabah Bank, Oriental Bank, Oriental Finance, Sabah Finance, International Bank Malaysia, MBf Finance, Bumiputra Merchant Bank, Phileo Allied Bank, Bolton Finance	Daim's allies
Bumiputra-Commerce CIMB	Hong Leong Bank, Hong Leong Finance, CCM	Renong/NST (linked to Daim)
Perwira Affin Bank	Arab-Malaysian Bank, Bank Utama	Malaysian government
Perwira Affin Merchant Bank, Affin Finance	Utama Merchant Bank, BSN Bank, BSN Finance, Arab-Malaysian Finance	
Public Bank Public Finance	Wah Tat Bank, Hock Hua Bank, Inter Finance, Advance Finance, Sime Merchant Bank	Teh Hong Piow
Southern Bank	Ban Hin Lee Bank, Perdana Merchant Bank, Cempaka Finance	Tan Teong Hean
Subsequent Ten		
Malayan Banking	Mayban Finance, Aseambankers Malaysia, PhileoAllied Bank, Pacific Bank, Sime Finance Bank, Kewangan Bersatu	Malaysian government
Bumiputra-Commerce	Bumiputra-Commerce Finance	Malaysian government
Bank	Commerce International Merchant Bankers	
RHB Bank	RHB Sakura Merchant Bankers, Delta Finance, Interfinance	Rashid Hussain*
Public Bank	Public Finance, Hock Hua Bank, Advance Finance, Sime Merchant Bankers	Teh Hong Piow

Arab-Malaysian Bank	Arab-Malaysian Finance, Arab-Malaysian Merchant Bank, Bank Utama, Utama Merchant Bankers	Azman Hashim
Hong Leong Bank	Hong Leong Finance, Wah Tat Bank, Credit Corporation Malaysia	Quek Leng Chan
Perwira Affin Bank	Affin Finance, Perwira Affin Merchant Bankers, BSN Commercial Bank, BSN Finance, BSN Merchant Bank	Malaysian government
Multi-Purpose Bank	International Bank Malaysia, Sabah Bank, MBf Finance, Bolton Finance, Sabah Finance, Bumiputra Merchant Bankers, Amanah Merchant Bank	Daim's allies
Southern Bank	Ban Hin Lee Bank, Cempaka Finance, United Merchant Finance, Perdana Finance, Perdana Merchant Bankers	Tan Teong Hean
EON Bank	EON Finance, Oriental Bank, City Finance, Malaysian International Merchant Bankers, Perkasa Finance	Malaysian government

* In 2003, Rashid Hussain relinquished control of RHB Bank to family members of Taib Mahmud, the Chief Minister of the state of Sarawak.

6.5.2. Selective Corporate Governance

Issues of ownership and control are central to corporate governance. A firm's shareholders have the right to how an organization's assets are used to assure themselves a good return on their investment. Yet the separation of ownership from control, in which managers, along with a board of directors vested with power to run a firm on behalf of shareholders, is the norm in most corporations (Berle and Means 1967; Scott 1997). Good corporate governance stems from directors following their fiduciary duty to run a corporation with shareholders' interests in mind. Following the Asian Crisis, when new regulations and institutions were introduced to enforce governance of the corporate sector in Malaysia, there were two key areas of concern. First, how should directors be selected and remunerated? Second, should banks or institutional investors, like pension funds or mutual funds, be actively managing firms in which they have investments and able to have some control over corporate activities like mergers and takeovers?

In 1998, the government established the Finance Committee on Corporate Governance, which eventually proposed the Malaysian Code of Corporate Governance, mainly to deal with problems in the corporate sector that were exposed by the crisis. This Code has two primary objectives: to encourage disclosure to ensure that investors are aware of how their company is being managed, and to remind company directors of their responsibilities. The four principles of corporate governance set out in the Code refer to: (*a*) effective leadership by directors of companies, (*b*) transparency in determining the remuneration of directors, (*c*) ensuring accountability of directors through adequate internal controls and an independent external audit, and (*d*) the promotion of dialogue between a company's management and its investors (Low, C.K. 2000b: 436–51).

The new regulations did not, however, provide for enforcement of corporate practices common in Malaysia but not accepted in other countries. For example, a majority shareholder in Malaysia can inject a privately held asset into a quoted firm; this practice is not permitted in the USA, as it is seen as a 'self-serving deal' (*The Edge*, March 31, 2003). This practice had led to several controversies, specifically during the 1980s when the KLSE emerged as an avenue for businessmen to raise funds quickly.

Institutions in Malaysia responsible for governance of the corporate sector, like the Securities Commission, have the capacity to perform effectively, and have a good reputation for regulating the equity and financial markets. In view of the executive hegemony over the state, however, the relevance and effectiveness of these institutions depend on the will of government leaders to enforce corporate governance. Regulatory institutions usually act independently, but are also used as tools by powerful politicians for vested interests. These politicians can determine if regulatory institutions should act against businessmen, even when there is evidence of corruption. By ostensibly enforcing corporate governance provisions, politicians in control of the executive have transferred corporate assets into the hands of their allies, as demonstrated by the bank consolidation exercise. Thus, although selective imposition of rules and regulations has helped create the impression of an increasingly well-governed corporate sector, irregularities continue to occur.

6.5.3. Corporate Restructuring and Changing Ownership and Control Patterns

Among the companies that encountered the most problems following the Asian Crisis were the largest quoted firms that were controlled through holding companies. Many of the groups that owned these firms were burdened with enormous debts and were subject to takeover and/or were restructured. The problems of these groups, especially in regard to overleveraging, suggest the danger of cross-shareholding and pyramiding. Although new regulations were introduced to enhance corporate governance and transparency, no attempt was made to curb these practices.

To curb intercompany loans within a corporate group, the KLSE issued new guidelines in 2002. For example, if the volume of the new loans crosses 5 percent of the lender's equity, an extraordinary general meeting has to be convened to approve the transaction (*The Edge*, January 6, 2003). Since it was common for holding companies to secure loans from their subsidiaries, some of which the former found difficult to service, these transactions did not serve the interests of minority shareholders.

Although the government has made it difficult for holding companies to get loans from subsidiaries, subsidiaries can still declare dividends as a means to channel funds to the parent firm through the interlocking relationships. These dividends can be used to reduce loans of holding companies. This mechanism is acceptable because minority shareholders also benefit from dividends.

Other corporate groups, although diversified, gained credibility by focusing primarily on one or two industries.[13] This change to a more focused approach to business is important because the aftermath of the Asian Crisis suggests that selective intervention failed, though not because these big firms did not get enough support from the state. The strategy of diversifying extensively through acquisitions rather than through long-term growth plans based on product development and market penetration no longer appears wise. Short-term financial gains and growth through debt, rather than through equity and reinvestment of profits, was not a viable way to develop modern industry. Firms that did not depend considerably on bank loans to develop their corporate base tended to cope better with the crisis.

In mid-2003, a study of the top 100 companies quoted on the KLSE indicated that the largest business groups did not have overwhelming control of the corporate sector. In fact, there was evidence of fairly wide dispersal of ownership of corporate equity of the top 100 quoted firms. In 2001, a list compiled by *Malaysian Business* (January 2, 2001) of the country's twenty wealthiest business people indicated that their combined wealth amounted to RM41.7 billion, only about 10 percent of the KLSE's market capitalization. None of these individuals appears to hold corporate equity in trust for influential politicians.

A list of the top ten KLSE firms, in terms of market capitalization, indicates that the government has majority ownership in seven. These firms include the largest bank, a utility company, a shipping line, and a gas producer. The other three firms in the top ten are Chinese-owned. Notably, none of these firms is owned either by a foreign enterprise or by a Bumiputera, despite substantial state support for the development of Malay capital.

The state's failure to develop Bumiputera entrepreneurs was due to how it attempted to do so. The government selected so-called 'winners' in a non-transparent manner and accorded them numerous concessions, particularly privatized projects, to facilitate their rapid expansion (see Jomo 1995). Since political patronage involved easy access to loans and other privileges, individuals benefiting from it appeared to exercise little caution in how they developed their companies. The state's failure to discipline this style of growth contributed to the rapid collapse of these firms when the Asian Crisis occurred.

In addition, leading Bumiputera businessmen's links to, and dependence on, state leaders meant their corporate activities were often influenced by politicians and affected by political crises. Firms benefiting from such patronage have often been taken over by other government allies when their own patrons fell out of power. Malay capitalists who have remained relatively independent have fared better.

The crisis also affected economic sectors that Bumiputera capitalists were actively involved in. This point highlights a crucial fact: no Malay firm listed in the KLSE top fifty has shown the capacity to venture successfully into manufacturing. Most have focused on finance, construction, property development, and telecommunications. Shamsuddin Kadir is probably the only Bumiputera actively involved in manufacturing, though none of his companies appear in the KLSE top fifty.

Although businessmen, particularly the Chinese, who had few or no links to politicians, appear to have retained control over their companies, mainly by conforming to state policies, the government has been able to remove corporate assets at will. Prominent businessmen such as Rashid Hussain, T.K. Lim, and Tong Kooi Ong have lost control of large, even thriving enterprises, because they were not allied with state leaders. In spite of the rise of huge enterprises by 2003, capitalists remain very subservient to the state. This subordination brings into question the sustainability of corporate enterprises, given the vulnerability of these firms to government power struggles.

6.6. CONCLUSION: CONTEMPORARY FEATURES OF CORPORATE MALAYSIA

Since the Asian Crisis, and the subsequent political and economic crises, corporate Malaysia has changed in important ways. Although Mahathir's policies strongly influenced the development of corporate Malaysia, the concentration of political power during his administration did not contribute to concentration of corporate equity in an elite group, primarily because of conflicts among political elites. Between 1997, when the currency crisis occurred, and 2001, Mahathir marginalized two influential politicians, Anwar and Daim, who had considerable indirect control over corporate Malaysia. The vast corporate assets owned by their business allies were reallocated to government institutions or private individuals. In October 2003, Mahathir stepped down as Prime Minister, handing over power to Abdullah Ahmad Badawi. Since the new Prime Minister has never shown any particular interest in most of Mahathir's pet projects, specifically the promotion of heavy industry and the development of Malaysian capitalists in control of huge conglomerates, the pattern of enterprise development during his tenure may differ significantly from that of Mahathir.

There are already signs indicating policy changes involving enterprise development. The Abdullah government has begun to shift support from conglomerates to small and medium-sized enterprises (SMEs). The new model for enterprise development for the government is that of Taiwan, whose economy is dominated by SMEs; nearly 98 percent of firms there fall into this category. The Taiwanese economy had also apparently weathered the currency crisis far better than a number of other countries in East Asia did. The Malaysian government has also encouraged firms to reduce their dependence on loans to generate growth. Corporate debt in Taiwan was among the lowest in East Asia, at about 30 percent of equity. In contrast, the corporate debt of South Korean companies was sometimes four times the value of these firms' assets.

Within the banking sector, there is speculation of another round of mergers that might result in just five or six anchor banks. The key issue is whether the government will drive this merger or if the initiative will come from owners of the ten anchor banks. Meanwhile, between mid-1997 and 2002, the volume of NPLs declined from 27 percent of total gross loans to 17 percent, reflecting growing stability within the consolidated bank sector (*The Star*, December 28, 2002).

Nevertheless, other features of corporate Malaysia might not change. Although Abdullah Badawi has stated his intention to end corruption, the existence of politically linked firms will likely continue. Abdullah's family has corporate interests and has benefited from privatized contracts. Moreover, structural reforms to enhance transparency and accountability in government are not being implemented. The continued concentration of power in the executive and the lack of autonomy of regulatory institutions to act against corruption and corporate activities that are not in the interests of shareholders do not serve to inspire confidence that genuine reforms are imminent in corporate Malaysia.

Appendix 6.1. Reputed political connections of prominent business figures in the mid-1990s

Name	Publicly-listed company	Background
Halim Saad	Renong United Engineers (M) (UEM) Kinta Kellas Time Engineering Ho Hup Construction Faber Group FCW Holdings Park May Crest Petroleum	Daim protégé. Halim publicly admitted in 1988 that he held UMNO's vast corporate holdings in trust for the party. He worked for Daim when the latter was in charge of Peremba, then a government-owned company.
Tajudin Ramli	Malaysia Airlines Malaysian Helicopter Services Technology Resources Industries	Daim protégé; worked for him in Peremba.
Wan Azmi Wan Hamzah	Land & General Rohas-Euco Industries Bell & Order Systematic Education Group RJ Reynolds	Daim protégé; worked for him in Peremba.
Samsudin Abu Hassan	Granite Industries Austral Amalgamated Dataprep Holdings	Daim protégé; worked for him in Peremba.
Ahmad Sebi Abu Bakar	Advance Synergy Prime Utilities United Merchant Group Ban Hin Lee Bank	Daim protégé, though once also associated with Anwar. Anwar's contemporary at the University of Malaya.
Tunku Abdullah	Malaysian Assurance Alliance Melewar Corporation George Town Holdings Aokam Perdana Malayan Cement MBf Capital MBf Holdings	Former UMNO MP; Mahathir's long-term close associate.
Yahya Ahmad (died 1997)	HICOM Holdings Diversified Resources Gadek (M) Gadek Capital Edaran Otomobil Nasional (EON) Perusahaan Otomobil Nasional (Proton) Kedah Cement Holdings Cycle & Carriage Bintang Golden Pharos Uniphoenix Corporation	Mahathir protégé. Anwar's school contemporary.

Tengku Adnan Mansor	Star Publications Berjaya Group Berjaya Singer Berjaya Industrial EMC Logistics Minho Dunham-Bush (M)	Former UMNO Youth Treasurer and Supreme Council member. Linked to Mahthir through close association with Vincent Tan.
Rashid Hussain	Rashid Hussain DCB Bank Kwong Yik Bank	Daim associate; also connected with Anwar
A. Kadir Jasin Nazri Abdullah Mohd Noor Mutalib Khalid Ahmad	New Straits Times (NSTP) TV3 Malaysian Resources Corp Malakoff Commerce Asset Holdings	Anwar supported their take-over of NSTP and TV3 in 1993. Kadir remains a Daim associate.
Abdul Mulok Damit	Pengkalen Industrial Holdings Construction & Supplies House	UMNO MP; Daim associate. Jointly owns these companies with Joseph Ambrose Lee.
Ishak Ismail	KFC Holdings (M) Idris Hydraulic Golden Plus Holdings Ayamas Food Corporation Best World Land Promet Pintaras Jaya Scientex Incorporated Gemtech Resources	Former secretary of Anwar's UMNO division.
Mohd Sarit Yusoh	KFC Holdings (M) Ayamas Food Corporation Golden Plus Holdings Malayawata Steel Khee San Goh Ban Huat Syarikat Kurnia Setia	Former political secretary to Anwar.
Amin Shah Omar Shah	PSC Industries Setron (M) Atacorp Holdings Kedah Cement Holdings Daibochi Plastic & Packaging Industry	Active in UMNO. Daim protégé.
Basir Ismail	Cycle & Carriage Ltd Cycle & Carriage Bintang Cold Storage United Plantations Fima Corporation	Mahathir's close associate.

(*continued*)

Appendix 6.1. (*Continued*)

Name	Publicly-listed company	Background
Mohd Noor Yusof	Datuk Keramat Holdings George Town Holdings	Former political secretary to Mahathir. Had majority ownership of UMBC before divesting to state-controlled Sime Darby.
Kamaruddin Jaffar	Sabah Shipyard Wing Teik Holdings Westmont Industries Inch Kenneth Kajang Rubber plc Mercury Industries	Kelantan UMNO leader; old Anwar confidante.
Kamaruddin Mohd Nor	Eastern & Oriental Dialog Group	Kelantan UMNO leader; old Anwar confidante.
Shuaib Lazim	Ekran George Town Holdings	Close associate of Mahathir and Daim. Former UMNO state assemblyman.
Anuar Othman	Konsortium Perkapalan	Ex-Daim protégé at Peremba; now associated with Anwar. Former UMNO business trustee.
Shamsuddin Kadir	Sapura Holdings Uniphone Telecommunications	Mahathir associate.
Hassan Abas	Cycle & Carriage Bintang	Daim protégé at Peremba.
Azman Hashim	AAMB Holdings Arab-Malaysian Corporation Arab-Malaysian Finance Arab-Malaysian First Property Trust holding company Arab-Malaysian Development South Peninsular Industries	UMNO member. Founding director of Fleet Holdings, UMNO's main investment.
Ibrahim Mohamed	Uniphoenix Corporation Damansara Realty	Mahathir associate.
Ibrahim Abdul Rahman	Industrial Oxygen Inc.	Anwar's father. Former UMNO MP.
Mirzan Mahathir	Mamee-Double Decker Lion Corporation Dataprep Holdings Konsortium Holdings	Mahathir's first son.

	KIG Glass Industrial Sunway Building Technology Worldwide Holdings Artwright Holdings	
Mokhzani Mahathir	Tongkah Holdings Technology Resources Industries Parkway Holdings Pantai Hospital UCM Industrial Corporation	Mahathir's second son.
Mukhriz Mahathir	Reliance Pacific	Mahathir's third son.
Ahmad Zahid Hamidi	Kretam Holdings	Anwar associate; UMNO Youth Head until Anwar's expulsion; MP.
Ting Pek Khiing	Ekran PWE Industries Pacific Chemicals Granite Industries Wembley Industries	Close Daim and Mahathir associate.
Vincent C.Y. Tan	Berjaya Group Berjaya Sports Toto Berjaya Singer Berjaya Leisure Dunham-Bush Hospital Pantai Sun Media Group Unza Holdings	Usually associated with Daim, but also Mahathir and Anwar.
T.K. Lim	Multi-Purpose Holdings Kamunting Corp. Magnum Corp. Bandar Raya Developments	Formerly close Daim associate, then linked to Anwar.
Joseph C.A. Chong	Westmont Westmont Land Asia Samanda Holdings Wing Teik Holdings	Associated with Anwar through Kamaruddin Jaffar.
T. Ananda Krishnan	Tanjong Binariang Pan Malaysian Pools Powertek Seri Kuda	Associated with Mahathir and Razaleigh.

Source: *KLSE Annual Companies Handbook* 21(1–4), 1996.

Appendix 6.2. Interlocking directorates in the top 100 KLSE companies, 2001

Name	Companies
Nuraizah Abu Hamid	Tenaga Nasional, Telekom
Md Yusof Hussin	UMW Holdings, Malayan Banking
Mohd Hilmey Mohd Taib	Malayan Banking, Kuala Lumpur Kepong (KLK)
Lau Yin Pin @ Lau Yen Beng	YTL Power International, Tenaga Nasional
Kamariah Hussain	Edaran Otomobil Nasional (EON), Tenaga Nasional
Mohd Hassan Marican	Petronas Gas, Petronas Dagangan, Malaysia International Shipping Corp (MISC)
Lim Goh Tong	Resorts World, Genting
Lim Kok Thay	Resorts World, Genting
Mohammed Hanif Omar	Resorts World, Genting, AMMB Holdings, Arab-Malaysian Finance
Alwi Jantan	Guinness Anchor, Resorts World
Siew Nim Chee	Malaysian Oxygen, Resorts World
Mohd Ali Hj Yasin	MISC, Petronas Dagangan
Wan Ali Tuanku Yubi	Sarawak Enterprise Corp, Malaysian Airline System (MAS), Cahya Mata Sarawak (CMS), MISC
Nik Mohamed Nik Yaacob	Sime Darby, Sime UEP Properties
Mohd Desa Pachi	Commerce Asset-Holding, Malaysia Mining Corp (MMC)
Nik Hashim Nik Yusoff	Utama Banking Group, Genting, Malayan United Industries (MUI)
Yeoh Tiong Lay	YTL Corp, YTL Power International
Francis Yeoh Sock Ping	YTL Corp, YTL Power International
Yeoh Seok Kian	YTL Corp, YTL Power International
Yeoh Seok Hong	YTL Corp, YTL Power International
Yeoh Seok Kah	YTL Corp, YTL Power International
Yeoh Soo Keng	YTL Corp, YTL Power International
Yeoh Soo Min	YTL Corp, YTL Power International
Michael Yeoh Sock Siong	YTL Corp, YTL Power International
Haron Mohd Taib	YTL Corp, YTL Power International
Yahya Ismail	YTL Corp, YTL Power International, Shell, Southern Bank, United Engineers (M) (UEM)
Raja Tun Mohar Raja Badiozaman	YTL Corp, YTL Power International
Thong Yaw Hong	Public Bank, KLK, MMC, Public Finance, Batu Kawan, Berjaya Land
Teh Hong Piow	Public Finance, Public Bank

Tay Ah Lek	Public Finance, Public Bank
Tengku Abdul Rahman ibni Sultan Hj Ahmad	Public Finance, Public Bank
Yeoh Chin Kee	Public Finance, Public Bank
Oh Chong Peng	Rothmans of Pall Mall, RHB Capital, Star Publications, Rashid Hussain, Powertek
Abdul Rashid Hussain	Rashid Hussain, RHB Capital
Seah Fook Chin	Rashid Hussain, RHB Capital
Chong Kin Leong	Rashid Hussain, RHB Capital
Clifford Francis Herbert	RHB Capital, MAS
Halim Saad	UEM, Renong
Syed Md Amin Syed Jan Aljeffri	KUB Malaysia, UEM
Mohd Zakhir Siddiqy Sidek	Renong, UEM
Chan Chin Cheung	Renong, Multi-Purpose Holdings
Vincent Tan Chee Yioun	Berjaya Land, Berjaya Group, Berjaya Capital, Berjaya Sports Toto, Digi Swisscom
Tan Kok Ping	Berjaya Sports Toto, Berjaya Group
Ng Foo Leong	Berjaya Land, Berjaya Sports Toto
Robin Tan Yeong Ching	Berjaya Sports Toto, Berjaya Group, Digi Swisscom
Robert Yong Kuen Loke	Berjaya Capital, Berjaya Land, Berjaya Sports Toto, Berjaya Group
Chan Kien Sing	Berjaya Capital, Berjaya Land, Berjaya Sports Toto, Berjaya Group, Digi Swisscom
Freddie Pang Hock Cheng	Berjaya Capital, Berjaya Sports Toto
Md Khir Johari	MUI, Magnum Corp
Lim Sze Guan @ Lim Kim Wah	Magnum Corp, Bandar Raya Developments
Mohd Ghazali Seth	Magnum Corp, Nestle, Carlsberg
Pee Ban Hock	Magnum Corp, Multi-Purpose Holdings
Lim Chiew	Magnum Corp, Bandar Raya Developments
Mohd Saleh Sulong	HICOM Holdings, EON, Perusahaan Otomobil Nasional (Proton), Kedah Cement
Tik Mustaffa	Proton, HICOM Holdings, Kedah Cement
Maznah Abdul Jalil	EON, HICOM Holdings, Kedah Cement, Proton
Mohd Nadzmi Mohd Salleh	Proton, RJ Reynolds
Lee Oi Hian	KLK, Batu Kawan
Yeoh Chin Hin	Batu Kawan, KLK
Charles Letts	Batu Kawan, KLK
Tengku Robert Hamzah	KLK, Batu Kawan
R. M. Alias	MMC, KLK, Batu Kawan

(*continued*)

Appendix 6.2. (*Continued*)

Name	Companies
Lee Hau Hian	KLK, Batu Kawan
Lee Soon Hian	KLK, Batu Kawan
Yeoh Eng Khoon	KLK, Batu Kawan
Quek Leng Chan	Hong Leong Bank, Hong Leong Credit, Hong Leong Indusries, Malaysian Pacific Industries (MPI), OYL Industries
David Edward Comley	MPI, Hong Leong Industries
Kwek Leng San	MPI, Hong Leong Industries
Mohd Shamsuddin Hj Mohd Yaacob	MPI, Malaysian Oxygen
Tan Keok Yin	MPI, Hong Leong Bank
Azman Hashim	AMMB Holdings, Arab-Malaysian Finance
Azlan Hashim	Arab-Malaysian Finance, AMMB Holdings
Mohd Tahir Hj Abdul Rahim	Arab-Malaysian Finance, AMMB Holdings
Mohd Rashdan Hj Baba	Arab-Malaysian Finance, AMMB Holdings, Unisem
Cheah Tek Kuang	Arab-Malaysian Finance, AMMB Holdings
Azlan Mohd Zainol	AMMB Holdings, Arab-Malaysian Finance
Chan Hua Eng	Malayan Cement, Lingui Developments, Carlsberg
Zain Azahari Zainal Abidin	Golden Hope Plantations, MMC
Mohammad Abdullah	Golden Hope Plantations, Malaysian National Reinsurance
Leong Wai Hoong	Tanjong, RJ Reynolds
Faisal Siraj	Kedah Cement, HICOM Holdings, EON
James Lim Cheng Poh	Hong Leong Bank, Hong Leong Credit
Seow Lun Hoo	Hong Leong Bank, Hong Leong Credit, Malaysian Resources Corp (MRCB)
Kwek Leng Seng	Hong Leong Bank, Hong Leong Credit
Yong Ming Sang	MUI, Star Publications, MAS
Khalid Hj Ahmad	Rashid Hussain, New Straits Times Press (NSTP), MRCB, Malakoff
Mohd Noor Mutalib	MRCB, NSTP, Malakoff
Ahmad Nazri Abdullah	MRCB, NSTP
Abdul Kadir Jasin	MRCB, NSTP
Ahmad Jauhari Yahya	Malakoff, MRCB
Mohd Osman Samsudin Cassim	Southern Bank, Berjaya Land
Mohd Ghazali Hj Che Mat	Malakoff, Kumpulan Guthrie, NSTP
Lin Yun Ling	Gamuda, Lingkaran Trans Kota Holdings

Ng Kee Leen	Gamuda, Lingkaran Trans Kota Holdings
Saw Wah Theng	Gamuda, Lingkaran Trans Kota Holdings
Tong Keng Tatt	TA Enterprise, Pan Malaysia Cement Works
Mustafa Mohd Ali	Sime UEP Properties, Batu Kawan
Syed Fahkri Barakbah	Sime Darby, Sime UEP Properties
Abdul Khalid Ibrahim	Highlands & Lowlands, Kumpulan Guthrie
Wong Chong Wah	Highlands & Lowlands, Kumpulan Guthrie
Ghazali Awang	Highlands & Lowlands, Kumpulan Guthrie
Geh Cheng Hooi	Star Publications, Tan Chong Motor Holdings, Lingui Developments, Hap Seng Consolidated
Jamiah Abdul Hamid	UMW Holdings, MMC
Azzat Kamaludin	NSTP, Affin Holdings
Ang Guan Seng	MUI, Perlis Plantations
Lodin Wok Kamaruddin	Affin Holdings, Ramatex
Tsuneo Horita	AMMB Holdings, Arab-Malaysian Finance
Lee Shin Cheng	IOI Properties, IOI Corp
Lee Cheng Leang	IOI Corp, IOI Properties
Lee Yeow Chor	IOI Corp, IOI Properties
Yeo How	IOI Corp, IOI Properties
John Madsen	Hap Seng Consolidated, Carlsberg
Anuar Mohd Hassan	Malaysian National Reinsurance, Malaysian Oxygen
Tajudin Ramli	MAS, Technology Resources Industries (TRI)
Abdul Rahman Hj Ismail	HICOM Holdings, TRI, BIMB Holdings
Jeffrey Alan Hedberg	Digi Swisscom, TRI
Abdul Rahim Hj Din	Berjaya Group, Digi Swisscom
Wan Abdul Rahman Wan Yaacob	Powertek, IJM Corp, MMC, Lingkaran Trans Kota Holdings
Khor Chin Poey	Perlis Plantations, PPB Oil Palms
Liang Kim Bang	Perlis Plantations, PPB Oil Palms, CMS
Ahmad Abdullah	Phileo Allied, Tan Chong Motor Holdings
Mohd Noor Yusof	Commerce Asset-Holding, KUB Malaysia
Anuar Hamdan	Multi-Purpose Holdings, Kamunting Corp, Bandar Raya Developments
Abdul Khalid Sahan	MMC, PSC Industries
Amin Shah Omar Shah	Kedah Cement, PSC Industries
Saw Huat Lye	Shell, Guinness Anchor
Jaffar Ahmad Indot	Guinness Anchor, Shell
Siti Ramelah Yahya	Kumpulan Guthrie, Highlands & Lowlands

(*continued*)

Appendix 6.2. (*Continued*)

Name	Companies
Danny Tan Chee Sing	Berjaya Capital, Berjaya Land, Berjaya Group
Mohammed Adnan Shuiab	Multi-Purpose Holdings, Berjaya Land
Mansor Salleh @ Md Salleh	Ban Hin Lee Bank, Berjaya Capital
Abdul Manap Ibrahim	WTK Holdings, Amsteel Corp
Omar Yoke Lin Ong	OYL Industries, Malaysian Oxygen
Abdul Rahman Sulaiman	Pan Malaysian Cement Works, MRCB
Nasruddin Mohamed	Amsteel Corp, IOI Properties, Hong Leong Industries
Wan Azmi Wan Hamzah	Amway Holdings, Land & General
Lim Ah Tam @ Lim Bok Yeng	Kamunting Corp, Bandar Raya Developments
Lim Thian Kiat	Kamunting Corp, Bandar Raya Developments, Land & General

Appendix 6.3. Ownership of the 50 largest companies in Malaysia, 1997 and 2001

Name of corporation (1997) (Owner)	Name of Corporation (2001) (Owner)
1. Telekom (Government)	1. Telekom (Government)
2. Tenaga Nasional (Government)	2. Malayan Banking (Government)
3. Malayan Banking (Government)	3. Tenaga Nasional (Government)
4. Petronas Gas (Government)	4. Petronas Gas (Government)
5. Genting (Lim Goh Tong)	5. Resorts World (Lim Goh Tong)
6. Resorts World (Lim Goh Tong)	6. Malaysia International Shipping Corporation (MISC) (Government)
7. Sime Darby (Government)	7. Sime Darby (Government)
8. United Engineers (Malaysia) (UEM) (Halim Saad)	8. Commerce Asset-Holding (Government)
9. Malaysia International Shipping Corporation (MISC) (Government)	9. Genting (Lim Goh Tong)
10. Renong (Halim Saad)	10. YTL Corp (Yeoh family)
11. Rothmans of Pall Mall (Foreign)	11. Public Bank (Teh Hong Piow)
12. Development & Commercial Bank (Rashid Hussain)	12. Rothmans of Pall Mall (Foreign)
13. Malaysian Airlines (Tajudin Ramli)	13. YTL Power International (Yeoh family)
14. AMMB Holdings (Azman Hashim)	14. RHB Capital (Rashid Hussain)
15. Public Bank (Teh Hong Piow)	15. United Engineers (Malaysia) (UEM) (Halim Saad – now under the state)
16. YTL Corp (Yeoh family)	16. Renong (Halim Saad – now under the state)
17. TR Industries (TRI) (Tajudin Ramli)	17. Berjaya Sports Toto (Vincent Tan)
18. Magnum Corp (T.K. Lim)	18. Magnum Corp (T.K. Lim – now controlled by Daim's allies)

19. Perusahaan Otomobil Nasional (Proton) (Yahya Ahmad)	19. Perusahaan Otomobil Nasional (Proton) (Government)
20. Nestle (Foreign)	20. Kuala Lumpur Kepong (KLK) (Lee family)
21. Edaran Otomobil Nasional (EON) (Yahya Ahmad)	21. Malaysian Pacific Industries (Quek Leng Chan)
22. Heavy Industries Corp of Malaysia (HICOM) (Yahya Ahmad)	22. Nestle (Foreign)
23. Golden Hope Plantations (Government)	23. AMMB Holdings (Azman Hashim)
24. Hong Leong Credit (Quek Leng Chan)	24. Malayan Cement (Foreign)
25. Kuala Lumpur Kepong (KLK) (Lee family)	25. Golden Hope Plantations (Government)
26. Guthrie (Government)	26. Tanjong (T. Ananda Krishnan)
27. Faber (Halim Saad, through Renong)	27. Edaran Otomobil Nasional (EON) (Government)
28. Hong Leong Bank (Quek Leng Chan)	28. Hong Leong Bank (Quek Leng Chan)
29. Berjaya Toto (Vincent Tan)	29. Sarawak Enterprise Corporation (Sarawak state government)
30. Commerce-Asset Holdings (Halim Saad, through Renong)	30. Malaysian Airline System (Tajudin Ramli – now government)
31. Hume Industries (Quek Leng Chan)	31. Malaysian Resources Corporation (Government)
32. Multi-Purpose Holdings (MPHB) (T.K. Lim)	32. Oriental Holdings (Loh family)
33. Tanjong (T. Anada Krishnan)	33. Southern Bank (Tan Teong Hean)
34. Malayan United Industries (MUI) (Khoo Kay Peng)	34. HICOM Holdings (De-listed)
35. Rashid Hussain (RHB) (Rashid Hussain)	35. Malakoff (Government, through MRCB)
36. Affin Holdings (Government)	36. Gamuda (Lin Yun Ling)
37. Leader Universal (H'ng family)	37. Unisem (Foreign)
38. Higlands & Lowlands (Government)	38. Hong Leong Credit (Quek Leng Chan)
39. Land & General (L&G) (Wan Azmi Wan Hamzah)	39. TA Enterprise (Tiah Thee Kian)
40. OYL (Quek Leng Chan)	40. Sime UEP Properties (Government, through Sime Darby)
41. AMCORP (William Cheng)	41. Jaya Tiasa Holdings (Tiong Hiew King)
42. AMSTEEL (William Cheng)	42. Kumpulan Guthrie (Government)
43. Perlis Plantations (Robert Kuok)	43. Lingui Developments (Yaw Chee Ming)
44. Lingui Developments (Yaw Chee Ming)	44. Petronas Dagangan (Government)
45. Malaysian Helicopter Services (MHS) (Tajudin Ramli)	45. UMW Holdings (Government)
46. Jaya Tiasa Holdings (Tiong Hiew King)	46. New Straits Times Press (Government, through MRCB)
47. Petronas Dagangan (Government)	47. Affin Holdings (Government)
48. Shell (Foreign)	48. Arab-Malaysian Finance (Azman Hashim)
49. Sri Hartamas (Loy Hean Heong)	49. Malayan United Industries (Khoo Kay Peng)
50. IOI Corporation (Lee Shin Cheng)	50. IOI Corporation (Lee Shin Cheng)

Sources: KLSE Annual Companies Handbook 1996, 2001.

NOTES

1. See Gomez (2002) for a detailed assessment of the tripartite linkage between state, business groups, and the financial sector in Malaysia, and East Asia more generally.
2. In 2002, the ethnic breakdown of the Malaysian population was 66.1 percent Bumiputera, 25.3 percent Chinese, 7.4 percent Indian, and 1.2 percent others (Malaysia, 2001: 89).
3. See Gomez (1999) for an in-depth study of the impact of the NEP on Chinese-owned businesses. This study provides detailed case analyses of Chinese enterprises to reveal the different methods used by their owners to develop their firms during the NEP's implementation.
4. See, for example, Gomez (1990), whose study of UMNO's corporate investment indicates the extensive use of nominee companies to hold equity acquired by the party.
5. For an assessment of Mahathir's view on the need to develop huge business enterprises, specifically by emulating the Japanese *sogoshosha* model, see Chee and Gomez (1994).
6. Gomez and Jomo (1999) study the rise of these politically well-connected businessmen.
7. By early 1996, the switch from a conglomerate pattern of growth to a more focused approach was noted among well-connected firms (see Gomez 2002). This switch was in response to Mahathir's call for companies to develop expertise and a reputation in a particular industry.
8. The holding company structure exists when a parent firm controls the composition of the board of directors, or controls more than half the voting power, or holds more than half of the issued share capital of another subsidiary. The holding company uses the system of pyramiding, which allows the owner to maintain control over corporations with a relatively small investment (Sieh 1982; Lim 1981).
9. The exchange rate then between the Malaysian ringgit (RM) and the US dollar was RM2.4 = US$1. Presently, the exchange rate is RM3.8 = US$1.
10. Between the early 1970s and late 1980s, UMNO had acquired a huge interest in firms involved in most sectors of the economy (see Gomez 1990). UMNO's prominent role in the corporate sector led to allegations of conflicts of interest and corruption when its companies secured major government contracts. When a UMNO faction formed a new party and claimed these corporate assets in 1990, Mahathir permitted the transfer of party-owned enterprises to private individuals closely aligned to Daim.
11. For details on the takeover of assets controlled by Anwar allies and Daim protégés, see Gomez (2001).
12. Quoted in Gomez and Jomo (1999: 188).
13. See Gomez (1999) for case studies on the Yeoh Tiong Lay (YTL) Corp, Kuala Lumpur Kepong Berhad (KLK), and Oriental groups, which profile the growth of these enterprises from the time of their incorporation. These studies indicate that their standing as leading Malaysian firms is due to their adoption of a predominantly vertical or horizontal pattern of growth.

7

Thai Business Groups: Crisis and Restructuring

Piruna Polsiri and Yupana Wiwattanakantang

Modern capitalization in Thailand began around 1900. Immigrant and local-born Chinese spurred its rise. In this chapter, we investigate how these families diversified their holdings and later started business groups. As argued by many scholars in the business group literature, market imperfections, political economy, and cultural heritage may have contributed to this development in Thailand, as they did in many other emerging economies (Granovetter 1994; Ghemawat and Khanna 1998; Khanna 2000; Khanna and Palepu 2000). In contrast, our analysis is based on the political economy approach, which emphasizes the close connections between businessmen and government officials (Hamilton, Zeile, and Kin 1990).

We also use our unique, comprehensive database to investigate the ownership, control structures, and financial characteristics of the top thirty business group affiliates. We focus on nonfinancial firms listed on the Stock Exchange of Thailand between 1995 and 2000. Our sample coverage cannot go beyond listed firms because data for nonlisted firms and data before 1995 are not available. This sample period lets us examine how business groups have been affected by the 1997 Asian Crisis and how they have responded to it. We also provide some background on the government's restructuring initiatives under the International Monetary Fund's (IMF) program and briefly examine operational and financial restructuring actions undertaken by business group firms.

Sections 7.1 and 7.2 discuss the origin and evolution of business groups. Section 7.3 illustrates the impact of the East Asian financial crisis on business groups, and presents governance and financial characteristics of listed firms that are affiliated with the top thirty business groups in the period before and after the crisis. Section 7.4 describes restructuring schemes introduced by the government and investigates restructuring activities undertaken by business group firms as well as the efficiency of such activities. We also consider some of the restructuring activities taken by some leading Thai business groups in this section. Section 7.5 provides a summary and conclusion.

7.1. THE EMERGENCE OF BUSINESS GROUPS

Until 1932, Thailand was under an absolute monarchy. The king, royal family members, and high-ranking nobles controlled all commercial transactions. Because of Chinese merchants' skills and experience in trading, the government promoted Chinese immigration. During 1820–70, the Chinese were given privileges, patronized with trading licenses, tax farms, and investment loans, and provided political support (Phongpaichit and Baker 1995). Under this patronage, these Chinese merchants did very well, especially at rice trading, which accounted for about 70 percent of all exports in the 1910s (Piriyarangsan 1983; Phongpaichit and Baker 1995). In the 1930s, the 'Big Five' families that dominated the rice trade were all Chinese. These families continue to lead prominent business groups.

After the absolute monarchy was overthrown in 1932, civil service officers and military officers took over. They helped shape the Thai economy. In this section, we describe how the new rulers developed economic policy, and how Chinese entrepreneurs built connections with them and established business networks. We also describe the interrelationships between the sociocultural environments, the state, and the capital market that played an important role in the emergence and evolution of Thai business groups.

Figure 7.1 summarizes these relationships. Under corrupt military regimes, only skillful businessmen that had close connections with the state became successful in expanding their empire. Also, when capital markets were underdeveloped, owning financial institutions was essential to obtain funding and business expansion. So, families that owned banks and the connected families grew tremendously during the 1960s to 1980s. Interestingly, new business groups emerged around the end of the 1980s. When the country was financially liberalized, families that gained access to foreign capitals and technology expanded rapidly.

7.1.1. The Political Background during 1932–73

From 1932 until 1947, the People's Party ruled Thailand. The development regime was nationalistic and attempted to increase Thai nationals' business participation and decrease the role of Chinese immigrants by promoting the

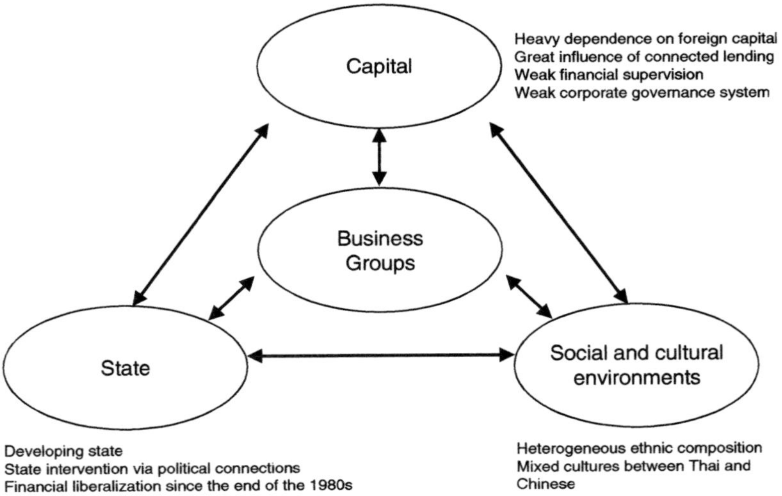

Figure 7.1. Thai institutional environments

former group's investments and restricting the latter group's trading activities. Nonetheless, the Big Five families had expanded their business networks to assist their rice trading. These businesses included rice milling, warehouses, shipping, banking, insurance, and foreign exchange dealing (Phongpaichit and Baker 1995). Further, the government's attempts to make native Thais more entrepreneurial did not succeed because Thais could easily live on the country's plentiful natural resources. Moreover, Thais regarded government jobs as more prestigious and secure than owning their own businesses (Phipatseritham and Yoshihara 1983). To limit Chinese dominance, the government set up many state-owned enterprises and semigovernmental companies, especially in trading and financial services. The government and the private sector jointly owned these semigovernmental firms. The private sector usually comprised People's Party members, government officials, and Chinese businessmen who had close relationships with People's Party members. People's Party members and their close associates (including the Chinese traders) also used their power to set up private companies (Piriyarangsan 1983; Phongpaichit and Baker 1995). Ironically, the government's policy to eradicate the small and medium-sized Chinese traders' economic power cemented the influence of big Chinese merchants.

In 1947, several military officers took over Thailand. Military officials maintained control until 1973, although a coup in 1957 meant that a second group of officials usurped power. During this period, the second regime did not renounce the 'state capitalism' policy of the People's Party, but they established more private companies and protected their affiliated business more vigorously than the People's Party members had (Piriyarangsan 1983).

Under the military regime, major profitable industries, namely sugar refining, tobacco, paper and plywood, and brewing, were monopolized by the state, which set up fifty-six state enterprises during 1947–56. The government also formed many joint-venture companies with leading Sino-Thai businessmen and had ownership and directorship in all thirteen commercial banks (Suehiro 1989).

It is thought, however, that the real objective behind this involvement in business activity was to generate funding to finance both personal and political activities of the officials who controlled the government (Riggs 1966; Piriyarangsan 1983; Hewison 1985, 2001). This objective became clear after 1951 when those in power no longer hid their interests. These individuals became extremely wealthy, and owned banking, trading, mining, manufacturing, construction, and services companies (Meechai 1983; Suehiro 1989; Sonsuphap 1996).

In general, the military government's pervasive control during this period created an uncertain business environment (Hewison 1985, 2001). Potential entrepreneurs feared that businesses they start might be taken over by the government or abolished if these firms were against the interests of important military officials (Hewison 1985; Suehiro 1989). For example, several big rice-trading families were suppressed when the People's Party lost power.

7.1.2. The Formation of Political Connections

To operate in the business environment, businessmen, especially those who owned larger firms, had to establish close ties with Thai rulers (Suehiro 1989). Sino-Thai businessmen provided the government ruling class not only capital but also the entrepreneurial and managerial expertise that government figures lacked. For example, several members of Big Five families were managing or executive directors of state-owned companies, and these families gave company shares and directorships to government officials. For example, the Lamsam family provided a directorship to Field Marshal Thanom Kittikachorn. In return, the Sino-Thai businessmen obtained security from political harassment and seizures of their assets (Suehiro 1989; Hewison 1989). They were also granted monopolistic rights, quotas, licenses, lucrative contracts, capital, foreign loans that the government guaranteed, and other privileges that competitors who lacked connections did not receive (Hewison 1985, 1989, 2001; Suehiro 1989). As noted earlier, however, these privileges lasted only as long as one regime maintained control since the Sino-Thai businessmen lacked connections with the new regime.

7.1.3. Political Connections and the Emergence of Business Groups during the 1950s

By the early 1950s, most of the business groups that now exist had emerged. As noted earlier, several rice-trading families already had sizeable concerns by this point. In the 1940s and the early 1950s, Chinese businessmen set up four banks that became economic juggernauts. These businessmen were skillful, but their strong relationships with the government were equally crucial to their success in expanding their business. For instance, Chin Sophonpanich adeptly managed his political network to make the Bangkok Bank not only the largest Thai bank but also the largest business group in Thailand for the next three decades (see Hewison 1985, 2001; Suehiro 1989; Bualek 2000). He appointed influential government officials to top positions within the bank, convinced the government to bail out the bank, and obtained various transactions from state-owned enterprises, including deposits and loans. Since then the Bangkok Bank has been the cornerstone of the Sophonpanich Group (Hewison 1989; Suehiro 1989; Bualek 2000). Even after the new military regime assumed power in 1957, Chin eventually reestablished a similar pattern of political connections that helped the bank maintain dominance.

7.1.4. The Development during 1960s until the mid-1990s: The Role of Connections and Foreign Capital

Even after the first National Economic Development Plan was implemented in 1961, close connections with the government remained essential to winning governmental contracts and financial support.[1] This plan first focused on industrialization, but began emphasizing exports in 1972. The Board of Investment (BOI) was established to promote investment. It has provided various investment incentives and privileges as well as tax exemptions to eligible companies based on their production capacities, thus favoring large firms. Because the project evaluation process was often not transparent, well-connected families, including those who owned business groups, received most of these privileges.

Moreover, big business groups likely obtained preferential funding from the Industrial Finance Corporation of Thailand (IFCT), a state-owned bank that was established in 1959 to spur industrialization by providing medium and long-term credit to industrial companies. Since family members from the big business groups that owned banks served as the IFCT's directors, Hewison (1985) concludes the IFCT likely gave preferential treatment to the owners of these business groups.

Due to the government's economic policies, well-connected families' businesses grew rapidly and emerged as new business groups. Some families, such as the Charoen Pokphand (CP) Group, which had focused on the agriculture industry and trading, shifted their investments to manufacturing industries (Suehiro 1989).

Until the early 1980s, the five business groups that grew most quickly all owned banks. Beyond their ties to the government, these groups probably grew because their control over capital meant that they were less financially constrained than were business groups that did not own financial concerns. According to Suehiro (1989), these five groups had about 281 affiliated firms in the beginning of the 1980s. For example, the Bangkok Bank group had diversified into the textile, food and beverage, trading, shipping, paper, and real estate industries. It owned eighty-three domestic affiliates and thirty-eight overseas affiliates. The Thai Farmers Bank group and the Bangkok Metropolitan Bank group had seventy-two and seventy-seven affiliated companies, respectively (Suehiro 1989).

Similar to many emerging economies, the expansion of Thai business empires was also attributable to foreign capital and technology (Suehiro 1989), which Thailand began receiving in the 1960s. These resources gave smaller business groups, which did not own financial institutions, needed funds and provided the technology they lacked. For example, Thai groups formed numerous joint ventures with Japanese automobile firms (Suehiro 1989). In the 1980s, many joint ventures were formed between local and Japanese firms to assemble goods not for local markets but exports in labor-intensive industries like textiles, automobiles, and electronics.

Financial deregulation and the development of the Stock Exchange of Thailand during the late 1980s, as well as the establishment of the Bangkok International Banking Facilities (BIBF) in the early 1990s, provided alternative sources of funds. Accordingly, business groups that did not own banks have used their increased access to capital to expand rapidly. Until the Asian Crisis in 1997, business groups in communications, media, electronics, manufacturing, and real estate grew more quickly than bank-dominated business groups did (Hewison 2000). Table 7.1 supports this argument. Panel A of this table presents the ranking of the top thirty business groups during the 1970s–90s.[2] Panel B focuses on the top thirty business groups in 1994. It presents the industries in which these groups have operated and the number of affiliated companies in the groups.[3]

Table 7.1. The top 30 business groups in Thailand

Panel A presents the ranking of business groups. The ranking in 1979 is taken from Suehiro (1989). The rankings in 1984, 1994, and 1997 are taken from Suehiro (2000). The 1979 and 1984 rankings are based on total sales of companies in the same group. The rankings of 1994 and 1997 are based on total sales of group affiliates that appear among the top 1,000 companies in Thailand based on sales. Panel B presents the owner family names of each of the top 30 business groups in 1994, and the business lines and the number of affiliated firms in each group. This information is taken from Brooker Group (2001).

Panel A: The rankings

	1979	1984	1994	1997
Ranking	Group name	Group name	Group name	Group name
1	Siam Cement (Siam Commercial Bank)	Bangkok Bank	Siam Cement (Siam Commercial Bank)	Siam Cement (Siam Commercial Bank)
2	Bangkok Bank	Siam Cement (Siam Commercial Bank)	Bangkok Bank	Bangkok Bank
3	Chawkwanyu	CP	CP	CP
4	Siam Motors	Metro	Thai Farmers Bank	TCC
5	CP	Thai Farmers Bank	Siam Motors	Thai Farmers Bank
6	Bangkok Metropolitan Bank	Bangkok Metropolitan Bank	Boon Rawd Brewery	Boon Rawd Brewery
7	Thai Farmers Bank	Siam Motors	TCC	Bank of Ayudhya
8	Metro	Soon Hua Seng	Sahapattanapibul	TPI
9	Boon Rawd Brewery	Sahapattanapibul	Thonburi Phanich	Siam Motors
10	Chaiyaporn Rice	Saha-Union	Sittipol	Central
11	Sahapattanapibul	Boon Rawd Brewery	Bank of Ayudhya	Sahapattanapibul
12	Sukree	Hong Yih Seng	Metro	Ital-Thai
13	Laemthong	Sukree	Osotsapa	Metro

(*Continued*)

Table 7.1. (*Continued*)

	1979	1984	1994	1997
Ranking	Group name	Group name	Group name	Group name
14	TPI	Siew	Cathay	MMC Sithipol
15	Bank of Ayudhya	Cathay	Central	Srifuengfung
16	Kamol Sukosol	Central	TPI	Taechaphaibun
17	Thai Rung Ruang	Laemthong	Ital-Thai	Saha-Union
18	Sittipol	Thai Rung Ruang	Saha-Union	Osotsapa
19	U Chu Liang	Kwang Soon Lee	Bangkok Metropolitan Bank	Sahaviriya
20	Kwang Soon Lee	Osothsapha	Shinnawatra	Shinnawatra
21	Soon Hua Seng	Yip In Tsoi	Sahaviriya	Thonburi Phanich
22	Ital-Thai	Mitr-Pol	Siam Steel Pipe	Soon Hua Seng
23	Saha-Union	Nanaphan	SP International	UCOM
24	Central	Sentagro	Soon Hua Seng	TPC
25	Cathay	Unicord	Land and House	Thai Union
26	Siew	Mah Boonkrong	Yip In Tsoi	Land and House
27	PSA	Wangkanai	Thai Life Insurance	Siam Steel Pipe
28	Wang Lee	Kamol Kij	Thai Summit	Thai Summit
29	Bangkok Rice	teck Bee Han	Bangkok Land	Betagro
30	Osothsapha	Kamol Sukosol	Thai Union	Mitr Phol

Panel B: Business lines

Ranking in 1994	Group name	Owner family name	Industries	No. of firms
1	Siam Cement/Siam Commercial Bank	Crown Property Bureau	Manufacturing; banking, finance and insurance; hotels, real estate development and construction; media/communication/advertising	29
2	Bangkok Bank	Sophonpanich	Finance and insurance; agri-industry and warehousing; health care services; real estate development; holding companies	46
3	CP	Chiarawanon	Agro-industry; aquaculture; chemicals; international trading; marketing and services; real estate and property development; industrial/commercial/petrochemicals; telecommunications/mass media	75
4	Thai Farmers Bank/Loxley	Lamsam	Banking, finance and insurance; trading; telecommunications/computers/media and advertising; manufacturing; hotels, real estate development and construction	43
5	Siam Motors	Pornprapha	Trading; recreation, transport and services; real estate development and construction; automotive industry/manufacturing; distribution; information technology/services	63

(*Continued*)

Table 7.1. (*Continued*)

Ranking in 1994	Group name	Owner family name	Industries	No. of firms
6	Boon Rawd	Piromphakdi	Liquor distilling and distribution; manufacturing; real estate and property development; holding companies	12
7	TCC/First Bangkok City Bank	Siriwattanapakdi	Liquor distilling and distribution; holding companies; banking, finance and insurance	60
8	Sahapattanapibul	Chokwattana	Consumer products; textile and garments; cosmetics and toiletries; footwear and rubber products; food processing and distribution; office equipment; machinery and electrical equipment; plastics products; advertising and design; property development; holding companies; finance	194
9	Thonburi Phanich	Wiriyaphan	Automotive; real estate development; tourism and transport; publishing	9
10	MMC Sittipol	Lee-issaranukun	Automotive; manufacturing	7
11	Bank of Ayudhya	Ratanarak	Banking, finance and insurance; manufacturing	25
12	Metro	Laohathai	Agro-chemicals; metals; agriculture and food industry; plastics; industrial chemicals; real estate development; warehousing	46
13	Osotsapa/Premier/GF Holdings	Osathanukhro	Manufacturing and distribution; real estate development and construction; trading; finance and insurance	97

14	Cathay/Thai-Asahi	Srifuengfung	Financial services; manufacturing; mining; marketing; shipping and transport; hotels, real estate development and construction	111
15	Central	Chirathiwat	Retailing; manufacturing; hotels, real estate development and construction; trading and distribution; finance and insurance	69
16	TPI/Hong Yiah Seng	Liaophairat	Petrochemical industry/oil retailing/ energy; finance and insurance; agro-industry and agricultural trading; textile	22
17	Ital-Thai	Kannasut	Construction; trading; manufacturing; hotels, travel and real estate development; food and beverages; telecommunications	37
18	Saha-Union	Darakanon	Manufacturing; distribution; real estate development; power generation	78
19	Bangkok Metropolitan Bank	Taechaphaibun	Banking and finance; hotels, real estate development and construction; transport; liquor distilling and distribution; manufacturing; holding companies	81
20	Shinnawatra	Shinnawatra	Computer and telecommunication; broadcasting	26
21	Sahaviriya	Wiriyaphraphaikit	Agriculture; computer and telecommunications; finance; steel manufacturing	58
22	Siam Steel Pipe/Siam Syntech	Leesawattrakun	Steel trading and manufacturing; construction/building systems; real estate development	35

(*Continued*)

Table 7.1. (*Continued*)

Ranking in 1994	Group name	Owner family name	Industries	No. of firms
23	SP International	Phornprapha	Automotive, assembly and distribution	11
24	Soon Hua Seng/Kaset Rung Ruang	Damnoencharnwanit	Import and export of agricultural products; agricultural milling; paper and pulp; cold storage and warehousing	23
25	Land and House/Quality House	Assawaphokhin	Hotels, real estate development and construction	26
26	Yip In Tsoi/Finance One	Yip In Tsoi, Chutrakul	Trading; finance and insurance; real estate development; manufacturing	24
27	Thai Life Insurance	Chaiyawan	Finance and insurance; real estate development	23
28	Thai Summit	Jungrungruenkit	Automotive; hotels and real estate development; finance and securities	28
29	Tanayong	Kanchanapat	Real estate, hotels and property management; finance; retail outlets and restaurants; holding companies	34
30	Thai Union	Charnsiri	N/A	13

Panel A reveals that even though the big three bank-dominated groups have remained in the top five business groups since the 1980s, other bank-dominated groups have been declining. Panel B suggests that similar to business groups in many emerging economies, the top business groups in Thailand are highly diversified and have many affiliates (see Chang 2003b). On average, the top five business groups owned 51.2 companies and the top thirty business groups owned 46.83 firms. The Sahapattanapibul Group had the highest number of companies, with 194 affiliates.

7.2. THE BUSINESS GROUPS IN THAILAND

First, we survey the characteristics of the top thirty business group affiliates. We then briefly discuss the causes of the 1997 Asian Crisis, focusing on Thailand. We also explore how this crisis affected the ownership, control structures, and financial characteristics of the top thirty business groups. Because there are no data for unlisted firms, our investigation covers only listed companies. Also, we focus only on nonfinancial firms.

7.2.1. The Characteristics of Business Groups

Panel A of Table 7.2 shows the number of (nonfinancial) firms affiliated with the top thirty business groups listed in the Stock Exchange of Thailand during 1995 to 2000. A firm is classified as an affiliate if its largest shareholder is a group's founding family. Compared to the chaebols in Korea, it is less common for Thai business groups to have their affiliates listed on the Stock Exchange. On average, the top five business groups had eight listed companies, while the top thirty business groups had 3.27 listed companies. Even the Sahapattanapibul group had only ten listed companies during 1996–7. There are also groups that do not list their companies. Among the top thirty groups, five groups did not have a single listed company.

Panel B of Table 7.2 reports the percentage of the firms' market capitalization relative to total market capitalization. Even excluding banks and financial affiliates, listed firms belonging to the top thirty business groups are relatively large. The market capitalization of the business group firms accounted for 29.82 and 25.67 percent of the total market capitalization in 1995 and 1996, respectively. With the crisis in 1997, affiliates' share of total market capitalization fell to 22.95 percent. This share subsequently increased to 26.71, 31.05, and 28.21 percent, respectively, in 1998, 1999, and 2000.

Table 7.2. The number of listed firms affiliated with the top 30 business groups and their market capitalization

Panel A presents the number of nonfinancial firms listed on the Stock Exchange of Thailand between 1995 and 2000 in which the largest shareholder is one of the families who own the top 30 business groups. Panel B presents the 'share of group-firm market capitalization', which is calculated as the percentage of market capitalization by group firms to total market capitalization.

Panel A: Number of nonfinancial listed firms

		1995	1996	1997	1998	1999	2000
Ranking	Group name	No. of firms	No. of firms	No. of firms	No. of firms	No. of firms	No. of firms
1	Siam Cement/Siam Commercial Bank	5	6	7	7	6	6
2	Bangkok Bank	2	3	3	3	3	4
3	CP	6	6	6	7	4	4
4	Thai Farmers Bank/Loxley	4	3	4	4	4	3
5	Siam Motors	0	0	0	0	0	0
6	Boon Rawd	0	0	0	0	0	0
7	TCC/First Bangkok City Bank	1	1	1	1	1	1
8	Sahapattanapibul	18	19	19	19	19	19
9	Thonburi Phanich	0	0	0	0	0	0
10	MMC Sittipol	2	2	1	1	1	1
11	Bank of Ayudhya	3	3	3	3	0	0
12	Metro	3	4	4	4	4	3
13	Osotsapa/Premier/GF Holdings	10	9	8	7	6	6
14	Cathay/Thai-Asahi	3	3	2	3	2	2
15	Central	4	6	6	6	6	5
16	TPI/Hong Yiah Seng	2	2	2	2	3	3
17	Ital-Thai	2	2	2	2	2	2
18	Saha-Union	5	5	5	5	5	5
19	Bangkok Metropolitan Bank	0	0	0	0	0	0
20	Shinnawatra	3	3	4	3	3	3
21	Sahaviriya	2	2	2	2	2	1
22	Siam Steel Pipe/Siam Syntech	2	2	1	1	1	1
23	SP International	0	1	1	1	1	1
24	Soon Hua Seng/Kaset Rung Ruang	1	1	1	1	1	1
25	Land and House/Quality House	3	4	4	4	4	4
26	Yip In Tsoi/Finance One	8	9	10	9	7	5
27	Thai Life Insurance	0	0	0	0	0	0
28	Thai Summit	0	0	0	0	0	0
29	Tanayong	2	2	2	2	1	1
30	Thai Union	1	2	2	1	1	1
Average number of firms per group		3.07	3.33	3.33	3.27	2.90	2.73

Panel B: Market capitalization

	1995	1996	1997	1998	1999	2000
Market capitalization by group firms (billion baht)	1,062.97	657.10	260.14	338.75	680.96	360.88
Total market capitalization (billion baht)	3,564.57	2,559.58	1,133.34	1,268.20	2,193.07	1,279.22
Share of group-firm market capitalization (%)	29.82	25.67	22.95	26.71	31.05	28.21
Number of firms	92	100	100	98	87	82

To investigate ownership and control structures, we constructed a comprehensive ownership database of nonfinancial companies during 1995–2000 that includes information on shareholders with at least 0.5 percent of a firm's shares.[4] The major source of these data is the I-SIMS database, which is produced by the Stock Exchange of Thailand. We also manually collected additional corporate ownership and board data, including a list of the firm's affiliated companies and shareholdings owned by these companies as well as relationships among major shareholders and board members from company files (FM 56–1) available at the Stock Exchange of Thailand's library and website. Our financial data also come from these sources.

Here we treat all family members as a single shareholder. We define the family relationship as those with the same surnames as well as those who are linked to the family by marriage. We traced the marriage relationship using various documents that provide a genealogical diagram of the top business group families (Pornkulwat 1996; Sappaiboon 2000a, 2000b, 2001; Brooker Group 2001). The related families via marriage are summarized in Table 7.3. This information indicates that the relationship via marriage might intensify business relationships; connected families appear to combine their businesses (Phipattseritham 1981; Suehiro 1989; Sappaiboon 2000a, 2000b, 2001).

In addition, we used the database provided by BusinessOnLine Ltd. (BOL) to trace the ultimate owners of private companies that appear as corporate shareholders of the sample firms. The BOL has a license from the Ministry of Commerce of Thailand to reproduce company information from the Ministry's database. This database contains major information on all registered companies in Thailand, which is reported annually to the Ministry. Accordingly, the ultimate owners of all privately owned companies that appear to be (domestic corporate) shareholders of listed firms in the sample are sought. The failure to search for the owners of these private companies would result in

Table 7.3. Family relationship between business groups

This table presents relationships between families that are tied via marriage with the top 30 business groups families. Note that we trace only the families who are shareholders of our sample firms, so the table might not include all the related families.

Ranking	Owner family name	Related families
1	Crown Property Bureau	—
2	Sophonpanich	Ramayarupa, Srifuengfung
3	Chiarawanon	—
4	Lamsam	Chatikavanij, Mokkawes, Chutrakul
5	Pornprapha	—
6	Piromphakdi	—
7	Siriwattanapakdi	—
8	Chokwattana	Dhanasarnsilp, Pavalolanvittaya, Kriang-pratana, Srirojanant, Punsak-udomsin
9	Wiriyaphan	—
10	Lee-issaranukun	Phannachet, Pisitkasem
11	Ratanarak	—
12	Laohathai	—
13	Osathanukhro	Phongsathorn, Prajuabmoh, Piya-oui, Thienprasidda
14	Srifuengfung	Panijcheeva, Sophonpanich
15	Chirathiwat	Boonyarat, Mongkolkiti, Eurwattanasakul
16	Liaophairat	—
17	Kannasut	Charanachitta, Rengpittaya, Terdprawat
18	Darakanon	—
19	Taechaphaibun	—
20	Shinnawatra	Damapong
21	Viriyapraphaikit	—
22	Leesawattrakun	Boonnamsap
23	Phornprapa	Narongdej
24	Damnoencharnwanit	—
25	Assawaphokhin	Harnpanich
26	Yip In Tsoi, Chutrakul	Chakkaphak, Chatikavanij, Srivikorn, Buranasiri, Sribunruang, Thavisin, Lam-sam
27	Chaiyawan	—
28	Jungrungruengkit	—
29	Kanchanapat	—
30	Charnsiri	Chan, Tangchansiri

the underestimation of the equity stake held by a firm's shareholders (see Khanthavit, Polsiri, and Wiwattanakantang 2003).

Table 7.4 presents summary statistics for several ownership and other governance variables for group and nongroup firms. The ownership of both group and nongroup firms is very concentrated in the largest shareholder's family. In group firms, the average voting rights held by the largest shareholder are 42.90, 44.1, and 46.28 percent in 1995, 1996, and 1997, respectively. The average cash flow rights held by the largest shareholder are 35.34, 37.44, and 38.65 percent in 1995, 1996, and 1997, respectively. The differences in the mean and median values for these figures are not always statistically significant.

We investigate the control structure that is used by the largest shareholder to control the firms. Following the literature, we consider three control mechanisms: pyramids, cross-shareholding, and direct shareholding. We define pyramid and cross-shareholding similar to how La Porta Lopez-de-Silanes, and Shleifer (1999) and Claessens et al. (2000) did. Specifically, pyramidal and cross-shareholding structures require that at least one public company appears in the chain of control, which effectively causes a disparity between cash-flow rights and voting rights.

The control structure of the business group firms is often via pyramids and cross-shareholding, apart from direct shareholding. Approximately 52, 54, and 56 percent of the business group firms use pyramidal shareholdings in 1995, 1996, and 1997, respectively. Cross-shareholding is used in about 18, 16, and 17 percent in 1995, 1996, and 1997, respectively. When compared with nongroup firms, the frequency with which business group affiliates use pyramid and cross-shareholdings is significantly greater (at the 1 percent level) for all years. Accordingly, the deviation of control from ownership, which is measured by the ratio of the cash flow rights to voting rights, is larger in group firms.

To illustrate how the control pattern is set up, we present the ownership structure of International Cosmetics in 1996 in Figure 7.2, which is taken from Wiwattanakantang (2001). This ownership structure illustrates direct equity and indirect equity via pyramidal and cross-shareholding. International Cosmetics belongs to the Sahapathanapibul Group, which was founded by the Chokwattana family. The family directly owns only 0.96 percent of International Cosmetics directly, but controls another 20.08 percent of the voting rights indirectly via the group's privately held holding companies. It also controls International Cosmetics by pyramidal shareholding via another three listed companies that it controls. International Cosmetics also holds 5.03 percent of Sahapathana Inter-Holdings. In total, Chokwattana family holds 48.58 percent of the voting rights in International Cosmetics.

Table 7.4. Governance characteristics

This table presents mean values of the governance variables of sample firms. The sample includes nonfinancial firms listed on the Stock Exchange of Thailand between 1995 and 2000. 'Group firms' refer to firms in which the largest shareholder is one of families who own the top 30 business groups. 'Nongroup firms' refer to firms in which the largest shareholder is not among families who own the top 30 business groups. ***, **, and * indicate that means are significantly different between group firms and nongroup firms at the 1%, 5%, and 10% levels, respectively, using heteroskedastic *t*-tests.

	1995		1996		1997		1998		1999		2000	
Variables	Group firms	Nongroup firms	Group firms	Nongroup firms	Group firms	Nongroup firms	Group firms	Nongroup firms	Group firms	Nongroup firms	Group firms	Nongroup firms
Cash-flow rights owned by the largest shareholder (%)	35.34**	40.13	37.44	39.67	38.65	39.97	38.33	40.29	37.49	39.45	38.59	39.67
Voting rights owned by the largest shareholder (%)	42.90	41.05	44.41*	40.89	46.28**	41.33	45.58*	41.73	44.16	40.69	45.03**	40.87
Percentage of firms with direct shareholdings	94.51	97.61	94.95	96.76	93.94	96.11	94.85	97.15	96.51	97.93	97.53	98.74
Percentage of firms in pyramidal structures	51.65***	9.57	53.54***	13.36	55.56***	15.18	53.61***	16.26	52.33***	14.46	45.68***	12.61
Percentage of firms with cross-shareholdings	17.58***	1.91	16.16***	2.43	17.17***	2.33	16.49***	3.25	15.12***	3.31	13.58***	2.10
Percentage of firms in which the largest shareholder is a top manager	37.36	43.06	33.33	40.65	35.35	42.19	38.54	43.27	39.53	39.17	40.74	36.55
Number of board positions	13.60***	10.58	13.76***	10.72	13.58***	10.64	13.83***	10.62	13.60***	10.30	13.53***	10.39
Number of board positions held by members of the largest shareholder	3.25***	2.20	3.32***	2.21	3.18***	2.21	3.11***	2.21	3.14***	2.08	3.14***	1.96
Number of firms	92	208	100	246	100	256	98	247	87	241	82	237

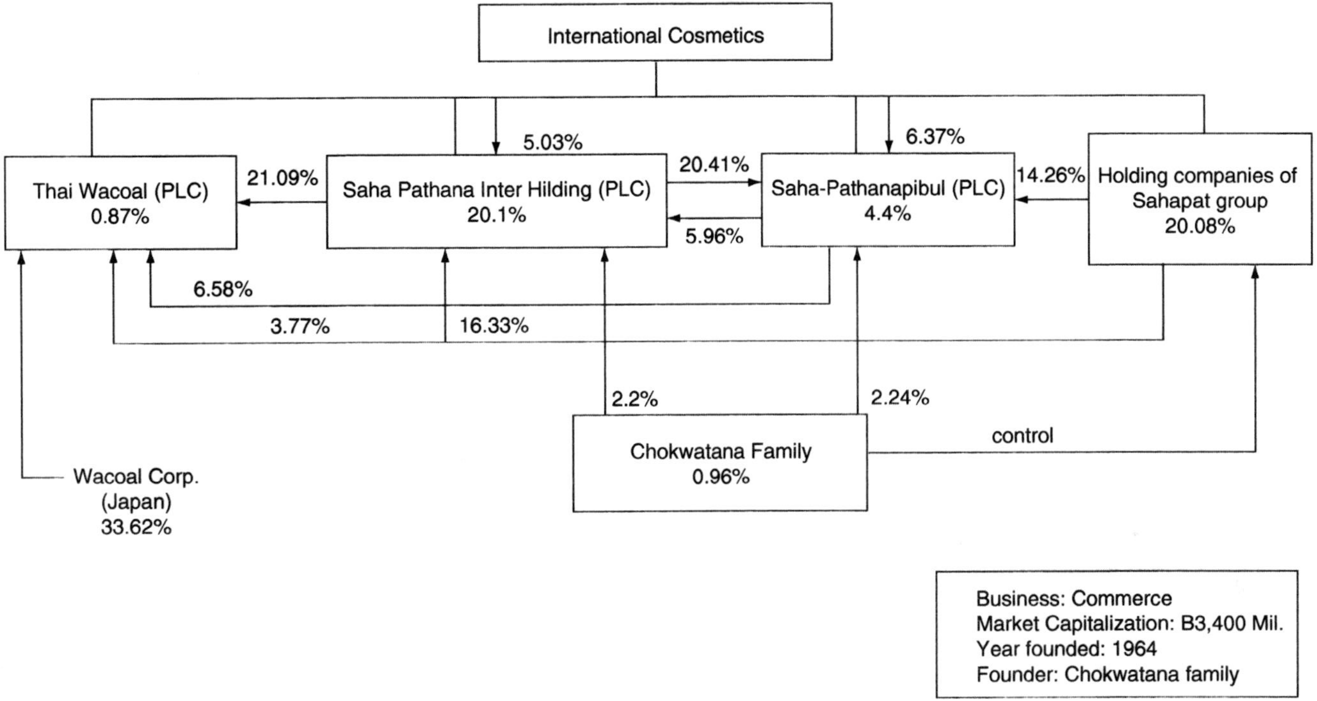

Figure 7.2. The ownership structure of International Cosmetics

Source: Wiwattanakantang (2001).

Table 7.4 also shows that the largest shareholders commonly hold positions as honorary chairman, chairman, executive chairman, vice chairman, president, vice president, chief executive officer, managing director, deputy managing director, and assistant managing director. Specifically, in about 37, 33 and 35 percent of the business group firms, at least one person from the largest shareholder's family serves in at least one such position in 1995, 1996, and 1997, respectively. Nongroup firms appear to have a similar pattern.

In addition, we find that the largest shareholder also sits in the board of directors. For group firms, there are on average 3.25, 3.32, and 3.18 members of the largest shareholder's family serving as board members in 1995, 1996, and 1997, respectively. The median numbers of persons are 3 for all the years. Board domination by the controlling family appears significantly more often in group firms than it does in nongroup firms.

Business group affiliates also have significantly larger boards than nongroup firms do. Business group firms have, on average, 13.60, 13.76, and 13.58 members on the board in 1995, 1996, and 1997, respectively. The median values are 13 for all three years. The median numbers of board members among nongroup firms is 10 during the same period.

Overall, these results suggest ownership of business group affiliates is concentrated in the hands of the founding family. Similar to chaebols, Thai business groups consist of legally independent companies that are affiliated to a common group name. These firms are centrally controlled through direct ownership, pyramidal shareholding, and cross-shareholding among member firms (see Pipattseritham 1984; Suehiro 1989). Founding family members also hold much of the decision-making and monitoring power in these groups.

In assessing the impact of the Asian Crisis on the top thirty business groups, we focus on these groups' capital structure since it has been argued that high debt ratios made Thai firms more vulnerable to the crisis. Table 7.5 shows the financial characteristics, financing structure, and performance of nonfinancial listed companies that are top thirty business group affiliates and those that are not. Regarding firm size, business group affiliates had two to three more total assets than nongroup firms did in all periods. There was no significant difference, however, between the financing structures of group and nongroup firms, and the debt levels of Thai group firms were much lower when compared with that of chaebols (see Chang 2003b). It should be noted, however, that the debt ratio shown Table 7.5 is only for listed companies.

On the other hand, after the crisis and the depreciation of the baht in July 1997, the debt ratios of both business group and nongroup firms increased. Furthermore, business group affiliates' profits decreased significantly. When

Table 7.5. Financial characteristics

This table presents mean values of the financial variables of sample firms. The sample includes nonfinancial firms listed on the Stock Exchange of Thailand between 1995 and 2000. All data are obtained from the I-SIMS database. Total capital is the sum of total debt and market value of equity. Tobin's Q is the ratio of the sum of total liabilities and market value of equity to book value of total assets. 'Group firms' refer to firms in which the largest shareholder is one of the families who own the top 30 business groups. 'Nongroup firms' refer to firms in which the largest shareholder is not among families who own the top 30 business groups. ***, **, and * indicate that means are significantly different between group firms and nongroup firms at the 1%, 5%, and 10% levels, respectively, using heteroskedastic t-tests.

	1995		1996		1997		1998		1999		2000	
Variables	Group firms	Nongroup firms	Group Firms	Nongroup firms	Group firms	Nongroup firms	Group firms	Nongroup firms	Group firms	Nongroup firms	Group firms	Nongroup firms
Total assets (million baht)	10,392.5***	4,801.1	12,174.9***	5,351.3	16,121.8**	5,906.7	15,662.9**	5,752.5	14,784.1**	5,850.0	14,651.4**	5,730.4
Total debt/Total assets	0.37	0.39	0.40	0.42	0.54	0.52	0.50	0.51	0.46	0.57	0.50	0.62
Short-term debt/Total assets	0.20	0.23	0.21	0.24	0.26	0.28	0.25	0.29	0.21*	0.33	0.19	0.28
Long-term debt/Total assets	0.18	0.17	0.19	0.18	0.28	0.24	0.25	0.23	0.24	0.24	0.31	0.34
Total debt/Total capital	0.39	0.39	0.50	0.48	0.66	0.66	0.64	0.62	0.52	0.57	0.57	0.56
EBIT/Total assets (%)	8.79	8.72	11.65	7.51	2.94	1.87	3.43	5.23	0.05	−4.20	3.08	−3.77
EBT/Total assets (%)	5.92	5.64	8.05	3.85	−1.56	−3.27	−3.17	−3.10	−5.49	−11.36	−2.10	−9.51
Industry-adjusted EBIT/ Total assets (%)	0.67	0.00	4.42	−0.11	−1.17	−3.31	−4.32	−1.76	−2.09	−6.56	−2.59	−8.89
Industry-adjusted EBT/ Total assets (%)	0.57	−0.19	3.90	−0.52	−2.13	−4.92	−5.39	−4.17	−2.41*	−8.82	−4.57	−11.20
Tobin's Q	1.34	1.37	1.07	1.16	1.02	1.04	0.98	1.04	1.19	1.22	1.08	1.38
Number of firms	92	208	100	246	100	256	98	247	87	241	82	237

interest expenses are deducted, the average business group continued to lose money through 2000.

7.3. THE ASIAN CRISIS AND THAILAND

There are many studies of the 1997 Asian Crisis (e.g. Corsetti, Pernti, and Roubini 1998; Krugman 1998a; Radelet and Sachs 1998; Department of Foreign Affairs 2000; Siamwalla 2001). In general, they have concluded that hasty financial liberalization without a comprehensive regulatory and supervisory framework, macroeconomic mismanagement by the government, large short-term debt owed to foreign investors, and inadequate corporate governance and regulations in the private sector were the Thai economy's underlying problems. Financial liberalization during the end of the 1980s and the early 1990s is often regarded as especially contributing to the crisis. In particular, the BIBF, which was set up in 1993 to serve as an intermediary between overseas lenders and local borrowers, facilitated foreign-dominated loans for both financial and nonfinancial companies. Most of these loans were not hedged from lenders' expectations of continued exchange-rate stability.

The growing mismatch in the currency denomination of banks' assets and liabilities is thought to have been another major cause of the banking crisis in 1996 and 1997 (Kawai and Takayasu 2000; Siamwalla 2001). Specifically, banks used deposits and unhedged short-term foreign currency loans for long-term loans in domestic currency. In addition, Thai banks and finance companies had many poor-quality loan portfolios due to risky lending, which was based on collateral and connections (Krugman 1998a; Charumilind, Kali, and Wiwattanakantang, forthcoming). There was a systematic failure of risk-management systems and controls underlying lending practices. When exports, real estate, and stock markets fell in 1996, many financial institutions became insolvent with huge amounts of nonperforming loans. The failure of the Thai government to deal with these problems precipitated the crisis in Thailand (Nukul Commission 1998; Flatters 1999). At the same time, increasing numbers of currency speculators bet against the baht (Siamwalla 2001). In response, massive capital flights began in late 1996 and continued until July 2, 1997, when the country's foreign exchange reserves were exhausted. In August 1997, the government signed the first Letter of Intent requesting the IMF's assistance. This speculation and capital flight weakened the cash flows of nonfinancial companies, which in turn further weakened the liquidity of financial firms.

7.3.1. Banking and Financial Sector Reforms

The IMF program attempted to stabilize the macro economy and restore financial market stability (Flatters 1999; Department of Foreign Affairs 2000; Kawai and Takayasu 2000). It proposed measures to improve the economic governance and competitiveness of Thai industries, develop social safety nets, and reform and rehabilitate the financial sector (Flatters 1999). To increase confidence in the banking industry, the government provided a blanket guarantee for depositors. To restore the effectiveness of the financial industry and increase financial sector transparency and competition, the government strengthened regulations, loan classification procedures, and capital requirements. In 1997 and 1998, several emergency amendments were passed to enable the Bank of Thailand to intervene promptly with nonviable financial institutions.

These reforms accompanied bank and finance company closures and nationalization. In addition, in order to assist recapitalization of financial services firms, the government increased the limit of foreign ownership in banks and finance companies from 25 to 100 percent for ten years. The government also injected 300 million baht into financial institutions that met specified conditions in August 1998 to expedite recapitalization of these firms, and it set up the Asset Management Corporation to help finance companies write off their bad loans. By the end of 2000, these measures had resulted in the closure of seventy-one out of ninety-one finance companies and four of fourteen domestic banks. Further two domestic banks had been taken over by the government and four banks had majority foreign ownership (Aunichitworawong, Souma, and Wiwattanakantang 2003). Most surviving financial institutions had recapitalized by obtaining direct equity investments from foreign partners and issuing shares and capital securities.

Table 7.6 presents banks' ownership structures 1996 and 2000. Interestingly, before the crisis the largest shareholder in twelve out of fourteen Thai commercial banks was either a single family or a group of families (see also Aunichitworawong, Souma, and Wiwattanakantang 2003). The largest shareholders of seven banks were the top thirty business group families. After the crisis, however, four families lost the control over the banks. The families that had remained the largest shareholders in Thai banks had done so by selling shares to other investors, many of which were foreign, and selling all or parts of their groups' noncore businesses (Hewison 2000).

Table 7.6. Ownership of commercial banks in 1996 and 2000

This table presents the name of the founders and the largest shareholders of all Thai commercial banks in 1996 and 2000. The information on the largest shareholders is obtained from Anuchitworawong, Souma, and Wiwattanakantang (2003).

			Largest shareholders		
Commercial banks as of 1996	Founding Year	Founders	1996	2000	Commercial banks as of 2000
Bank of Ayudhya	1945	Panomyong and Luprasert	Ratanarak	Ratanarak	Bank of Ayudhya
Bangkok Bank	1944	Leelanuch and Sophonpanich	Sophonpanich	Sophonpanich	Bangkok Bank
Bangkok Bank of Commerce	1944	Pinitchonkadee and Intaratoot	Tantipipatpong	Closed down in 1998	Krungthai Bank
Bangkok Metropolitan Bank	1950	Euawattanasakul, Srifuengfung, Techapaibul, and Setthapakdee	Techapaibul, Siriwattanapakdee	State (intervened in 1998)	Bangkok Metropolitan Bank (HSBC)
Bank of Asia	1939	University of Moral Science and Politics	Phatraprasith	ABN Amro Holding	Bank of Asia
Bank Thai	1998	State	—	State	Bank Thai
First Bangkok City Bank	1955	Tan Keng Kun	Siriwattanapakdee	Closed down in 1998	Krungthai Bank
Krungthai Bank	1966	State	State	State	Krungthai Bank

Laem Thong Bank	1948	Nanthapiwat	Chansrichawala	Closed down in 1998	UOB Radanasin Bank
Nakornthon Bank	1933	Wang Lee	Wang Lee	Standard Chartered Bank	Standard Chartered Nakornthon Bank
Siam Commercial Bank	1906	Crown Property Bureau	Crown Property Bureau	Crown Property Bureau	Siam Commercial Bank
Siam City Bank	1941	Nirandorn	Srifuengfung and Mahadamrongkul	State (intervened in 1998)	Siam City Bank
UOB Ratanasin Bank	1998	State	—	United Overseas Bank	UOB Ratanasin Bank
Thai Dhanu Bank	1949	Thaveesin	Tuchinda and Rasanon	DBS Bank	DBS Thai Dhanu Bank
Thai Farmers Bank	1945	Lamsam	Lamsam	Government of Singapore International Corporation	Thai Farmers Bank
Thai Military Bank	1957	Army, Navy, Airforce	Army, Navy, Airforce	Army, Navy, Airforce	Thai Military Bank
Union Bank of Bangkok	1949	Mahakun and Visutthipol	Cholvijarn	Closed down in 1998	Bank Thai

7.3.2. Corporate Sector Reforms

To refurbish the corporate sector's balance sheets, the government promised the IMF that it would facilitate corporate restructuring. The major reforms included amending bankruptcy and foreclosure laws, establishing an effective bankruptcy enforcement framework, developing a structured out-of-court procedure for voluntary debt restructuring, streamlining institutional arrangements for corporate debt workouts, and establishing an effective legal scheme for asset recovery through court-based bankruptcy and court-controlled debt restructuring or reorganization (Department of Foreign Affairs 2000; Flatters 1999; Kawai and Takayasu 2000). The government has also implemented reforms to strengthen boards of directors, the institutional framework for accounting and auditing practices, the quality and reliability of company information, and minority shareholder rights (Department of Foreign Affairs 2000).

In addition, the Corporate Debt Restructuring Advisory Committee (CDRAC) was set up in June 1998 to oversee and facilitate voluntary debt restructuring negotiations under a market-oriented framework. Members of the CDRAC include both creditor and debtor associations, although de facto the CDRAC's process covers only creditors who are financial institutions (Kawai and Takayasu 2000; Dasri 2001). CDRAC and the March 1999 bankruptcy law amendment accelerated corporate-debt restructuring. About 400,000 classified loans, totaling 2.6 trillion baht, were restructured under the CDRAC process as of August 1999. Among them, 700 cases were large distressed loans that exceeded 500 million baht. By the end of 2000, cases totaling 1.1 trillion baht had undergone the CDRAC process (Bank of Thailand 2000). According to the World Bank's survey, which covered about 400 nonfinancial firms, CDRAC helped reduce corporate debt significantly (Department of Foreign Affairs 2000; World Bank 2000).

7.4. BUSINESS GROUPS AFTER THE CRISIS: EXTENSIVE RESTRUCTURINGS

Increased debt and reduced profitability after the East Asian financial crisis and baht devaluation induced Thai firms to restructure extensively. In this section, we investigate restructuring activities undertaken by the top thirty business group firms. The data on restructuring actions are collected from the company daily news database at the website of the Stock Exchange of Thailand, company annual reports, and financial statements.

7.4.1. Restructuring Activities of Business Groups

Following the literature (John et al. 1992; Ofek 1993; Kang and Shivdasani 1997; Lai and Sudarsanam 1997; Denis and Kruse 2000; Kang et al. 2001; Baek et al. 2002), we categorize restructuring actions into, (a) operational actions and (b) financial actions. Operational actions include the following three actions. First, *asset downsizing* occurred when a firm sold assets (e.g. financial securities, land, properties, and stakes in other businesses or joint ventures), closed a plant, reduced production capacity, discontinued or suspended production, or shut down a division, office, branch, or subsidiary. We do not include employee layoffs because data about them are not available. Second, *expansion* occurred when a firm engaged in a joint venture or strategic alliance, fully or partially acquired other businesses, diversified into new businesses, constructed new facilities, established a new division, office, branch, or subsidiary, expanded existing production facilities, or invested in existing subsidiaries. Third, *top management turnover* occurred when at least one top manager was replaced. The top management positions include chairman of the board, president, vice president, chief executive officer, managing director, and deputy managing director.

Financial actions occurred when a firm had a dividend cut by reducing or discontinuing the dividends it had been paying, restructured debt by reducing its required interest or principal payment on a debt agreement, extending a debt maturity, exchanging equity securities (common stocks or securities convertible to common stocks) for debt or giving creditors equity securities, and appointing a financial advisor to assist in debt-restructuring process, or raised capital by issuing debt and securities such as new loans, debentures, common stocks, and hybrid securities, including preferred stocks, warrants, and convertible debentures.

Table 7.7 reports the frequency of restructuring actions undertaken by the top thirty group firms during 1996–2000. We also provide the information for nongroup firms for a comparison. In general, group firms restructured more than nongroup firms did in all years. The differences are statistically significant at the 5 percent level, however, only in 1997.

Interestingly, the most common restructuring activity was expansion. Even after the crisis, many business group affiliates expanded after they raised capital and reduced their total assets (two of the other most common activities). In addition, although most group affiliates cut dividends in 1997, relatively few did in subsequent years. In sum, group affiliates responded to the Asian Crisis by initially cutting dividends and then raising external capital and restructuring debt.

Table 7.7. Restructuring activities during 1996–2000

This table presents the frequency of restructuring activities taken by sample firms. The sample includes nonfinancial firms listed on the Stock Exchange of Thailand (SET) between 1997 and 2000. Figures in 'group firms' columns are the percentage of firms undertaking a restructuring action to the number of total group firms. 'Group firms' refer to firms in which the largest shareholder is one of the families who own the top 30 business groups. 'Nongroup firms' refer to firms in which the largest shareholder is not among families who own the top 30 business groups. Figures in 'nongroup firms' columns are the ratio of the number of firms undertaking a restructuring action to the number of total nongroup firms. The '*p*-value' columns report *p*-values of the test of difference in the proportion of firms undertaking restructuring actions between two group firms and nongroup firms.

	1996			1997			1998			1999			2000		
Restructuring actions	Group firms	Nongroup firms	*p*-value	Group firms	Nongroup firms	*p*-value	Group firms	Nongroup firms	*p*-value	Group firms	Nongroup firms	*p*-value	Group firms	Nongroup firms	*p*-value
Any restructuring actions	94.95	91.50	0.23	92.93	85.55	**0.03**	72.16	59.76	**0.03**	75.58	66.53	0.11	74.07	66.39	0.19
Any operational actions	84.85	82.59	0.60	65.66	54.30	**0.05**	52.58	42.28	**0.09**	58.14	43.39	**0.01**	58.02	48.32	0.13
Asset downsizing	18.18	23.89	0.23	17.17	20.62	0.45	24.74	18.29	0.20	25.58	21.90	0.50	27.16	21.85	0.35
Expansion	83.84	78.95	0.28	55.56	45.14	**0.08**	40.21	28.86	**0.05**	44.19	26.86	**0.01**	40.74	30.25	**0.10**
Management turnover	2.02	4.45	0.21	18.18	5.06	**0.00**	12.37	9.35	0.43	15.12	12.40	0.54	16.05	12.61	0.46
Any financial actions	72.73	56.68	**0.00**	80.81	70.82	**0.04**	42.27	36.99	0.37	51.16	43.39	0.22	46.91	43.70	0.62
Dividend cut	51.52	39.68	**0.05**	67.68	57.98	**0.09**	10.31	14.23	0.31	9.30	9.92	0.87	18.52	13.03	0.26
Debt restructuring	0.00	2.02	**0.03**	0.00	3.50	**0.00**	7.22	8.94	0.59	8.14	12.40	0.24	14.81	17.65	0.55
Capital raising	47.47	33.60	**0.02**	46.46	31.52	**0.01**	29.90	21.14	**0.10**	43.02	27.27	**0.01**	34.57	30.25	0.48

A substantial increase in the number of firms restructuring debt since 1997 might be attributable to the passage of the Amendment to Bankruptcy Act (No. 4) on March 4, 1998. The amendment contains the legal framework designed for a court-supervised debt restructuring or reorganization of a company. It resembles the Chapter 11 provisions in the USA. The new law allows a distressed company to recuperate its business and protects the interests of a company's creditors (Pornavalai 1999; Wong, Phunsunthron, and Sucharikul 2000).

Finally, it is worth noting that top management turnover increased substantially after the crisis hit. Specifically, the turnover rate rose from 2.02 percent in 1996 to 18.18 percent in 1997, and exceeded 12 percent for the whole sample period. This finding suggests that long-term distress forced Thai firms to remove their managers.

7.4.2. The Effects of Restructurings

In this section, we investigate the results of the restructuring implemented by major business groups by comparing performance before and after this restructuring occurred. Performance is measured by the ratio of earnings before interest and taxes (EBIT) to total assets. To control for industry effects, we computed industry-adjusted changes in the operating performance from the year in which firms restructured to the two subsequent years. We calculated the industry-adjusted change in operating performance as a change in the ratio of EBIT to total assets for a sample firm minus a median change in the ratio of EBIT to total assets for its industry.

We calculated mean and median changes in the operating performance from Year 0 (in which a restructuring is undertaken) to two years following Year 0 (denoted by Year 1 and Year 2, respectively). The results shown in Table 7.8 indicate that operating performance improved after restructuring occurred. When the performance measure does not control for the industry effects (unadjusted changes in operating performance), debt restructuring has the most pronounced favorable effect. Specifically, firms that restructured debt in Year 0 exhibited significantly positive mean and median changes in the ratio of EBIT to assets from Year 1 to Year 2 and from Year 0 to Year 2. When the industry effects are controlled, group firms had significantly positive changes in operating performance for the first and second year subsequent to a restructuring. Overall, the mean (median) value of industry-adjusted changes in the ratio of EBIT to total assets from Year 0 to Year 1 is 2.51 percent (1.68 percent), which is significant at the 1 percent level.

Consistent with the general results and adjusting for industry effects, except for dividend cuts and debt restructuring, group affiliates that adopted other

Table 7.8. Operating performance following restructuring activities

The table presents changes in (industry-adjusted) operating performance following restructuring activities taken by business group firms. The sample consists of nonfinancial firms listed on the Stock Exchange of Thailand (SET) between 1996 and 2000 in which the largest shareholder is one of the families who own the top 30 business groups. Change in EBIT/total assets is calculated as the ratio of EBIT to total assets for the current year minus the same ratio for the previous year. Industry-adjusted change in EBIT/total assets is calculated as change in EBIT/total assets is calculated as the ratio of EBIT to total assets for a sample firm minus median change in EBIT/total assets for its industry. Year 0 denotes the year in which restructuring actions are taken. Medians are reported in brackets below the means. ***, **, and * indicate that means (medians) are significantly different from zero at the 1%, 5%, and 10% levels, respectively, using *t*-tests (Wilcoxon signed-ranks tests).

	Change in EBIT/Total assets			Industry-adjusted change in EBIT/Total assets		
Type of actions	Year (0, 1)	Year (1, 2)	Year (0, 2)	Year (0, 1)	Year (1, 2)	Year (0, 2)
Any restructuring actions ($n = 365$)	0.14	0.65	0.80	2.51***	0.93	0.99
	[−0.33]	[0.82]	[0.96]	[1.68]***	[0.19]	[0.44]**
Any operational actions ($n = 283$)	0.24	0.57	0.81	2.66***	0.70	1.02
	[−0.47]	[0.93]	[0.76]	[1.50]***	[0.14]	[0.50]**
Asset downsizing ($n = 96$)	1.21	1.03	2.23	4.17**	0.85	2.12
	[−0.55]	[1.43]	[1.90]	[2.11]***	[0.22]	[0.55]
Expansion ($n = 238$)	−0.57	0.33	−0.24	1.85**	0.38	0.19
	[−0.87]	[0.98]	[0.54]	[1.13]***	[0.21]	[0.55]*
Management turnover ($n = 54$)	2.13	0.39	2.52*	4.38***	1.67	2.74**
	[1.38]	[−0.05]	[1.41]	[2.70]**	[0.02]	[0.45]
Any financial actions ($n = 267$)	0.46	0.79	1.24	2.48***	1.42	1.59
	[−0.23]	[0.77]	[1.41]**	[1.80]***	[0.25]*	[1.09]***
Dividend cut ($n = 145$)	0.75	−1.47	−0.72	1.06	0.57	0.61
	[−0.05]	[−0.79]	[0.56]	[0.00]	[0.14]	[1.15]**
Debt restructuring ($n = 25$)	0.38	10.73***	11.11*	3.49	8.57**	7.95
	[−3.94]	[5.72]***	[3.89]**	[−0.36]	[2.52]**	[2.11]
Capital raising ($n = 180$)	1.65	0.24	1.89	4.32***	0.71	2.12
	[0.21]	[1.04]	[2.09]**	[3.43]***	[0.43]	[1.40]***

types of restructuring positively and significantly improved performance change in the year following the restructuring. We also find that, except for asset downsizing and debt restructuring, the performance of firms that adopted other types of restructuring significantly increased two years after the restructuring.

7.5. SUMMARY AND CONCLUSION

This chapter has investigated the top thirty business groups in Thailand. It focused especially on how these groups formed, groups' characteristics before the Asian Crisis, and the effects of the crisis and these groups' responses. Thai business groups emerged around the end of the 1940s. Political connections, as well as foreign capital and technology were crucial to their emergence. Further, financial regulations affected the growth of business groups that did not own financial firms relative to those that did. Our analysis has indicated that Thai business groups are similar to business groups in many emerging economies, especially in regard to the high concentration of ownership and control in the hands of these groups' founding families.

The East Asian financial crisis has had significant adverse effects on Thailand. On a positive note, the Thai government undertook various effective legal measures to remodel the country's institutional environment. These changes have induced big business groups to change somewhat. Further, many of these groups have restructured significantly since the crisis, and these measures have improved firms' performance.

Nonetheless, many business group affiliates had not restored profitability by 2000. In addition, many business groups have lost their financial bases, and hence will probably not be able to obtain funding easily as they did when they owned banks and financial institutions. To obtain external funding from capital markets, business groups need to continue to improve their corporate governance and become more transparent.

NOTES

1. The Plan was supervised by the National Economic Development Board. Its chairman was Thailand's prime minister. The Plan's single goal was to accelerate economic growth through centralized planning. It emphasized public investment in Thailand's infrastructure industrial development in the private sector. The Plan

also focused on accumulation of physical capital assets. Since 1972, the plan has been called the National Economic and Social Development Plan (*Source*: Office of the National Economic and Social Development Board).

2. As far as we know, there are no statistics for business groups in Thailand before 1979. Phipattseritham (1981) and Suehiro (1989) are the first studies.
3. This ranking was based on sales. It was done by Suehiro (2000). This ranking includes only firms that appeared on the list of the top 1000 companies in 1994 that was published by Advance Research Group (1995). Therefore, it may not include all the groups' affiliates.
4. Previous research (e.g. Claessens, Djankov, and Lang 2000; Mitton 2002; Lemmon and Lins 2003; Lins 2003) uses ownership databases that include only shareholders with at least 5 percent of the equity in a firm.

8

Indonesian Business Groups: The Crisis in Progress

Alberto D. Hanani

Definitions of business groups share common features. Yet they are somewhat idiosyncratic in identifying characteristics that apply only to business groups in specific countries. This chapter will use a definition that fits the Indonesian context, but is largely similar to ones employed by other authors in this book. In Indonesia, 'business group' is virtually interchangeable with 'conglomerate' since most Indonesian business groups comprise strategically and technologically unrelated companies. Regardless of how diversified they are, most Indonesian business groups are controlled and managed by their founders and the founders' families and longtime friends. There is little formal, professional management of these groups.

As noted in Chapter 1 of this volume, business groups often play important roles in developing economies by overcoming imperfect factor markets. They can, for instance, enable member firms to share risk by mitigating the volatility of income flows and by reallocating money from one affiliate to another in times of distress. Yet the governance systems in these groups are often deeply flawed (Dewenter, Novaes, and Pettway 1999; Nam 2001). They could not check overleveraged business expansion and inefficient investment because they lacked internal mechanisms to monitor management. In addition, founding families and their associates have frequently used their control over business groups to expropriate wealth from minority shareholders (Chang 2003a). In Indonesia, the ruling government behaves similarly in regard to the approximately 165 state-owned enterprises in which it has a controlling interest.

To date, the role business groups played in the Asian Crisis has been relatively neglected by policy initiatives and research. For instance, even though the corporate governance of business groups has been studied intensively, these studies have remained largely at the macro-policy level. This chapter attempts to fill that gap by reporting some early observations on

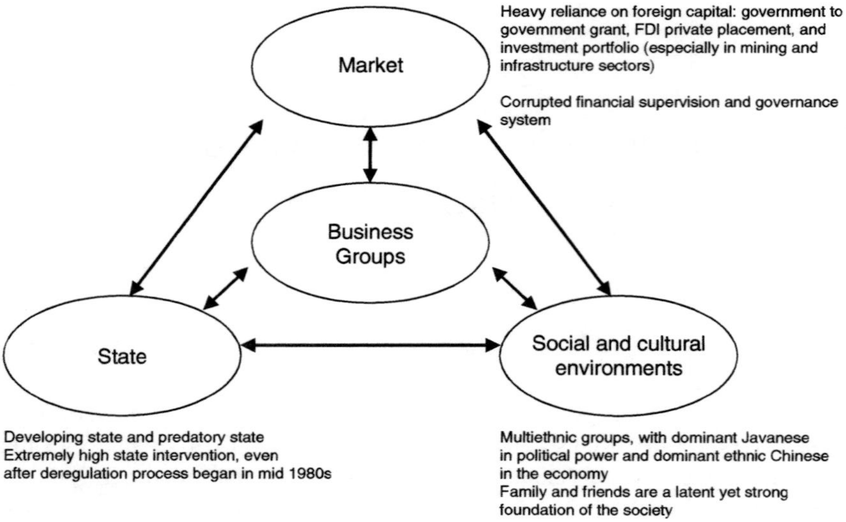

Figure 8.1. Indonesian institutional environments

how several large Indonesian business groups have been adapting to the new business environment in the postcrisis era. The following sections outline the relevance of theories about business groups to the Indonesian context, discuss the history of Indonesia's economy, and consider the role business groups have played in Indonesia before and after the Asian Crisis. This analysis pays special attention to two dominant categories of Indonesian business groups, the private Suharto-linked business group and the state-owned enterprise business group.

8.1. THEORETICAL FOUNDATIONS AND THE INDONESIAN CONTEXT

The comparative institutional framework adopted in this book (see Chapter 1) identifies four major forces—markets (especially, capital markets), the state, social and economic environments, and business groups (entrepreneurs), and their respective relationship with each other, as the most important influences on national economies. These forces can help a developing economy like Indonesia's grow and become more efficient, so long as the state manages the conflicting interests of capital and business groups, by giving sound references and acting as trustworthy guardian for both sides—i.e. the capital and entrepreneurs (see Figure 8.1). When the state fails to do so, external shocks such as the Asian Crisis may jeopardize the stable relationships between these forces. For example, capital markets in many East Asian countries, including Indonesia, failed to work because family-based business groups and government officials were too closely connected. In other words, the State guarded the interest of family-business groups at the expense of the interest of the capital.

Consequently, such business groups tend to expand their businesses carelessly, expecting their home government to bail them out if they failed. In turn, foreign creditors often placed a high premium of entrepreneurial rent on these political connections in assessing the chances of being repaid. Over time, these arrangements were inherently unstable and helped precipitate the Asian Crisis.

Furthermore, the socioeconomic environment is another significant force that has great yet subtle influence on relationships among the state, markets, and entrepreneurs, and this socioeconomic environment force built a solid path-dependent institution in Indonesian context that evolved rather slowly even throughout the period of Indonesia's rapid development program. For instance, familism and favoritism based on personal contacts characterize strongly all relationships among the state, markets, and entrepreneurs, as societal trust is very low between 'strangers'. This environment of exclusive societal trust among family and friends is hard to dissolve, and an introduction of a new kind of institution such as good corporate governance will only be adopted very slowly. Therefore, the 'old' corporate control mechanism of cross-shareholdings and cross-management team between (extended) family members and friends in Indonesian business groups cannot be completely replaced by any other institution in the near future.

The next section examines the history of these forces and their relationships in Indonesia, in order to explain how they evolve and sustain through years until present time and beyond.

8.2. HISTORICAL BACKGROUND AND LEGACY OF THE INDONESIAN ECONOMY: STATE DOMINANCE

8.2.1. Brief Historical Background of Indonesia

Indonesia is one of the most culturally diverse nations in the world. It is a vast archipelago comprising over 17,000 islands that span 5,000 kilometers across the equator, running from the west coast of Malaysia past the north coast of Australia. The islands of Sumatra, Kalimantan, and West Papua are the largest in the archipelago, yet are dwarfed in importance by Java, home to around 60 percent of the country's population, which totals over 220 million, and is the site of Indonesia's capital, Jakarta. There are approximately 300 different ethnic groups spread throughout the islands, with a matching number of languages and dialects. Ethnic Javanese constitute around 45 percent of the population, making them the dominant group, not only in number but also in political power.

The archipelago originated from several Hindu kingdoms that ruled parts of what was to become Indonesia in its precolonial period. The history of Indonesian business is, in a nutshell, one of failed transformation. Historical opportunities disappeared as often as they have arisen. During the fifteenth and sixteenth centuries, for example, one port after another emerged and prospered in different islands of the archipelago.

The age of commerce ended when Dutch trading houses forcefully monopolized Southeast Asian trade. Local traders sank into oblivion. Divided as they had been all along, local rulers were content with petty bribes. Batavia, which later became Jakarta, was the seat of Dutch colonial power from the arrival of the Dutch Indies Company (VOC) in the early 1600s.

The first stirrings of nationalist sentiment emerged on Java in the early twentieth century. A group of Dutch-educated nationalists, led by Sukarno, founded the Indonesian Nationalist Party (PNI) in 1927. The Dutch moved quickly to suppress the movement, arresting the leadership and exiling Sukarno to southern Sumatra.

World War II was a turning point in Indonesia's colonial history. The Dutch surrender to the invading Japanese army in 1942 destroyed the notion that colonial rule was invincible. As the war in the Pacific ended in 1945, the Dutch attempted to reclaim their colonial territory, but Indonesian nationalism had strengthened considerably. On August 17, 1945, just three days after Japan surrendered, Sukarno and other nationalists declared an independent 'Republic of Indonesia'. Four years of struggle ensued before the Dutch retreated completely. In 1949, the colonial era ended and Sukarno assumed power.

Despite Sukarno's considerable personal charisma, his regime was characterized by political and economic chaos. In part it arose from the number and diversity of groups vying for power. The Indonesian Communist Party (PKI), the nationalists, two organized Muslim groups, and the military all contested the political order. Major political changes occurred in the mid-1960s. It began with a failed coup attempt on September 30, 1965. Although responsibility for this attempt was never been clearly established, the military, led by Major General Suharto, blamed the Communist Party. This event appeared to act as a trigger, setting off a wave of mass killings that raged through the remainder of 1965 and continued into early 1966. In 1968, Suharto replaced Sukarno as President and established the 'New Order'.

The New Order inherited a dire economic legacy. The Sukarno government had expropriated all foreign assets and established state control over most markets, including foreign trade and bank credit. The economy was characterized by regulation and state controls. Exports were stagnant, factories were operating at a fraction of capacity, and inflation was rampant. The government was running a huge budget deficit, foreign debt was over US$2 billion, and interest on the debt was more than Indonesia's total export revenues.

The Suharto government issued new policies that encouraged foreign direct investment (FDI), principally in natural resource exploitation. It also reformed the banking sector, permitting the operation of both state and private banks. In the early 1970s, foreign exchange controls were abolished and the complex structure of multiple exchange rates was reformed. By 1971, the rupiah was fully convertible at a fixed rate of 415 to the US dollar and banks were free to offer foreign currency deposit accounts. The three largest islands were rich in natural resources, including the second-largest tropical rainforest in the world, and extensive oil, gas, and mineral reserves. Indonesian oil contributed significantly to economic growth and provided capital for development.

The fall in oil prices between 1982 and 1986 forced new changes. The rupiah was devalued by 28 percent in 1983 and an additional 31 percent in September 1986, when the exchange rate reached 1,644 to the US dollar. In late 1988, the Indonesian government announced further major reforms. Politically protected trading and distribution companies had stifled competition, leading to high prices and manufacturing industries that could not compete in international markets. Key import monopolies were dismantled to allow easier and cheaper imports of intermediate goods required for export production. Regulations on foreign investment were relaxed and simplified to attract new capital and technology. The government also lifted limits on licenses for private and foreign banks, opening up what had been a closely regulated industry. The number of private banks, many owned by ethnic Chinese, more than doubled to 135, and eighteen new foreign banks were licensed, both due to the October 1988 banking sector deregulation.

Indonesia's economy grew at a real annual rate of 9 percent in the 1980s and 7.9 percent from 1990 to 1996. Per-capita gross domestic product (GDP) surpassed US$1,000 for the first time in 1995, as compared to US$70 when Suharto became President. Unemployment in 1996 was 4.5 percent, and the workforce totaled 85 million. The World Bank predicted that Indonesia would become the fifth largest economy in the world by 2020. Inflation was low and the currency was stable.

According to the World Investment Report 1997, Indonesia was the third-largest FDI recipient in the Asia Pacific.[1] From 1994 to 1996, approved FDI averaged over US$31 billion annually. In the first half of 1997, approved FDI in Indonesia totaled US$16 billion.[2] Yet the International Monetary Fund (IMF) annual report for the year ended April 30, 1997[3] identified the continual excess demand for funds and large capital inflows as important policy challenges. To maintain rapid and sustainable growth, the IMF believed substantial reform, especially in the financial and banking sector, was essential. In particular, it urged the Indonesian government to resolve the problem of insolvent banks and to recover nonperforming loans in order to reduce the vulnerability of the economy to shocks and to lessen moral hazard. Despite these recommendations, the overall tone of its report was generally positive, and the relationships among the capital markets, the state, and business groups, remained strong.

8.2.2. Economic Legacy of Indonesian History

When Indonesia was declared independent in 1945, it enacted a socialist constitution. This constitution, which remains in force today, favors state ownership and control over important sectors of the economy. The private sector is to be allowed to participate only in areas of minor importance. Needless to say, demarcating important economic sectors *ex ante* is impossible, and the relative importance of sectors changes over time.

In practice, since Indonesia became independent, all five governments have gone well beyond the 'gas and water socialism' originally proposed in the 1940s. In effect, the Indonesian state has continued to play the same central role in Indonesian business life that it did under Dutch rule. There are many Indonesian state enterprises in the plantation, hotel, commercial banking, trading, and mining industries.

Whatever their stated political ideologies, all Indonesian governments have been anticompetitive. By and large, the Indonesian elite considers competition as a nice concept, yet does not care to practice it. Economic policies are full of holes through which anticompetitive practices and conduct can creep in, including the deregulation policies discussed in the next section.

8.3. DEREGULATIONS ESTABLISH THE 'FAMILY AND FRIENDS' INSTITUTION

The anticompetitive legacy has meant that there is no clear divide between the Indonesian state and business groups. The New Order government introduced relatively liberal laws governing foreign and domestic private investments in 1967 and 1968. These laws started a slow transition toward a market economy, a trend that accelerated between 1983 and 1997. It was during this second period that Indonesia came closest to a market economy, albeit a highly imperfect one, due to the embedded anticompetitive mindset. Yet during this period of deregulation, a rather different Indonesian institution emerged, which I call the 'family and friends institution'. In turn, this new institution produced two types of major (or dominant) Indonesian business groups—state-owned business groups and Suharto-linked business groups.

8.3.1. Financial Sector Deregulation

Banking sector deregulation occurred in 1988. Many of the local banks established between then and 1996, however, were merely subsidiaries of a few large business groups. They served mainly as vehicles for mobilizing funds to support these groups' insatiable appetite for expansion.

Furthermore, the capital market was overhauled at the end of 1989. Requirements for share listing were relaxed. The Capital Market Agency deliberately stimulated entry to the stock exchange first, hoping that compliance with the principles and rules of good corporate governance could be enforced once a company was listed. Stock market frenzy swept over Indonesia. The number of listed companies rose from twenty-four in 1988 to 306 by 1997. With the help of aggressive marketing, which in many cases involved dubious practices, groups created the impression that the demand for shares was large and rising. These groups also engineered financial data to make owning stock in them very tempting. By doing so, they mobilized substantial funds and lost only a little control. With the proceeds from share listings, the founding owners embarked upon new expansion projects with little oversight.

In a nutshell, the relationship with finance that typifies East Asian nations was exaggerated in Indonesia. On the surface, it appeared the New Order government had created a favorable business environment. Yet this environment favored some far more than it did others.

8.3.2. Real Sector Deregulation

Through deregulation, the Indonesian government transferred power over most of the economy from the state to the private sector. Yet the only major beneficiaries of this transfer were a few private business groups, which were controlled mainly by the family and friends of senior government officials. As the economy was privatized, politically well-connected people entered business at an unprecedented pace and scale as the government transferred rent-generating assets to business groups. Values of ongoing projects were highly inflated so that the new owners could cash in once bank credits were disbursed. Hence, although deregulation had supposedly occurred, business groups were unfamiliar with the true power of competition until the Asian Crisis hit Indonesia.

8.3.3. Two Types of Major Indonesian Business Groups

Private Indonesian business groups typically own businesses in distribution and retailing, banking, insurance and other financial services, plantations, forestry concessions, property, and manufacturing. Their sales are concentrated in the domestic market. Within each group, competition is severely suppressed through horizontal, vertical, and diagonal integration. Transfer pricing between two or more businesses in the same group may be deployed. A firm in a downstream industry may have an unfair advantage over competitors through better access to intermediate products, which are controlled by an affiliated firm.

There were about 300 major private business groups in 1996 (Indonesian Business Data Center 1997). Although ordinary citizens founded many of them, larger groups benefited immeasurably from their founders' close ties to the Suharto regime. Suharto's family and his Chinese friends controlled most of these groups. Members of other ethnic groups who owned companies were also quite close to Suharto, his family, or his allies. Not surprisingly, these connections became the focus of considerable criticism.

8.3.4. Suharto-linked Business Groups: The Children, Old Buddies, Foreign Investors, and Yayasan

Suharto granted his children, friends, political allies, and business partners many significant licenses, monopolies, and government contracts through numerous presidential decrees. Those who were granted such privileges

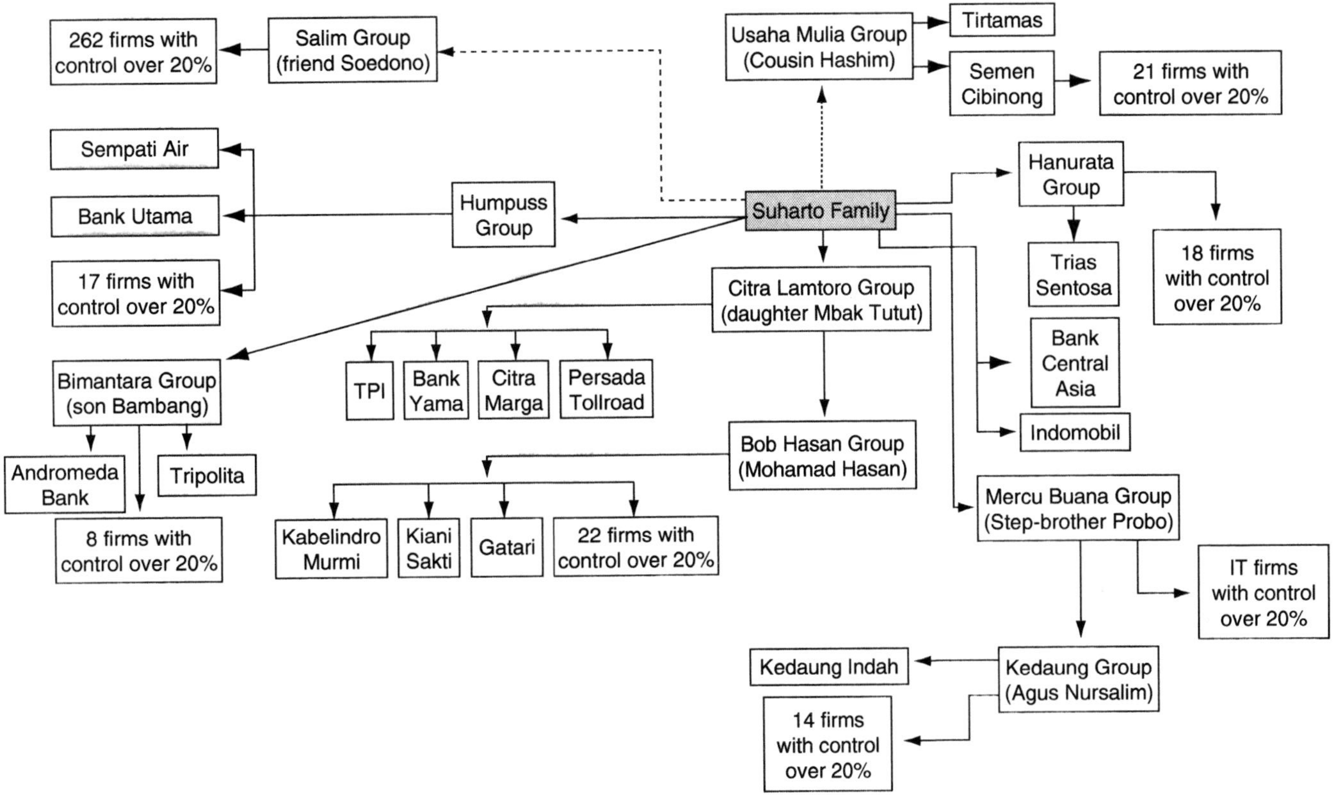

Figure 8.2. Suharto business groups (before 1998)

Sources: Stjin Claessens, Simeon Djankov and Larry H. P. Lang (Feb. 1999). Who Controls East Asian Corporations? Financial Economics Unit. Financal Sector Practice Department, World Bank.

started business groups that diversified into virtually every sector of the Indonesian economy. Sometimes these groups, such as Humpuss Group—the one begun by Suharto's youngest son—required costly government bailouts in order to survive. Other groups were more successful. Most notably, the Salim Group reportedly accounted for 5 percent of Indonesia's GDP. Liem Sioe Liong, whose rise began as a supplier to the Indonesian army in the 1950s under the patronage of then Colonel Suharto, controlled this group.

Major companies such as Deutsche Telekom, Siemens, Hyatt, and Hyundai frequently invested in or were joint venture partners of these groups. Critics argued that such partnerships with Suharto's children were essential prerequisites for winning major contracts from the Indonesian government. Members of the Suharto family were often given shares in foreign ventures in Indonesia, from which they collected substantial dividends, without paying for them.

Suharto's *yayasans*, or 'presidential foundations funded by voluntary contributions for charity', collected levies on numerous items ranging from utility bills to movie tickets. Although the foundations did some good work such as building schools and hospitals, they also reportedly bought votes for Suharto's political party Golongan Karya (GOLKAR), and served as Suharto's personal banks for projects that enriched his children or partners.

Figure 8.2 provides a glimpse of Suharto-linked business groups, but it is not exhaustive. Between 1988 and 1996, the average sales of Suharto-linked business groups were substantially greater than were those of independent business groups. In 1996, average sales per year of Suharto-linked business groups were around Rp1.2 trillion, while those of independent private business groups are averaged less than Rp700 billion.

8.3.5. State-owned Enterprise Business Groups: Twin Sister of Indonesian Private Business Groups

Even though deregulation has decreased the state's dominance of the economy, state-owned enterprises (SOEs) are still major contributors to the national economy. At the end of 1995, there were 165 Indonesian SOEs. They had diversified into many related and unrelated sectors under the supervision of 'technical' departments. For instance, the Ministry of Finance (MOF) supervised thirty SOEs, which collectively had the most assets. SOEs controlled by the Ministry of Mining and Energy (MME) included Pertamina, Indonesia's National Oil Company.

As of 1995, there were fifty-eight SOEs with subsidiaries and affiliates. Unlike private business groups, these SOEs did not use cross-shareholding mechanisms, as government institutions controlled all of them. Taken together, they had 459 subsidiaries and affiliates with total assets of Rp343.3 trillion. SOEs' sales growth fluctuated during 1990–6, registering an average annual rate of 10 percent. Similarly, SOEs' growth in terms of net profits and assets was erratic, but averaged 24 percent and 31 percent, respectively, between 1993 and 1995. These growth rates were low compared to those for listed companies during the same period.

Assuming a fixed ratio of value added to sales (as high as 30 percent), the SOEs' value added as a percentage of GDP ranged from 6 to 8.7 percent in 1990s. This figure was relatively high compared to the 3.7 to 7 percent for publicly listed companies. This ratio decreased, however, from 8.7 percent in 1990 to 6 percent in 1996, indicating SOEs' declining importance.

8.3.6. Economic Performance of Indonesian Business Groups

In 1997, the 300 major conglomerates owned 9,766 business units, which were mostly private companies. Their total sales increased from Rp90.1 trillion in 1990 to Rp234 trillion in 1997. Assuming a constant ratio of value added to sales (as high as 30 percent), conglomerates' contribution to GDP increased from 12.8 percent in 1990 to 13.4 percent in 1994, but dropped to 11.2 percent in 1997. This indicator reflects that the family and friends institution fit into the Indonesian business landscape for a long time, but was becoming less fit by the time the Asian Crisis hit. Why did this institution fit during one period and not in another? To answer this question, we consider corporate control and governance as an explanatory variable for the vulnerability of Indonesian business groups founded under the family and friends institution.

8.4. INDONESIAN BUSINESS GROUPS IN CRISIS: CORPORATE CONTROL AND GOVERNANCE

Governance was certainly not the only important factor behind the crisis, but it was partially responsible for the crisis' severity. Even listed companies ignored governance issues before the crisis. Family-run business groups were at best indifferent to these issues. Management, which was dominated by majority owners, flagrantly exploited small investors.

8.4.1. Corporate Control and Governance of Indonesian Business Groups Before Crisis

Corporate ownership in Indonesia is highly concentrated. The Jakarta Stock Exchange (JSX) was dormant for a long time. Even today, fifteen years after the capital market deregulation of 1989, there are only 337 listed companies. These firms constitute a very small part of business in Indonesia, as reflected by a market capitalization of only US$65 billion in 2004. Although about 90 percent of the 337 listed companies belong to business groups (either as subsidiaries or as parent companies) and 93.4 percent of total market capitalization in 1997 is represented by group-affiliated firms, the number of listed companies within each business group is limited, and the proportion of shares they floated in the market rarely goes beyond 20 percent. In all these listed companies, founders are the majority owners. In the compulsory two-board system, the majority owner or a chosen relative is usually chief executive officer (CEO). The majority owner may choose a nonrelative executive to chair the Executive Board and/or the Commissioners Board, but these outsiders must have demonstrated unquestionable loyalty to the majority shareholder.

Managers seem more likely to behave opportunistically as their power within the firm they manage increases. In turn, this power becomes more concentrated where majority ownership and management are consolidated. Such is the case in most Indonesian business groups, be they private or public. Several forms of abuse are common.

First, political alliances between entrepreneurs and government officials frequently lead to violations of regulations meant to promote prudent business practices. As noted earlier, banks owned by business groups typically act as 'cashiers' that provide credit to companies within their group. Prudent credit analysis tends to be ignored. In addition, controlling shareholders in business groups that have ties to government officials often give these officials (or their family members) a small portion of shares. Such gifts ensure they will continue to receive protection and certain privileges.

As do founding families in other East Asian nations, controlling shareholders in Indonesian business groups frequently use cross-shareholding to strengthen their control over affiliated companies. Indonesian law does not restrict this practice, and it is difficult to obtain data on cross-shareholding. This practice reflects the relative lack of trust Indonesians have in those who are not family members or close friends.

It is generally believed that cross-shareholding between financial and nonfinancial companies is common. This practice has the potential to create serious problems. Banks in which there is cross-shareholding by business group affiliates, for example, must consider not only their own interests but also those of the entire group. Bank Papan Sejahtera and Bank Niaga are cases in point. After the crisis, they were liquidated and recapitalized after being acquired by the Tirtamas Group, which owns a publicly listed cement company, Semen Cibinong.

8.4.2. Indonesian Business Groups' Vulnerability during the Asian Crisis

When the Asian Crisis hit Indonesia in mid-1997, the national monetary authority first tried to defend the domestic currency, the rupiah, by widening the intervention band from 5 to 12 percent while maintaining its managed floating rate system. This intervention quickly proved ineffective; the rupiah fell by 6 percent against the dollar on July 21, 1997, the biggest one-day fall in five years. Finally, the Indonesian monetary authority realized that the system could not cope with the continuing pressure on the currency, as the risk of losing all foreign exchange reserves to prop up the rupiah was too high. On August 14, 1997, the monetary authority adopted a free-floating exchange rate system. Nonetheless, the rupiah's value fell further, eventually decreasing from Rp4,950 per dollar to Rp15,000 per dollar by the height of the crisis in June 1998, although it later stabilized at about Rp8,500. At that exchange rate, it is estimated that half of Indonesian corporations became technically insolvent.

The macro impact of the financial crisis on the Indonesian economy was devastating. In 1998, Indonesian GDP contracted by 13 percent and the inflation rate reached almost 60 percent. All sectors except utilities contracted, with revenue in the construction and finance sectors decreasing by 36.5 percent and 26.6 percent, respectively, as the most hit sectors in Indonesia.

At the micro level, this crisis was amplified both by a severe drought-related supply shock and the decay of political and business institutions. The costs of inputs skyrocketed. Firms were forced to pass on the bulk of this increase to buyers through higher prices, and workers were forced to ask for major increases in nominal wages to compensate for the steep reduction in their real income. As a consequence, the cost of goods sold rose tremendously while accrual interest costs more than tripled. Along with the dramatic rises in market prices, corporate sales plunged and the majority of business groups lost money. Most of these groups were fighting for their survival, especially those in which cross-shareholding was common. In turn, this situation strained the family and friends institution. Indonesia's ethnic diversity has compounded social strain. Reflecting the ongoing tensions between these different ethnicities, the number of 'mixed groups' had declined from eighty-six in 1988 to sixty-eight in 1996. These groups supplied about 20 percent of Indonesia's total sales in 1988 but only 14 percent by 1996. The drop might indicate the increasing social polarization along ethnic lines, and it has created a lot of social tension. This indicator shows clearly the vulnerability of trust in business that has been built solely on the strength of the family and friends institution. Eventually, this polarization may threaten social stability, and this factor eventually helped to accelerate the dissolution of Suharto-linked business groups.

Having experienced all these troubles, the Indonesian government, as well as most Indonesian business groups, began considering how to make the business landscape more robust to future environmental shocks. The solution is most likely found in market institutions, or at least more market-friendly institutions. We examine this issue in the next section.

8.5. GOVERNMENT RESPONSES TO THE CRISIS: RESTRUCTURING AND REFORMATION

8.5.1. Corporate Restructuring: Banking and Nonbanking Sectors

The Indonesian Bank Restructuring Agency (IBRA) was established in early 1998 by Presidential Decree No. 27/1998 as the government's response to the crisis, and has been dismissed by February 27, 2004 (by Presidential Decree No. 15/2004). Its main task is to administer the blanket guarantee program and to restructure and revitalize banks. The IBRA then developed and undertook an integrated and comprehensive series of activities consisting of bank liability programs, bank restructuring, bank loan restructuring, shareholder settlements, and the recovery of state funds. Until 2004, the IBRA was the most powerful force in Indonesian corporate restructuring.

The MOF, the Financial Sector Policy Committee (FSPC), whose members include the economic minister of Indonesia, and the Independent Review Committee (IRC), which includes representatives from the IMF, the World Bank, and Asian Development Bank (ADB), supervise the IBRA. The FSPC has also established an audit committee within the organization and monitors both its performance and its compliance not only to prevailing policies but also to the principles of good corporate governance and transparency.

A brief summary of a few major Indonesian business groups that were restructured significantly through IBRA follows.

8.5.2. Banking Sector Restructuring: Recapitalizing and Selling

The bank recapitalization program was run under the Joint Decree of Minister of Finance and the Governor of Bank Indonesia. Government-run recapitalizations were done in the form of stock/bond placements. Independent experts and eligible shareholders determine the amount of recapitalization. To avoid moral hazard, the government participated in recapitalization for any given bank only once.

Banks were then reclassified into three categories according to their capital adequacy ratio (CAR) during 1998. As a result, seventy-three banks with CAR of 4 percent or higher (class A banks) are allowed to operate normally without obligation for recapitalization. Nine banks with CAR between −25 to 4 percent (class B banks) are allowed to operate with an obligation to recapitalize aimed at a CAR of 4 percent by April 21, 1999. The owners of Class B banks need to provide in cash 20 percent of capital needed, while the rest will be borne by the government using bonds. Nine class B banks are taken over by IBRA, and thirty-eight banks of class C and class B banks were closed.

Bank Mandiri was by far the largest case of restructuring. Bank Mandiri is a product of the government's wholesale restructuring of Indonesia's banking system following the 1997–8 Asian financial crisis. Bank Mandiri was formed through the merger of four state banks. It was incorporated in October 1998 and began operations in August 1999, after the four banks were merged. Bank Mandiri was required to restructure most of the four banks' assets before the government would undertake the recapitalization. It met this condition by restructuring over Rp18.9 trillion in nonperforming loans and transferring Rp77.37 trillion in bad debts to IBRA at zero value. In return, the MDF issued a series of recapitalization bonds totaling Rp175.3 trillion. These bonds are now assets of Bank Mandiri and, at the same time, obligations of the Government of the Republic of Indonesia. The bonds, as obligations of the Republic of Indonesia, give Bank Mandiri a solid asset base that is independent of private sector credit risk.

Bank Mandiri now is Indonesia's largest bank with total assets as of June 30, 2001 of Rp251 trillion, representing 23 percent of the assets in the banking system. It has turned its balance sheet around, its profitability, and its way of doing business to become the preferred bank in Indonesia. It has streamlined its processes, reduced its operating expenses, laid off employees, and developed a rigorous process for restructuring nonperforming loans. As of July 11, 2003, its market capitalization of Rp13.5 trillion was 4 percent of the JSX's total capitalization.

8.5.3. Restructuring in Nonbanking Sectors: The Market and Institutional Framework for Corporate Control

Overall, the IBRA's effort to restructure nonfinancial firms has been less successful. In its over 100 attempts to use bankruptcy proceedings to speed the liquidation of debtor's assets, for instance, the court has decided in favor of debtors over 90 percent of the time. The slow progress in restructuring is at least partially attributable to the embarrassingly poor performance in law enforcement.

Nor has the IBRA succeeded in deriving significant revenues from the immediate sales of peripheral assets that are largely immaterial to corporate survival. IBRA was quick to organize such sales through competitive auctions. It was reported to have secured good prices for the peripheral assets. The proceeds from the sales of these assets were negligible, however, relative to the total assets involved in corporate restructuring.

In addition, although the FSPC has derived a collective settlement for the thousands of individuals and small business debtors that includes relatively deep debt reductions and discounts on accrued interest, the total amount of these loans is negligible relative to the total amount of bank loans. In effect, this solution was more a symbolic gesture of favoritism toward small and medium-sized businesses than it was a substantive step in restructuring.

The main results of corporate restructuring process in the private sector are likely to come about only with time. The government initiated new legislation to strengthen the market institutions, including the antitrust law (1999), a municipal autonomy legal framework (1999), an anticorruption law (1999 and 2001), and anti-money laundering provisions (2002). Having suffered badly from the crisis, good governance is more valued. Nonetheless, the real challenge for Indonesia is to enforce this legislation consistently and persistently. It is, however, unrealistic to expect quick progress. Therefore, it is hard to secure a commitment to competition in Indonesia. Law enforcement has barely improved.

In the long run, there is no substitute for competition and a reliable legal system if good corporate governance is to be sustainable. Otherwise, the family and friends institution will return. In other words, regardless of the emergence of liberal democracy in Indonesia and the rapid progress of globalization, market institutions will not be established unless there is strong political will to allow competition and install a reliable legal system.

8.6. BUSINESS GROUPS' RESPONSE TO THE CRISIS: FINANCIAL ENGINEERING AND REFOCUSING

There are only four major business groups' responses that will be exemplified here. All of them are Suharto-linked business groups. In the case of Lippo Group and Astra International Group, they were not linked directly to the former president's family business, yet they are connected through the family and friends institution to Suharto-linked business groups. Moreover, the SOE's response to crisis is not discussed in depth here, as they have not yet made any significant actions—apart from the privatization plan announcement.

8.6.1. Salim Group: Financial Engineering Through Special Purpose Vehicle

Bank Central Asia (BCA) rose to prominence under the 32-year rule of former President Suharto and became the pre-eminent financial symbol of his New Order regime. The bank was founded by Liem Sioe Liong, also known as Sudono Salim, whose sprawling Salim Group dominated the country's economic landscape like no other—at one time contributing 5 percent of Indonesia's economic output. BCA helped power the growth of Salim Group companies in instant noodles, cement, and flour milling. A very close relationship with Suharto was an essential element of the group's success. Two of the former president's children owned 30 percent of the bank.

When the Asian financial crisis brought down Suharto, in May 1998, it took Salim Group with him. Like many other Indonesian banks, BCA had violated the law by lending excessively to companies belonging to Salim Group. BCA was rescued with a capital injection from the government of Rp28.5 trillion. Another Rp61 trillion worth of Government bonds was used to wipe clean the bank's loans to Salim Group companies. As a result, BCA was handed over to IBRA, which was given 93 percent of the share of the bank. The remaining 7 percent stayed with the Salim family, but the Indonesian Finance Ministry has asked them to sell it.

When BCA was restructured (see the material on bank restructuring earlier), many of Salim Group's companies were transferred to the IBRA. In addition, PT Holdiko Perkasa (Holdiko) was formed to arrange the settlement between the Salim Group and the IBRA with regard to liquidity credits provided to BCA and the additional loans given by BCA to Salim Group affiliates that exceeded the legal lending limit. Holdiko's main task is to sell all of its shareholdings in these companies and subsequently direct all sales

President Director & Chief Executive Officer
Eva Riyanti Hutapea

Director & Deputy Chief Executive Officer
Cesar M. dela Cruz

Chief Operating Officer—Branded	: Iwan Arsianto, Aufrans
Chief Operating Officer—Commodity	: Gaotama Setiawan, Richard Kastilani
Chief Financial Officer	: Lanasastri Setiadi, M.P. Sibarani
Chief Administration Officer	: Indra Josepha

DIVISIONAL MANAGEMENT

Noodles	Taufik Wiraatmadja Lanny Hendarsin*	Treasury	Sri Dewi Subijanto Thomas Thjie*
Commodity		Controller	M.P. Sibarani Romeo L. Bato*
Edible Oils and Fats		Information Technology	Jun Urmeneta
Trading & Plantation	Richard Kastilani	Corporate Purchasing	Lanasastri Setiadi
Branded	Ongkie Tedjasurya	Technical Project Development	Gaotama Setiawan
Flour	Franky Welirang	Corporate Personnel	Indra Josepha
Baby Foods	Andy Setiadi	Investor Relations	Djoko Wibowo Mulyawan Tjandra*
Foods Seasonings	Eliezer Hardjo	Public Relations	Indra Josepha Sri Bugo Suratmo*
Snack	Lanny Hendarsin	Business Development	Eva Riyanti Hutapea
Biscuit	Andy Setiadi	Corporate Legal	M.P. Sibarani
Dairy Products	Lanny Hendarsin	Corporate Audit	M.P. Sibarani
International	Aufrans	Management Service and Business Analysis	Jun Urmeneta
Distribution	Hendro Gunarto		
Packaging	Aswan Tukiaty George Abraham*	Research and Development	Dr. Chu Hsiung Tzeng
Food Ingredients	Aufrans Edwin Salazar*		

* Deputy Division Head

Figure 8.3. Organization and management structure of PT. INDOFOOD SUKSES MAKMUR (Year 2000)

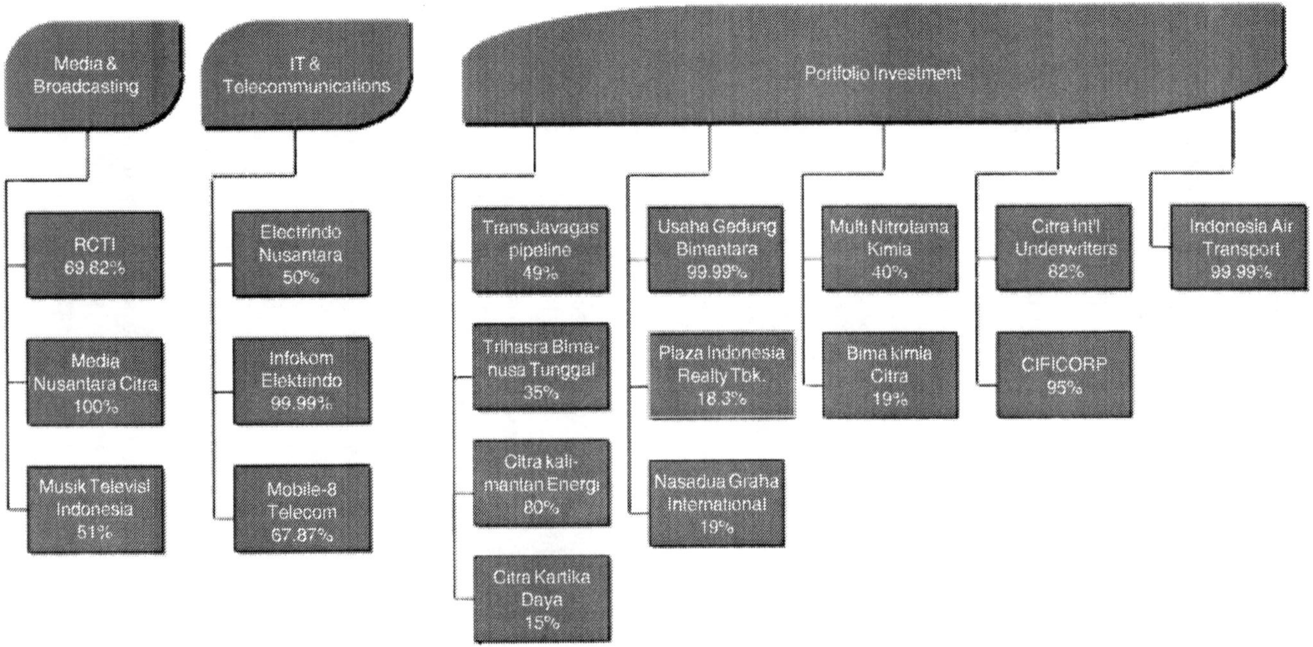

Figure 8.4. Corporate structure of BIMANTARA (Year 2003)

Table 8.1. PT Bimantara Citra shareholders

	Amount	Proportion (%)
Founders:		
PT Astriland	126,015,600	12.35
PT Rizki Bukit Abadi	53,550,000	5.25
PT Matra Teguh Abadi	10,165,200	1.00
PT Internusa Rizki Abadi	4,171,666	0.41
PT Persada Giri Abadi	0	0.00
Subtotal Founders	193,902,466	19.00
Public:		
Major Investor:		
PT Bhakti Investama Tbk	383,739,500	37.60
Almington Assets Ltd.	141,150,000	13.83
Astoria Development Ltd.	60,409,800	5.92
Subtotal Investor	585,299,300	57.35
Minor Investor	241,454,178	23.66
Subtotal Minor Investors	241,454,178	23.66
Total	1,020,655,944	100.00

As of July 31, 2003

proceeds to IBRA, which has the right to appoint the majority of Holdiko's management and direct its asset disposal efforts. Holdiko intends to sell 107 companies in the industries/sectors shown in Figure 8.3.

Nonetheless, the Salim Group retained its most valuable assets, such as PT Indofood Sukses Makmur, which is attempting to become a major food and beverage concern in Asia. In addition, Salim Group plans to raise capital to fund the expansion of promising businesses and reduce debt. Further, the separation of ownership and control in many of its subsidiaries is viewed as one of the group's strengths. Through these means, Salim Group will likely become stronger.

8.6.2. Bimantara: Refocusing The First-Family Business

Bimantara was founded in 1981, by one of Suharto's sons. It began as a trading company, but diversified into many unrelated sectors, including media and broadcasting, telecommunications, infrastructure, transportation and automobiles, chemicals, hotels and property, and financial services. In

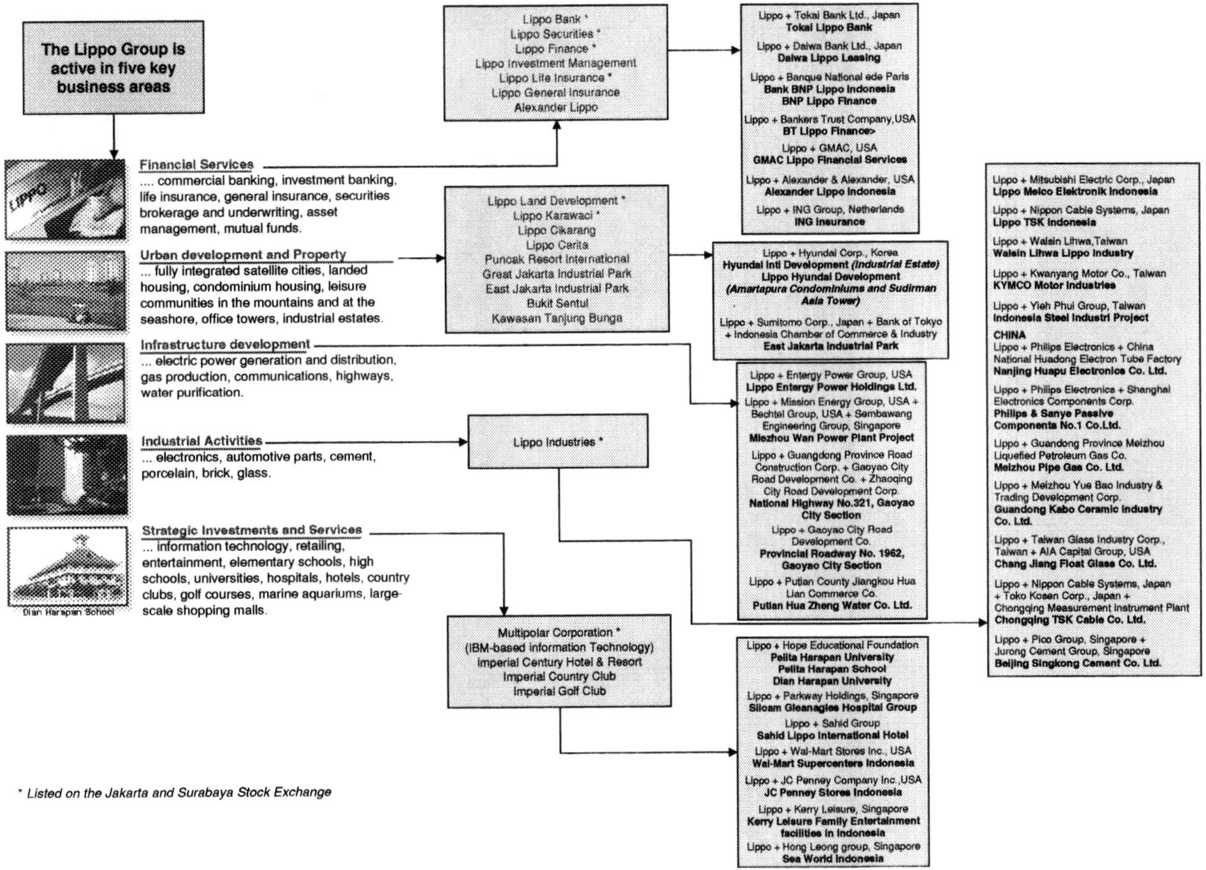

Figure 8.5. Corporate structure of Lippo Group (Year 2002)

July 1995, Bimantara floated 200 million shares (around 20.8 percent of its paid-in capital) on the Jakarta and Surabaya Stock Exchanges.

The Asian Crisis drove the group to restructure its businesses. In 1999, the new management board decided to restructure the group's business portfolio and its debt. It sold many of its assets at that time, and in 2000 refocused its businesses into three business groups: (a) Media and broadcasting, (b) Transportation and logistics, and (c) Telecommunications. Any subsidiary that does not belong to one of these three groups is to be managed only as an investment portfolio. Bimantara also completed its debt restructuring by the end of 2000. Since then, it has continued to shed noncore businesses and develop core enterprises (see Figure 8.4).

Despite these efforts, and their results in terms of shareholders' composition, as depicted in Table 8.1, the public believes that Suharto's family still somehow controls this business group behind the scenes. There is no formal evidence to prove or disprove this speculation, but elite business people and fund managers in Jakarta do not deny this possibility.

8.6.3. Lippo Group: Recapitalization and Financial Engineering

The Lippo Group, founded by Mochtar Riady, developed Lippo Bank into the top five biggest private banks in Indonesia. It established Lippo Land Development in 1991 and built up an extensive portfolio of commercial and residential real estate. At one point, Lippo Group had more than 165 affiliated companies in Indonesia, China, and the USA.

It was widely assumed that this empire was on the verge of collapse when the Asian Crisis struck. It seemed dangerously vulnerable to astronomical interest rates and inflation, and mountains of bad debt at Lippo Bank. Further, Lippo Bank's customers had a run on the bank, almost bringing it down (see Figure 8.5).

Lippo Bank was the first bank to be recapitalized by the state. The Riady family lost control of it when the government effectively nationalized it by taking a 59 percent stake in return for a US$700 million bailout. Nonetheless, the group survived by streamlining its infrastructure, raising cash, and selling off assets. Even though Riady's family is no longer the majority shareholder in Lippo Group, it still exerts substantial influence over its operations and strategic decisions. The group structure depicted in Figure 8.5 shows clearly the wide business interests of the Riady family, yet it is not obvious how the family can control those businesses without holding majority stakes in them.

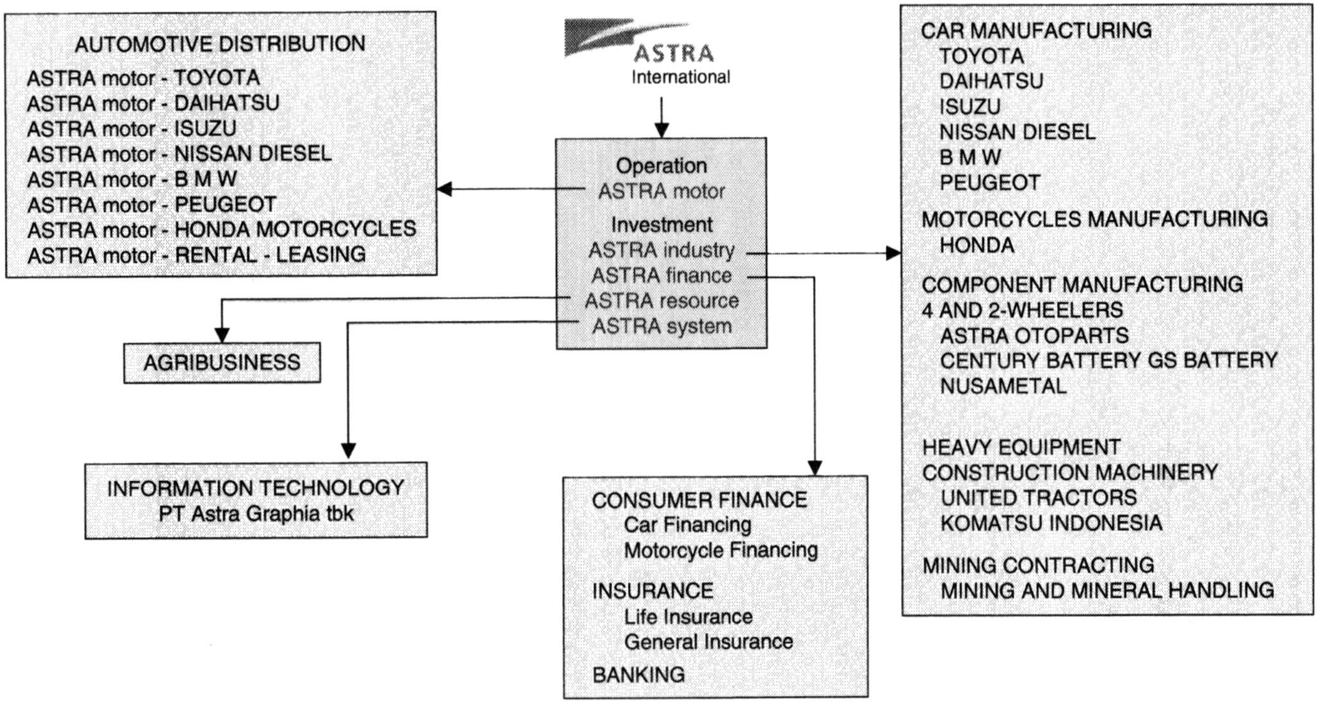

Figure 8.6. Corporate structure of PT Astra International Tbk (Year 2003)

Table 8.2. PT Astra International shareholding structure

No.	Name of Investors	Latest Known Holdings	Proportion (%)
1	Cycle & Carriage (Mauritius) Ltd.	1,408,975,504	35.06
2	JPMCB-US Resident (Norbax Inc.)	327,450,242	8.15
3	Others	2,282,113,370	56.79
	TOTAL	4,018,539,116	100.00

(As of August 31, 2003)

8.6.4. Astra International Group: Debt Rescheduling, Divesting, and Help from the Market

The Astra Group began in 1957 as a small trading company. When Indonesia's economy was first liberalized in the late 1960s, Astra International quickly established relations with Japanese companies, including Toyota Motor Company. Within a short period of time, Astra International emerged as Indonesia's largest importer and assembler of motor vehicles. The company profited greatly from the protectionist policy of import substitution. The brands that Astra International represents in Indonesia widened to include reputable European brands (see Figure 8.6).

Capitalizing on the motor vehicle business and a good management team, Astra International diversified into a wide range of businesses, becoming the second largest Indonesian business group in terms of assets and earnings. Indeed, Astra International was, and is, consistently regarded as Indonesia's best-managed company among the country's largest business groups.

Today, PT Astra International Tbk is a public company with six business divisions: automotive, financial services, heavy equipment, agribusiness, information technology, and infrastructure. During its development, the company has formed strategic alliances with reputable international corporations in its efforts to expand business opportunities.

Listed on the Jakarta and Surabaya Stock Exchanges, Astra International was Indonesia's fifth largest business group before the Asian Crisis began, with total assets of US$8 billion. It had diversified into trading, chemicals, metal processing, financial services, and plantations. It was severely affected by the crisis, as car sales decreased by as much as 90 percent in 1998. Astra International lost Rp3.7 trillion in 1998, while its total borrowing increased from Rp5.8 trillion in 1996 to Rp17.1 trillion in 1998, reflecting the adverse impact of the devaluation on corporate debt. Nevertheless, Astra International was relatively lucky compared to many other large business groups. The car market recovered in 1999 and Astra Group's net income was Rp1.5 trillion, facilitating a return to a decent level of equity. Further, the group's reputation of good corporate governance was of great value when Astra International had to restructure its debt.

Astra International's response to the crisis was demonstrated by a credible commitment to repay its debts. It was among the first debtors to come to a settlement. It managed to convince its creditors that it needed to retain its core assets. Its restructuring effort combined sales of noncore assets, debt rescheduling, and equity reinforcement by the group's joint venture partners. As a result, the composition of Astra International's ownership was also changed, as depicted in Table 8.2.

8.7. CONCLUSION

As mentioned earlier, several new legislation initiatives by the government have been launched in order to strengthen the market institutions, including the antitrust law (1999), a municipal autonomy legal framework (1999), an anticorruption law (1999 and 2001), and anti-money laundering provisions (2002). Nonetheless the real challenge for Indonesia is to enforce these legislations consistently and persistently. It is, however, unrealistic to expect quick progress. Douglas North—a Nobel prize winner in institutional economics—reminds us that old institutions survive even after a revolution. Therefore, the business environment is unlikely to change dramatically anytime soon.

Most of these Indonesian industrial elite came from families with strong links to the Suharto's New Order government and have developed their business groups throughout the last 20 to 30 years. Partly as a result of various government policies, the Indonesian industrial sector became quite diverse. At the beginning, most of the companies were small. They mainly produced consumer goods and employed the bulk of the industrial labor force. Over time, many companies and business groups grew large through their government connections and then became the dominant forces in their respective industries. This business evolution has produced the precrisis institutional framework as well as business model that may not be easily reformed. Traditional role of the state as a 'bridge' between capital and entrepreneurs, and these 300 business groups' dependency an government protection may not be gone soon.

Nonetheless, the Asian Crisis badly hurt most of the business groups that had grown rapidly during the late 1980s and early 1990s. Because of corporate restructuring, founding families no longer own many of their business groups' subsidiaries. Some business groups, including Bank Mandiri, Salim Group, Bimantara Group, Astra International Group, and Lippo Group, have transformed their corporate structures and survived the economic turmoil. Some of the founding owners of these groups have used financial engineering to enhance their groups' strength and prospects for survival, some others have successfully refocused their businesses.

I predict that for the next several years, Salim Group will remain a vital part of the Indonesian market economy and most likely it will have a new business model. I also believe the Bimantara and Astra International Groups will continue to become less diversified and more focused. Lippo Group and Bank Mandiri will likely remain more or less the same in terms of diversification level and their corporate governance practices. Other business groups will follow and resemble one of these major paths.

Meanwhile, the government cannot create mature market institutions in the Indonesian business environment overnight. Parallel mechanisms are necessary to ensure honesty. Regardless of what is going on in the business environment, paying attention to the internal organization of business groups is worth the effort. Owners and management can also be inspired to discover voluntarily the merits of good corporate governance, market competition mechanism, and law enforcement. Although the family and friends institution may completely disappear eventually, its legacy will remain for at least one or two generations. And SOEs will be one kind of its legacy.

NOTES

1. United Nations Conference on Trade and Development (1997). *World Investment Report 1997: Transnational Corporations, Market Structure and Competition Policy.* United Nations, Switzerland, p. 78.
2. Bank Indonesia (1998). *Approved Foreign Direct Investment Projects by Sector.* December 1998. [http://www.bi.go.id/intl/stats/T30603.rep.January1999]
3. International Monetary Fund (1997). *Annual Report of the Executive Board for the Financial Year Ended April 30, 1997.* Washington DC, pp. 80–1.

Part III

New Horizons for Business Groups in East Asia

9

Chinese Business Groups: Their Origins and Development

Donghoon Hahn and Keun Lee

In China, business groups emerged in the mid-1980s. There are now thousands of Chinese business groups. Because they emerged as the Chinese economy evolved from a planned to a market economy, they are distinct from their Korean and Japanese counterparts in several important ways, including their origins and their ownership structure. In part, these differences are attributable to the Chinese government's policies towards business groups, which have been influenced by the successes and failures of business groups in Japan and Korea. For instance, following the Asian Crisis, Chinese policymakers observed that while China needed business groups to develop its economy, but that these groups should not expand or diversify too much (Lee and Woo 2002).

Chinese business groups have been formed through various ways, by various entities, and for various reasons. While most of the Chinese business groups are state owned, there are private business groups as well. Some types of business groups were formed under strong government initiative for restructuring and reforms, and some others were formed voluntarily by the enterprises for efficiency or for insider control purposes.

The characteristics and the origins of the Chinese business groups can be attributed to the distinctive institutional factors as are sketched in Figure 9.1. First, given the tradition of local self-sufficiency, each province or locality tended to promote the horizontal associations of enterprise since the late 1970s, which had become the forerunners of the business groups. 'Horizontal' refers to the relatively equal status among the enterprises constituting the association, and does not necessarily mean them belonging to different business sectors. Enterprises in the same business sector often formed horizontal associations to share brands, marketing channels, or production facilities. In other instances, enterprises in supplier and buyer relationships formed a horizontal association. Sometimes these associations linked civilian and military units, as well as industries, universities, and research institutes.[1] By forming associations, the enterprises expected to fill the gaps in markets that were insufficiently developed. Second, the central government as a developmental state played an important role in promoting some big business groups as it considered the business groups a useful device for economic catch-up as in the past Korea and Japan. The State Council designated and allowed specific business groups special benefits and privileges. Also, many cities, provinces, or ministries wanted to promote their own business groups by various mechanisms which often included transformation of the former government units in charge of state-owned companies into holding companies. Third, with the emergence of a more market-oriented economic system emphasizing competition and profitability, the former state-owned enterprises (SOEs) began to establish subsidiaries or joint venture companies in new and more profitable areas of business by establishing spin-off companies and/or forming alliance with domestic or foreign business partners, which paved another and more voluntary way to the formation of business groups.

To date, there have been several studies of Chinese business groups (Chi 1996; Hahn 1997; Keister 1998, 2001; Hahn and Lee 1999; Lee and Woo 2002). Several of these used data only for listed companies (Hahn 1997; Hahn and Lee 1998, 1999; Lee and Hahn 2003; Lee and Woo 2002). In contrast, our chapter uses more updated and comprehensive data, including those for unlisted firms that belong to listed business groups. We also examine how the Chinese government's actions and reactions have influenced these groups' development.

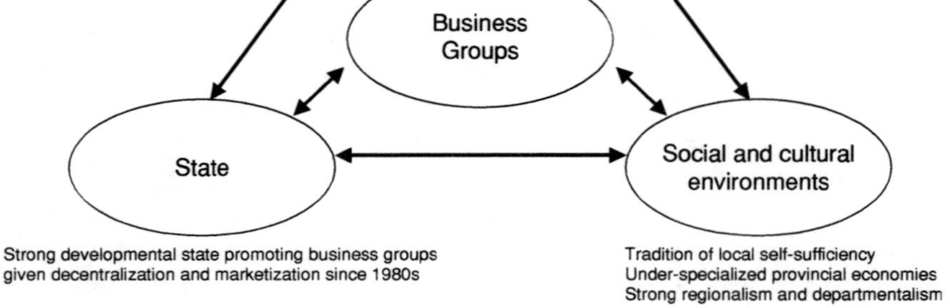

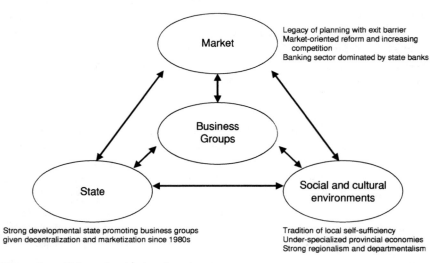

Figure 9.1. Chinese institutional environments

Table 9.1. Basic statistics of Chinese business groups

(Unit: 100 million yuan)

		1997	1998	1999	2000
Number of groups		2,369	2,472	2,757	2,655
Assets	Total amount	50,347	66,994	87,323	106,984
	Average	21.3	27.1	31.7	40.3
Sales revenue	Total amount	28,205	35,077	43,766	53,260
	Average	11.9	14.2	15.9	20.1

Source: National Bureau of Statistics, China, *Zhongguo daqiyejituan* (Chinese Big Enterprise Groups) (2000), China Statistics Press, 2001.

In China, a business group, regardless of whether it has capital ties among the member firms, is supposed to be approved by the relevant government organization and registered with the State Administration for Industry and Commerce. Registration lets a group be officially acknowledged and enjoy preferential treatment. Of course, besides those registered business groups, there are also many business groups that are not registered with the government. In this chapter, because of the limitations in data availability, we focus on the business groups registered with the government, which include both listed and unlisted companies. There are 2,655 business groups registered in China in 2000 (see Table 9.1).

In Section 9.1, we consider the many ways the Chinese government has influenced the rise of Chinese business groups. We then discuss the origins and evolutions of Chinese business groups in Section 9.2. Section 9.3 highlights the diverse paths firms and SOEs have taken to form business groups. We then identify the important characteristics of these groups in Section 9.4, and conclude our analysis with a brief summary in Section 9.5.

9.1. THE ORIGIN: FROM HORIZONTAL ASSOCIATIONS TO BUSINESS GROUPS IN THE 1980s

Other contributors to this book have emphasized the interplay between East Asian governments' actions and the rise of business groups in these nations. There are several reasons why this interplay has been extraordinarily complex in China. Reflecting China's long and uneasy transition from a centrally planned to a market economy, the demarcation between private and public enterprise is not well defined. The jurisdiction that multiple government bureaucracies have over businesses, as well as the government's ongoing attempts to use business groups to further social policies, also make it difficult to characterize the operations of all Chinese business groups with any one statement.

From 1949 onward, China's legacy of government planning and control at multiple levels influenced the context in which business groups emerged. Before the economic reforms of the late 1970s, enterprises tended to be vertically integrated and underspecialized. This is the tendency of the so-called *xiaoerquan daerquan* (small but doing everything, big so doing everything) in Chinese as every enterprise wanted to produce as diverse a variety of outputs as possible. During Mao's rule, the government emphasized regional self-sufficiency. Every local government had a full set of industries, so enterprises were small and there was substantial duplication of investment. Because central planning resulted in unreliable distribution channels and underdeveloped factor markets, enterprises tried to produce as diverse a variety of outputs as possible to protect themselves from supply shortages. In addition, there was a one-to-one match between government ministries and broad industry categories (e.g. light industry ministry, chemical industry ministry). Each ministry controlled state-owned firms in the corresponding industry. Consequently, several ministries usually exerted control over different parts of the same enterprise. Local governments also had jurisdiction over these enterprises.

9.1.1. Horizontal Associations of the Enterprises

When economic reforms began, enterprises enlarged their scope of integration to include other independent enterprises belonging to the same industry, other industries, or other localities, adding further to the overlay of government control. Accordingly, there was rarely one party that could assume full responsibility and decision-making over any one enterprise. Not surprisingly, such enterprises were quite inefficient.

Given this situation, a horizontal association of enterprises started to be formed by organizations of relatively equal status in the same or different business sectors. For example, enterprises in the same business sector formed a horizontal association to share brands, marketing channels, production facilities, or enterprises in supplier and buyer relationships formed a horizontal association. Sometimes, a horizontal association of enterprises was extended to include associations between civilian units and military units, as well as associations between industries, universities, and research institutes.[2] In other words, enterprises used these associations to fill the gaps in markets that were insufficiently developed.

In the early 1980s, on witnessing the appearance of the horizontal associations, the Chinese government encouraged more enterprises to form such associations. It thought the horizontal association was a good solution to the lack of efficient resource allocation mechanisms as China underwent the transition from a planned to a market economy, and that it could help improve the organizational structures of enterprises, particularly those of the earlier mentioned *xiaoerquan daerquan* in the under-specialized provincial economies. The Chinese government promulgated the regulation, 'Provisional Rules on Promoting Economic Associations' in 1980, with the intent of promoting the formation of horizontal associations. Later, in 1986, the Chinese government promulgated another regulation, 'Rules on Several Problems in Further Promoting the Horizontal Economic Associations'.

9.1.2. Contract-based Business Groups

As early as 1987, however, it became evident that the horizontal association form had several limitations. The opportunity cost of maintaining cooperation among the affiliated members had increased, while alternative sources of supply and marketing had emerged. Also, the loose organizational nature of the horizontal associations, which were not based on share ownership or any central authority, could not provide member companies with various benefits available to a normal business group, such as intragroup resource allocation, economy of scale and scope, reduction in transaction costs, and group-level strategic planning. Furthermore, these associations had faced many difficulties because of the unclear division of rights and responsibilities among member firms.

Thus, as an attempt to solve the problems arising from the absence of leadership, the horizontal associations had built internal hierarchies, turning themselves into business groups that had a clear power structure. The government also promoted this change in horizontal associations. During 1987 and 1988, when 'the business group fever' was rampant, many horizontal associations changed into business groups and new business groups were formed. The business groups formed in this structure had a core company at the first tier, closely related companies at the second-tier, semi-closely related companies at the third tier, and a loosely related tier of companies at the bottom. These groups were based on contracts rather than on cross-shareholding among member firms. Contract-based governance seemed to partly solve the problem of the absence of coordinating leadership.

The position of the Chinese government was that restructuring of the SOEs into groups could solve several problems of the Chinese economy, especially the problem of inefficient SOEs (State Council of China 1997; Lee and Hahn 2004), such as providing scale economies and increasing specialization. The government also believed business groups could help it implement industrial policies more effectively. Looking at the experience of Korea and Japan, Chinese government officials felt that it would be less costly and more efficient to implement industrial policies if a few big business groups led the economy (Lee 1992). These officials also thought that supervision of SOEs would be improved if there was only one body that possessed full decision-making rights and responsibilities for monitoring the SOEs.

Consequently, the Chinese government enacted the regulation, 'Several Suggestions on Forming and Developing Business Groups', in 1987. This regulation defined the standards a business group should meet and suggested the organizational structure a business group should have (i.e. the four-tier system of companies noted earlier). It also stipulated preferential policies for business groups, such as the right to set up finance companies (*caiwu gongsi* in Chinese) that can play the role of intragroup banks. Large national-level business groups were granted the province-level status in state plans, that is, they were treated like provinces when the government made state plans. In order to enjoy preferential treatment, however, newly formed business groups had to register with the State Administration for Industry and Commerce. Not surprisingly, many enterprises formed business groups. In addition, many business groups were built forcefully by administrative measures.

In this period, many industry-specific administrative units or bureaus (*xingzhengxing hangye zonggongsi* in Chinese) that had been built to control firms belonging to the industries in provinces or cities were transformed into business groups (Hahn 1997). In the prereform era, the Chinese government set up industrial administrative companies to control the SOEs belonging to the specific industries. However, these companies were neither industry associations that were organized voluntarily by firms nor holding companies that own shares of the affiliate firms. They played only a limited coordinating role, and their control over the affiliate firms was very weak. When the government began favoring business groups, these companies very quickly changed into and registered as business groups. As a natural result of this wave, many of the business groups formed via this path lacked centripetal force and were not operating as organic entities, which gave credence to the assertion that 'nine out of ten groups are empty'. This problem still exists to a certain extent in some Chinese business groups.

9.1.3. Business Groups with Equity Ties

With further development of markets, which resulted in the rise of opportunity costs for maintaining business groups, the weak cohesiveness of business groups was again revealed. Since around the second half of 1988, business groups formed through contracts have begun to turn into equity-based business groups as *ex post* shareholding relationships among member companies have been established. Measures such as spin-offs, mergers and acquisitions (M&As) of shares through administrative ways, were used to achieve this restructuring objective. When enterprises built up new business groups, they began to rely mainly on shareholding relationships, not contracts. The hierarchical structure of business groups has not changed, but the classification of member companies into different tiers now depends upon the share distribution and the nature of interactions among member companies. Both contract-based groups and shareholding-based groups are now common. The state-owned business groups take either of these two forms, whereas other types of business groups (i.e. private business groups and collective business groups) are usually formed when member firms create equity ties.

9.2. BUSINESS GROUPS IN THE 1990s AND 2000s

9.2.1. Experimental Business Groups Promoted by the State Council

In 1991, the State Council designated fifty-seven business groups as experimental groups that are specially promoted and privileged. In 1997, the experiment was extended to include 120 groups (State Council of China 1997). The Chinese government hoped to use this experiment to create giant business groups. The experimental business groups were granted various privileges in investment decision-making, financing, foreign trade, debt–equity swap, capital injection, and so on. Table 9.2 shows that, as of 2000, the 119 experimental business groups occupy 4.5, 42.2, and 42.9 percent, respectively, of the number, the asset size, and the sales revenue of all the officially registered business groups.[3]

We would like to note that the emergence of horizontal associations of enterprises and business groups in China is a bottom-up 'induced institutional innovation' driven by market forces rather than a top-down 'imposed institutional innovation'. This pattern of induced change is consistent with the typical implementation process of major economic reform measures in China. The government, on detecting the emergence of new voluntary

Table 9.2. Distribution of Chinese business groups by administrative level of state organs that gave approval to the business groups (2000)

(Unit: billion yuan, %)

	Number of groups		Assets			Major sales revenue		
	Number	Share	Amount	Share	Average	Amount	Share	Average
The State Council (Experimental Groups)	119	4.5	4,515	42.2	37.9	2,287	42.9	19.2
Relevant Ministries of the State Council	136	5.1	2,301	21.5	16.9	775	14.6	5.7
Provincial governments	1,212	45.6	2,438	22.8	2.0	1,350	25.4	1.1
Relevant Bureaus of provincial governments	754	28.4	754	7.0	1.0	467	8.8	0.6
Others	434	16.3	692	6.5	1.6	447	8.4	1.0
Total	2,655	100	10,700	100	4.8	5,326	100	2.0

Source: National Bureau of Statistics, China, *Zhongguo daqiyejituan* (Chinese Big Enterprise Groups) (2000), China Statistics Press, 2001.

Note: 'Others' means the business groups that have assets and sales revenues each in excess of 500 million Yuan.

economic institutions and trying some experiments with these new forms, fully endorsed and promoted them. One may note that many major economic reform measures promoted by the Chinese government, such as household responsibility system reform in agriculture,[4] corporatization of the SOEs, and establishing the Shenzhen and Shanghai Stock Exchanges, were bottom-up initiatives that were subsequently promoted by the government. Most major economic reforms have been induced rather than imposed because the government had no blueprint at hand for economic reforms, and enhancing the incentives of economic entities through liberalization was the only way they could adopt (Lee, Lin, and Chang 2005).

9.2.2. Strategic Restructuring and the Business Groups

Business groups are also formed out of various strategic considerations. Starting in the early 1990s, the Chinese government began to promote the creation of big business groups with the intent of strengthening Chinese firms' international competitiveness. To create big business groups, the Chinese government promoted M&As among big firms in a policy initiative called a 'strong–strong combination' (*qiangqiang lianhe* in Chinese). Administrative forces were often used in this process. For example, Shanghai

Baosteel Group, the biggest business group in the Chinese iron and steel industry with thirty-six iron and steel subsidiaries, was formed in 1998 through mergers and restructuring of Shanghai Metallurgical Holding Group and Shanghai Meishan Group with the former Shanghai Baoshan Iron & Steel Corporation as its core (i.e. parent) company. The biggest difficulty in forming this group was the different affiliations of the involved firms. The Shanghai city government controlled the first two groups, whereas the central government controlled the latter two. It took extensive negotiations before the Shanghai city government finally agreed to the merger of the firms.

On the local level, some business groups are formed by the local governments with the intent of enhancing enterprise performance by using existing managerial talent across a wider array of businesses in order to respond to the increasing market competition of the 1990s. Good managerial talent is in very limited supply in less-developed countries, especially in local regions in China. Some local governments restructured the SOEs under their supervision into several business groups. In 1993, Siping county in Liaocheng city, Shandong province restructured twenty-nine SOEs under its supervision into five business groups, based on these groups' industrial categories, in order to share both established brands and managerial talent (Lee 1998).

Business groups are also sometimes formed because of public policy considerations, rather than economic efficiency. Regarding the SOEs that are under their supervision, Chinese local governments have conflicting objectives: the promotion of profitable enterprises and social stability. As market competition increases and many SOEs' profitability decreases, local governments are often more concerned about the consequences of massive layoffs, such as social unrest. Accordingly, local governments tend to emphasize their responsibility to maintain social stability. As a result, to deal with unprofitable enterprises, they often opt to merge these enterprises with better-performing enterprises, in 'forced marriages' (*lalangpei* in Chinese), rather than having them go bankrupt. In this process, new business groups are formed or existing business groups are expanded.

9.2.3. Government Reform and the Business Groups

Business groups in China were also created as the government and the SOE supervision systems were restructured. In the prereform era in China, each ministry (bureau) was assigned the right and responsibility to control the SOEs in the corresponding industry. A SOE was supervised both by multiple ministries (*tiao* in Chinese) and the local government (*kuai* in Chinese), that is, a system called vertical and horizontal segmentation (*tiaokuai fenge* in Chinese). As noted earlier, this lacked a decision-making body that had full responsibility and power in monitoring the enterprise. Since the initiation of government reform in the 1990s, these ministries (bureaus) lost control over the firms and were integrated into the State Economy and Trade Commission as the constituent bureaus (sections). Some transformed themselves into state holding companies, and the firms that used to be under their jurisdiction were turned into the affiliate firms.

However, this system failed because the State Economy and Trade Commission had a conflict of interest. It was both the supervisor of the SOEs and the government agency responsible for the SOEs' performance. In line with the initiative to separate the government from the enterprises, the Chinese government established the State Asset Administration Commission in the mid-1990s to supervise the SOEs. Actually, the State Asset Administration Commission was launched through a restructuring and expansion of the existing State Asset Administration Bureau, which had been in charge only of administrative matters regarding state-owned land assets. The State Asset Administration Commission was entitled to exercise full rights regarding the supervision of the SOEs. However, the State Asset Administration Commission was criticized for pursuing its own self-interest and was consequently liquidated. Later, a new state asset management system, the State Asset Supervision and Administration Commission, was established. The Commission at the central government level was launched recently in 2003, and commissions are being built at local levels.

Throughout the whole process of the government reform and the supervision of the SOEs, the core issue of the state property management system has been who should be the personified shareholder for state-owned shares. In this regard, grouping of the SOEs was perceived as one solution, and the business groups were supposed to claim property rights on behalf of the abstract owner, the state. This idea was first suggested by scholars and government officials in the mid-1990s, when the State Asset Administration Commission was launched. The government intended to form a monitoring system that would maintain control of state property, which consists of three layers: the top authority, which bears the ultimate responsibility regarding state enterprise supervision at the first layer, the state holding companies or the business groups at the second layer, and the corporatized firms at the third layer (McNally 1997).

This idea was realized through transforming the government ministries or bureaus into business groups on the central and local levels. Many big business groups were formed this way. First, mostly on the central level, industry administration companies (*hangyexing zonggongsi* in Chinese) were granted shares of the affiliated SOEs and were changed into business groups. Since the 14th term, the Chinese Communist Party declared in the plenary meeting of the central committee that the existing national industry administration companies should be restructured into holding companies, the central and local governments began to promote the transformation of industry administration companies into holding companies (The Central Committee of the Chinese Communist Party 1993). This was the second wave to transform the industry administration companies into business groups. The government attempted to form business groups that could play the role of holding companies with shares of the subsidiaries. Actually, the industry administration companies had been formed through restructuring of government industry ministries. The first business groups approved by the State Council in 1994 included China Petroleum and Chemical Company, China Nonferrous Metals Company, and China Aviation Industrial Company. The biggest business group now in China, the State Power Corporation, is the most distinguished example of the groups that were formed this way.

Second, the industry ministries or bureaus at the central and local levels were transformed into business groups. A typical case of this form of restructuring involves Shanghai City, Shenzhen City, and Wuhan City (Huchet 1998). These cities established the earlier mentioned three-tier system for state asset management. In Shanghai, bureaus in charge of commerce were transformed into Shanghai First Department Store Group, Shanghai Hualian Group, and Shanghai Friendship Group. Bureaus in charge of industries were transformed into holding companies in 1995, and later all the government bureaus were changed into business groups, including holding companies. In Shenzhen, the three-tier system was set up through the transformation of government bureaus in 1995 (Hahn 1997). The major function granted to the above business groups on the national and local levels was to hold shares of the subsidiaries, although some groups are pure holding companies that conduct no business of their own. The rest are business holding companies that have their own businesses.

As of now, the newly launched State Asset Supervision and Administration Commission of the State Council controls the 188 enterprises or business groups. Like the central government, major local governments have also established the three-tier SOE management system. In the localities that have not yet launched the State Asset Supervision and Administration Commission, the SOE are under the control of the treasury bureaus.

9.2.4. Prevention of Monopoly and the Business Groups

The latest motive for forming business groups is the prevention of monopoly and improvement of industrial organization. From the mid-1990s, as firms rushed to form business groups, concerns emerged about markets becoming monopolistic or oligopolistic. This concern was especially pronounced for industries that were prone to natural monopoly, as well as key industries like civil aviation, petroleum, and petrochemicals. This kind of debate is of course deeply related to debates about the most-desirable industrial organizational structure. The worry about the harmful effects of the big business group strategy finally resulted in the launch of several business groups that led to the partition of the industries.

In 2001, with the intent to abolish monopoly and promote market competition, the central government separated the civil aviation industry into three groups: (*a*) China Aviation Group, (*b*) China Eastern Aviation Group, and (*c*) China Southern Aviation Group. In order to get rid of China Telecom's monopoly in telecommunications, the government separated its resources in northern China and merged them with China Jitong and China Netcom to launch the new China Netcom. It has thus created a competitive situation where four groups compete with each other, namely China Telecom, China Ironcom, China Unicom, and China Netcom (the Federation of Chinese Enterprises and the Association of Chinese Entrepreneurs 2002).

9.3. DIVERSE PATHS TOWARD THE BUSINESS GROUPS IN CHINA: MARKET COMPETITION AND FIRMS' RESPONSES

Chinese business groups have had distinct origins and are evolving in multiple ways. A survey conducted by the Chinese Academy of Social Sciences found that three paths typify the evolution of most Chinese business groups: spin-offs, M&As, and joint ventures. In Table 9.3, the 100 enterprises out of the sample of 670 enterprises answered that they had conducted organizational change that had lead to a business group. The most common change was the establishment of subsidiaries through spin-offs.

Spin-offs sometimes involve the establishment of new firms with both the parent firm's money and investments from independent companies. We consider spin-offs that involve investments from more than one firm to be joint ventures. Spin-offs and joint ventures are shown as paths 1 and 2,

Table 9.3. Enterprise grouping in China

	Very important	Important	Modest	Total scores	No. of enterprises responding
Question 1: Have you conducted any of the following since the 1990s?					
1. M&A of other firms		25	25%		
2. Forming a joint-venture with other companies		29	29%		
3. Establishing spin-off firms or subsidiaries		64	64%		
Total No. of enterprises responding:		100	118%		
Question 2: What are the main reasons for establishing a spin-off or subsidiary?					
1. To reduce surplus workers problem	30	51	31	223	112
2. To pool capital to expand the scale	28	55	27	221	110
3. To utilize the current assets in a more flexible way	30	50	31	221	111
4. To further reduce the interference from the state	10	16	84	146	110
5. To enhance accountability	8	19	83	145	110

Note: Total scores are calculated with 3 points assigned to 'very important', 2 points assigned to 'important,' and 1 point assigned to 'modest' answers.

Source: Results of the 1996 Survey of the 670 state-owned enterprises done by the Chinese Academy of Social Sciences.

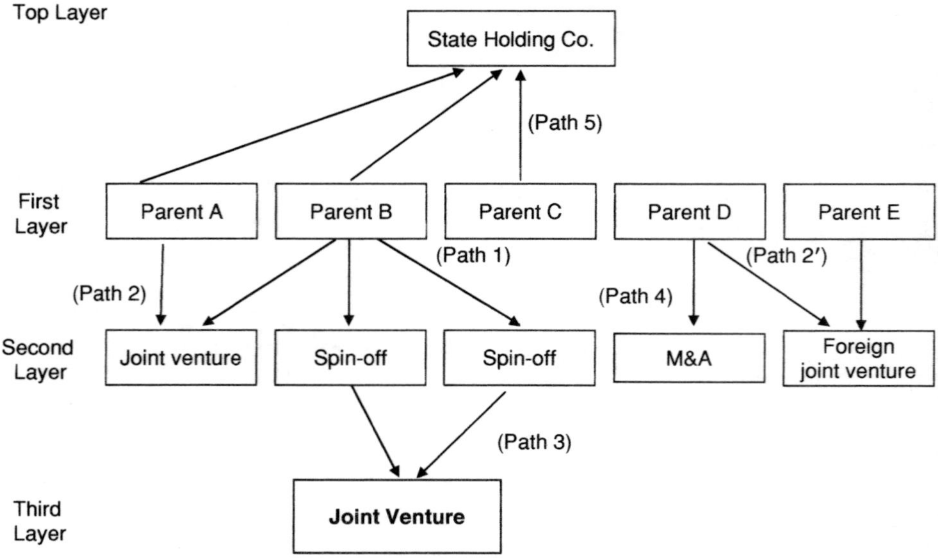

Figure 9.2. Diverse paths toward grouping in China

respectively, in Figure 9.2. Increasingly, there are cases of grouping that involve joint ventures with foreign partners, as in path 2′.

Many Chinese business groups form second-tier subsidiaries that are wholly owned and controlled by the parent company (see Lee and Woo 2002). Below this layer, as represented by path 3, two subsidiaries from the same business group sometimes form joint ventures with each other or with other firms. The business grouping via the three paths discussed previously represents spontaneous growth of a parent firm at the first layer into a business group comprising firms in the second and third tiers.

Although these group forms can be regarded as responses to market forces, there are other, less economically viable forms of groups, such as state-led M&As, as well as those that involve the formation of state holding companies above the firms in the first tier (paths 4 and 5, respectively). Path 4, denoting the state-led M&As, typically represents the administratively arranged merger of unprofitable SOEs by bigger or better-performing SOEs that are 'forced' by the state to merge with the less-successful SOEs. Path 5 typically represents the transformation of a former government bureau in charge of all the SOEs in a specific branch of industry into a state holding company, as in the case of Shanghai city reported in McNally (1997). It could also represent the administrative combination of several SOEs in several sectors, as found in Wuhan city (Huchet 1998). Paths 4 and 5 are more controversial as business groups formed through these paths originated from bureaucratic interests rather than economic efficiency considerations.

9.3.1. Spin-offs and Joint Ventures

Firms sometimes conduct spin-offs and change themselves into holding companies to increase efficiency and respond to market competition. Given the Chinese legacy of a planned economy, exit from unprofitable lines of businesses is very difficult, especially in regard to employment. A subsidiary can help resolve this difficulty by providing alternative means to deal with surplus and retired workers and thereby save money. For instance, one paper company solved its retired worker problem by setting up a new service firm and placing these workers in it (Lee 1998). This happened when the company was turned into a joint venture with a foreign partner. The parent company promised limited five-year subsidies to this new firm so that the workers might be motivated to work harder.

In addition, when a new subsidiary takes the form of a joint venture, it can often take advantage of pooled capital, equity, or brand names. Even when the parent owns the subsidiary outright, the subsidiary's new status can help it circumvent interference from state bureaucrats. It can also offer greater incentives to its employees and subject these individuals to more accountability and transparency.

On the negative side, firms sometimes set up new subsidiaries to make their operations less transparent rather than to add value. Building groups through spin-offs often involves irregular diversion of the parent firms' resources to the benefit of subsidiaries. Such diversions can provide a way to expropriate state property in the form of asset stripping, tax evasion, debt reduction, and dividend manipulation. As SOE reforms give managers and firms more autonomy, this problem is almost certain to increase in the future (Hahn and Lee 1999).

9.3.2. Mergers and acquisitions

Recently, the frequency of M&As in China has increased greatly, which goes against the usual trend of M&As being widespread mostly in mature market economies. The most prominent motivation for M&As is in industries like household electric appliances and beer that are characterized by intense market competition. Firms in such industries want to increase market share and scale economies, develop national brands, and capitalize on the superior managerial talent in certain firms (Hahn 2002). In household appliances, for instance, the concentration ratios for the largest five to seven firms now range from 50 to 72 percent for refrigerators, air conditioners, and washing machines (Wang and Kang 2001). Haier Group, for instance, is the sixteenth largest business group in terms of sales in China and is the biggest business group in the Chinese household electric appliances industry. It exemplifies this trend of expansion by M&As. It has merged firms with good technological capabilities that have foundered because of bad management, and revived them with better management, controls, and corporate culture.

9.3.3. Strategic Alliance and Virtual Grouping

Brand names are also sometimes the justification for such grouping. As brands become more important in China, some firms have sought to capitalize on another firm's good reputation by licensing that firm's brand name. In these transactions, the brand-owner firm usually examines the quality of the firm that hopes to borrow its brand name, including the applicant's production facilities, level of product quality control, and management capability. If the applicant passes the test, it is entitled to use the brand name for its own products. In return for sharing the brand name, the brand-owner firm usually takes a negotiated proportion of the profit or company shares. Sometimes these brand-sharing relationships evolve *ex post* into a closer relationship between firms through the sharing of managerial skills. Such arrangements are most common in industries that are extremely competitive and have substantial excess capacity (Hahn and Lee 1998).

9.4. THE CHARACTERISTICS OF CHINESE BUSINESS GROUPS: AN APPRAISAL

In this section, we focus on business groups registered with the government. There were 2,655 administratively approved business groups in China as of 2000. Of course, there are also many business groups that are not approved by or registered with the government, but have capital ties among the affiliate firms, such as more privately owned business groups that flourish in coastal areas like Shenzhen. We do not discuss unregistered groups because there are insufficient data about them.

9.4.1. Size

The total assets of these groups were about 10.6 trillion yuan and the total sales revenue was about 5.3 trillion yuan. Their average assets and sales revenue were about 4 billion and 2 billion yuan, respectively.[5] Table 9.4 shows the distribution of the enrolled business groups by asset size and sales revenue. Nine business groups have more than 100 billion yuan in assets and account for 38.4 percent of the total assets and 29.5 percent of the total sales revenue of all the enrolled business groups. Sixty-six groups have more than 10 billion yuan in both assets and sales, and account for 56.1 and 52.7 percent, respectively, of these figures for enrolled business groups. Most business groups have between 50 million and 5 billion yuan, but there are groups that have less than 50 million yuan in assets and/or less than 10 million yuan in sales.

Appendix 9.1 and Table 1.1 show the size of the biggest Chinese business groups relative to the largest international firms. In 2003, twenty Chinese

Table 9.4. Size distribution of Chinese business groups (2000)

(Unit: %)

	Number of groups		Assets		Sales revenue	
	Number	Share	Amount	Share	Amount	Share
Asset size (100 million yuan)						
1,000–	9	0.3	41,092	38.4	15,720	29.5
500–1,000	15	0.6	10,021	9.4	4,090	7.7
100–500	105	4.0	20,236	18.9	11,432	21.5
50–100	159	6.0	10,926	10.2	5,988	11.2
5–50	1,389	52.3	22,533	21.1	14,367	27.0
0.5–5	912	34.4	2,158	2.0	1,639	3.1
−0.5	66	2.5	19	0.0	23	0.0
Sales revenue (100 million yuan)						
100–	66	2.5	60,053	56.1	28,042	52.7
50–100	85	3.2	10,672	10.0	5,818	10.9
5–50	1,156	43.5	29,628	27.7	16,941	31.8
1–5	860	32.4	5,621	5.3	2,227	4.2
0.5–1	237	8.9	618	0.6	174	0.3
0.1–0.5	182	6.9	297	0.3	54	0.1
−0.1	69	2.6	95	0.1	3	0.0
Total	2,655	100	106,984	100	53,260	100

Source: National Bureau of Statistics, China, *Zhongguo daqiyejituan* (Chinese Big Enterprise Groups) (2000), China Statistics Press, 2001.

business groups were ranked in the *Fortune* Emerging Market 200 enterprises, but most of them are in finance or trade, and/or have government monopolies. This brief international comparison emphasizes the relatively small size of these groups, despite the Chinese government's active efforts to expand them.

9.4.2. Ownership and Administrative Level

Table 9.5 shows the distribution of ownership types of parent firms and their control over subsidiaries. In the majority (61 percent) of business groups, the parent firms are state owned. These firms keep absolute control over their subsidiaries or 'son' companies. This dominant type accounts for 92 percent of the total assets and 86.7 percent of the total sales revenue of all the registered business groups in China. 'Mother' companies denote parent firms that own at least 50 percent of a 'child' firm at the second tier (Lee and Woo 2002). This pattern contrasts with that of chaebols, in which the founding families control many affiliates by a combination of direct and circular shareholding among the core and noncore affiliates (see Chapter 3 of this book).

Table 9.5. Distribution of Chinese business groups by ownership of the parent companies (2000)

(Unit: million yuan, %)

	Number of groups		Assets		Major sales revenue	
	Number	Share	Amount	Share	Amount	Share
Absolute control, state ownership	1,605	60.5	98,472	92.0	46,152	86.7
Relative control, state ownership	130	4.9	1,849	1.7	1,337	2.5
Absolute control, collective ownership	331	12.5	2,825	2.6	2,758	5.2
Relative control, collective ownership	77	2.9	440	0.4	405	0.8
Others	512	19.3	3,397	3.2	2,608	4.9
Total	2,655	100	106,984	100	53,260	100

Source: National Bureau of Statistics, China, *Zhongguo daqiyejituan* (Chinese Big Enterprise Groups) (2000), China Statistics Press, 2001.

Notes:
1. 'Absolute control' means the state that the parent firm holds more than 50% of the shares; whereas 'Relative control' means the state that the parent firm holds less than 50% of the shares but has a plurality of shares.
2. 'Others' includes private firms and Sino-foreign joint ventures.

In sum, the state-owned business groups account for 65.4, 93.7, and 89.2 percent of the total number, total assets, and total sales revenue of the Chinese business groups. These figures indicate that state-owned business groups are substantially larger than other types of Chinese business groups.

As of 2000, there are 119 business groups that were designated as experimental business groups by the State Council. They held 42.2 percent of the total assets and 42.9 percent of the total sales revenue of the enrolled business groups.[6] There are also business groups that have been approved by relevant ministries of the State Council that are in charge of approving business groups. They accounted for 5.1 percent of the total number, 21.5 percent of the total assets, and 14.6 percent of the total sales revenue of the enrolled business groups.[7] The firms in the second group are smaller than those in the first group. The average size of the business groups approved by the State Council was about 37.9 billion yuan in assets and 19.2 billion yuan in sales revenue. The corresponding figures for the business groups approved by the relevant ministries in charge were 16.9 billion and 5.7 billion yuan, respectively. Business groups approved by the provincial governments are much smaller than these first two sets of business groups are.

9.4.3. Intragroup Organization and Parent–Subsidiary Relation

Table 9.6 shows the size distribution of parent firms and their subsidiaries. As of 2000, there were 2,155 parent companies and 21,948 son companies, indicating the average number of the subsidiaries in each business group was 8.3. The asset leverage multiplier (the sum total of assets held by all the subsidiaries divided by that of the parent company) and the sales revenue leverage multiplier between the subsidiaries and the parent firms were 1.7 times and 5.3 times, respectively. These figures mean that in relative terms, business groups are creating more revenue from the subsidiaries than they are from the parent firms, which implies that many parent firms are more like holding companies. This finding is consistent with 'asset diversion' (Lee and Hahn 2003), in which parent companies divert their best assets to their son companies, which are less subject to outside monitoring.

The intragroup size distribution between the parent firms and the subsidiaries shows a big difference between business groups with the SOEs as the parent firms and business groups with 'wholly state-owned with great autonomy'[8] enterprises as the parent firms. The latter group denotes SOEs that are 100 percent owned by the government and are granted special autonomy and privileges. The leverage multipliers of the regular SOEs are much bigger than those of the 'great autonomy' enterprises are, which means more business is

Table 9.6. Size comparison between the parents and the subsidiaries by type of the parent firms (2000)

(Unit: million yuan, times)

Types	Number of firms			Assets			Major sales revenue		
	P	S	T	P	S	T	P	S	T
State-owned	538	6,805 (12.6)	7,343	25,034	42,002 (1.7)	67,036	3,955	40,359 (10.2)	44,314
Wholly state-owned with full autonomy	696	2,067 (3.0)	2,763	13,883	9,007 (0.6)	22,890	3,706	3,616 (1.0)	7,322
Limited liability	665	6,392 (9.6)	7,057	4,080	10,631 (2.6)	14,711	1,472	6,249 (4.2)	7,722
Shareholding	438	1,562 (3.6)	2,000	3,526	14,601 (4.1)	18,126	1,706	6,299 (3.7)	8,004
Sino-foreign joint venture	43	1,747 (40.6)	1,790	476	3,771 (7.9)	4,247	319	3,462 (10.9)	3,781
Hong Kong, Taiwan, and Macau	28	597 (21.3)	625	197	1,219 (6.2)	1,416	72	755 (10.5)	827
Others	247	2,778 (11.2)	3,025	909	1,742 (1.9)	2,651	707	1,775 (2.5)	2,483
Total	2,655	21,948 (8.3)	24,603	48,105	82,973 (1.7)	131,078	11,937	62,515 (5.3)	74,452

Source: National Bureau of Statistics, China, *Zhongguo daqiyejituan* (Chinese Big Enterprise Groups) (2000), China Statistics Press, 2001.

Notes:

1. 'P', 'S', and 'T' stand for 'Parent', 'Subsidiaries', and 'Total', respectively.
2. 'Others' includes collective firms and private firms.
3. Figures in the parentheses are the leverage multipliers between the parent and the subsidiaries. For example, in the assets column in the bottom row showing the total, 1.7 means that the sum total of assets held by all the subsidiaries are 1.7 times bigger than that of the parent companies.

happening in the parent firms in the great autonomy firms than it is in the regular SOEs. Also, Sino-foreign joint ventures (including firms from Hong Kong, Taiwan, and Macau) have bigger leverage multipliers than business groups of other types do.

The cohesiveness of Chinese business groups, or lack thereof, also bears mentioning. Many of the registered business groups originated as contract-based business groups, and there are also many (enrolled) business groups formed through the leadership of the government, but without capital ties. Although contract-based business groups are changing into business groups that have intragroup capital ties, the controlling power of the parent firms over the subsidiaries is still very limited. Chinese business groups are generally not that cohesive, as some of them are not based on capital ties and only loosely or administratively connected as discussed in the Sections 9.2 and 9.3. As is shown in Table 9.7, the share of the business groups that have established capital ties between the parents and the subsidiaries is increasing. It has now reached 87.2 percent in 2000 from 81 percent in 1997.

Table 9.8 shows the control of parent firms over their subsidiaries, with the parent firms classified according to their affiliation with the government at diverse levels. In the bottom row, about 83.9 percent out of the 1,943 business groups in the sample have parent firms involved in the important decision-making of their subsidiaries. In appointing managers and deciding profit distributions, however, only 67.9 and 57.5 percent, respectively, of the parent firms are involved.

What is noteworthy in Table 9.8 is the finding that the parent firms of business groups affiliated with the central government (the State Council) are less involved in important decision-making in the son companies than the parent firms supervised by the lower-level or local governments are. For example, whereas about 68 percent of the parent firms affiliated with the State Council intervened in the decision-making of the son companies, about 80 percent of the parent companies affiliated with the provincial government intervened. This fact is consistent with the observation that the central

Table 9.7. Number of business groups with parent–subsidiary capital ties (2000)

	1997	1998	1999	2000
Number of groups with capital ties	1,916	2,063	2,346	2,316
Total number of groups	2,369	2,472	2,757	2,655
Share	81.0%	83.5%	85.1%	87.2%

Source: National Bureau of Statistics, China, *Zhongguo daqiyejituan* (Chinese Big Enterprise Groups) (2000), China Statistics Press, 2001.

Table 9.8. Involvement of the parent firms in the son company management by the type of state organs that gave approval to the business groups (2000)

(Unit: %)

State Organs that Gave Approval	Number of groups	Major decision-making		Manager appointment		Use of profits	
		Number	Share	Number	Share	Number	Share
The State Council	56	38	67.9	43	76.8	34	60.7
Relevant Ministries of the State Council	102	82	80.4	77	75.5	66	64.7
Provincial governments	927	777	83.8	620	66.9	514	55.5
Relevant Bureaus of Provincial gov't	548	462	84.3	358	65.3	306	55.8
Others	310	272	87.7	221	71.3	198	63.9
Total	1,943	1,631	83.9	1,319	67.9	1,118	57.5

Source: National Bureau of Statistics, China, *Zhongguo daqiyejituan* (Chinese Big Enterprise Groups) (2000), China Statistics Press, 2001.

Note: 'Others' means the groups that were approved by the below-Province level governments.

government promoted the business groups as a way to reform the overall administration of SOEs, and was less motivated to manage them directly.

9.4.4. Diversification

According to an analysis of Chinese business groups based on the data of listed companies, Chinese business groups are relatively less diversified than Korean chaebols are (Lee and Woo 2002). In most state-holding companies and business groups built through state-led restructuring, the main purpose of building business groups was to capitalize on scale economies and better supervise the SOEs. Hence, most of these groups did not focus on diversifying. In addition, many of the Chinese business groups that pursued diversification in the early 1990s retreated to their traditional core lines of business after they faced fierce market competition (Lee and Woo 2002).

In China, business groups that diversify tend to do so into related rather than unrelated fields. Of the acquisitions of nonlisted firms by listed firms in 1997, the portions of horizontal, vertical, related, and unrelated diversification were roughly 40, 20, 20, and 20 percent, respectively (Huang 2000), indicating the great majority of M&As in China involves horizontal–vertical integration and related diversification. In this respect, Chinese business groups are more viable than their Korean or Japanese counterparts, although they are also more vulnerable to sector-specific shock because of their greater specialization.

9.5. SUMMARY AND CONCLUSION

Business groups in China first appeared as the Chinese economy underwent a transition from a planned economy to a market economy. Their emergence is attributable largely to the disorders of resource allocation during this transition. Later, firms in these groups changed the nature of their ties, and eventually established capital ties among the member firms. Other private business groups have been formed through diverse paths, including contracts, spin-offs, and joint ventures, M&As, and brand name sharing.

The role of the Chinese government regarding the development of business groups was to approve them quickly *ex post* and to promote them through experiment, like other major economic reform measures. In this sense, the emergence and evolution of most Chinese business groups is another case of bottom-up innovation rather than top-down innovation. State-led grouping, which has entailed the restructuring of SOEs, has been another path to the formation of business groups.

The intragroup ownership structures of Chinese business groups are more like Japanese vertical keiretsu than they are like Korean chaebols or Japanese horizontal keiretsu, which use cross-shareholding.[9] In China, some used to argue that cross-shareholding in business groups was a good practice. When chaebols were blamed for the Asian Crisis in Korea, however, this suggestion lost impetus. Thus, we believe that as far as intraorganizational capital structure is concerned, the Chinese business groups are more viable than Korean chaebols are.

The Chinese business groups are in an early stage of development. Despite the government's efforts to make them large, they are still relatively small, and centered on the state-owned business groups approved by the central government. Moreover, some business groups are very loosely organized.

Nevertheless, we believe the business group form has long-term viability in China. On average, these groups are less diversified and more focused than other business groups in Asia are. As noted by Lee and Woo (2002), however, Chinese business groups might be more vulnerable to firm-specific or sector-specific risk than chaebol affiliates are because they are less diversified. In contrast, chaebol affiliates are more vulnerable to major shocks like the Asian Crisis. Such vulnerability should be taken as an ominous sign for firms in

Appendix 9.1 Top 30 Chinese business groups in terms of sales volume (2000)

(Unit: 100 million yuan, persons)

Business groups	Sales revenue	Assets	Employees
State Power	3,728	12,407	842,848
Sinopec	3,686	5,353	1,168,464
China National Petroleum	3,470	6,565	1,140,472
China Telecommunications	1,723	5,276	588,882
China Mobile	1,246	3,215	111,666
COFCO (China Oil and Food)	1,052	377	20,111
Baoshan Steel	685	1,729	118,442
Guangdong Power	616	1,503	40,661
China First Auto Works (FAW)	592	547	120,823
Putian Information Industry	465	351	32,816
China Ocean Shipping and Transportation (COSTCO)	464	821	52,966
Shanghai Electric Appliances	440	873	175,675
China Construction Engineering	439	684	233,479
Haier	406	132	21,297
China Xinjian	379	612	707,970
Capital Steel	300	551	154,992
Legend	285	136	12,000
China Unicom	278	1,456	87,872
CITIC	276	3,586	53,829
Sinochem	270	296	6,281
Shanghai Auto Industry	263	302	58,422
Dongfeng Automobile	259	465	104,602
China Wukuang	248	182	1,702
Yuxi Hongtashan Tobacco	246	437	8,109
Shanghai Tobacco	221	172	7,376
Anshan Steel	208	675	153,053
Wuhan Steel	207	490	146,062
China Electronic and Information Industry	198	341	29,319
Dongfang International	195	114	3,551
TCL	179	110	29,146
Total	23,024	49,758	6,232,888

Source: Chinese Federation of Enterprises, *Zhongguo Qiye Fazhan Baogao* (A Report on the Development of Chinese Enterprises), Enterprise Management Publishing House, 2002.

developing countries, but fierce competition in Chinese domestic markets would not allow excessive diversification. In addition, consistent with our view of competition in China, we believe the more focused nature of Chinese business groups is attributable to how competitive Chinese markets are. Accordingly, we believe the formation, structure, and properties of the Chinese business groups are economically rational.

NOTES

1 and 2. The horizontal associations had no name, whether official or not, and so there does not exist any aggregate statistical data or report on a specific case of the horizontal association.

3. There were minor changes in the number of experimental business groups.
4. The individual household responsibility system was voluntarily and unlawfully adopted in a County of Anhui province in place of the former collective farming. On detecting the stunning success of this change in agricultural system, the Chinese government gave a quick approval to it in limited regions, and finally promoted the new system nationwide.
5. The coverage of the data used in this chapter includes the subsidiaries that are either in absolute control or in relative control. 'Absolute control' means that the parent firm holds ownership of the subsidiary in excess of 50 percent, whereas 'relative control' means that the parent firm is the plurality shareholder of the subsidiary but owns less than 50 percent of the shares of the subsidiary. Subsidiaries in which the parent firm has neither the majority nor the plurality of shares are not included in the data of the subsidiaries.
6. There are minor year-to-year changes in the number of the experimental groups directly approved by the State Council because some groups fail to satisfy the government requirement to maintain this status.
7. 'The ministries of the State Council in charge' means the ministries that are in charge of administrative approval of the business groups, including the State Development and Reform Commission the former State Economy and Trade Commission, and so on. Without the approval from the appropriate ministries, registration with the State Administration for Industry and Commerce is not allowed.
8. Besides the two major forms of modern corporations (i.e. joint-stock corporations and limited-liability corporations), it is an exceptionally accepted as a special form of modern corporations by the government. Firms of this type are relatively big SOEs and are distributed mainly in industries that the government believes it needs to control.
9. Japanese business groups can be classified into two categories, vertical keiretsu and horizontal keiretsu, according to their organizational and industrial structures. The horizontal keiretsu have circular capital ties among the affiliate firms and much diversified industrial structures. For example, Mitsubishi, Sumitomo, Mitsui belong to this category. The vertical keiretsu have hierarchical organizational structures among the member firms and focused industrial structures. Toyota and Sony belong to this category.

10

Conclusion: The Future of Business Groups in East Asia

Sea-Jin Chang

10.1. THE POSTCRISIS EVOLUTION OF BUSINESS GROUPS IN EAST ASIA

The Asian Crisis had a significant impact on the nations discussed in this book. Banks and other financial institutions quickly became insolvent, and heavily indebted industrial firms, many of which were affiliated with the business groups in this region, went bankrupt. Interest rates and exchange rates skyrocketed. Unemployed people filled the street. Although the crisis affected Thailand, Indonesia, Korea, and Malaysia most directly, other East Asian countries, such as Singapore, that depended heavily upon intraregion trade were also hurt by this crisis.

The individual country chapters in this book examined the impact of the Asian Crisis on the institutional environments and business groups in these countries. Each showed how states, markets, and sociocultural environments have interacted with business groups in the aftermath of the crisis. The analyses in these chapters suggest three general conclusions, which will be discussed later. First, despite the hardships associated with the crisis, most business groups in East Asia remained intact and showed they were robust to external shocks. Second, the business groups of each country developed in very divergent ways in response to the crisis. Third, several affected nations changed their institutional environments following the crisis. They enhanced corporate governance and tightened capital market supervision. These changes will have long-term ramifications for business groups in this region.

10.1.1. Robustness of Business Group Structure

A critical commonality emerging from these chapters is the robustness of the business group structure. One might have expected this crisis would have wiped out debt-ridden business groups in the affected countries and that the postcrisis restructuring programs initiated by the International Monetary Fund (IMF) and World Bank would have instituted a corporate governance system similar to the Anglo-Saxon model. Despite adverse conditions, most business groups in this region did not collapse. Many remained intact and some even prospered. In countries not directly affected by the crisis, such as Taiwan and China, business groups kept growing.

Although financial crisis, accounting changes, and foreign influence caused upheaval in some groups, other fundamental business group practices persisted either because they had real benefits or better matched a given institutional environment. According to market imperfection theorists, business groups thrive when markets are imperfect. When capital markets and intermediate goods markets malfunction, business groups fill this gap by internalizing their business transactions. As long as markets remain imperfect, business groups in East Asia will prosper. In addition, East Asian business groups may be socially and culturally embedded in the specific countries where they operate. Keiretsu may be based on the close exchange relationships embedded in Japanese society. Similarly, Korean and Taiwanese groups might fit the patrimonial and patrilineal cultures of their respective countries. The conflicts between indigenous locals and ethnic Chinese in other Southeast Asian countries might impel existing groups either to promote local indigenous capital or to protect their own interests. Continued government intervention, even after the crisis, also distorts the market, thus providing business groups with chances to create value.

The robustness of the business group structure suggests accounts of globalization's impact have often been exaggerated (Ohmae 1990; Guéhenno 1995). Globalization theorists have argued that global convergence of markets and business organizations will occur due to intensified global competition. The postcrisis restructuring of business groups provides further evidence that changes attributed to globalization are more evolutionary than revolutionary (Campbell 2004).

10.1.2. Divergent Development Paths

The individual country chapters reveal that business groups in each country have responded to the Asian Crisis differently. Government in each country perceived problems of varying magnitudes, and had different levels of capabilities to implement changes. Business groups fiercely resisted any changes that would undermine their resources and power bases. The incumbent institutional infrastructures, culture, social norms, and ethnic conflicts in each country further constrained actors' choices. The outcomes of such constraints are divergent development paths (Whitley 1999).

Japan differs from other East Asian countries in that the state did not seriously attempt to break up, weaken, or restructure business groups; these groups themselves simply were not an issue in the reform agenda of the Japanese government. It is impossible to think of entrepreneurs on a group-wide level in Japan because groups had no center and instead comprised more informal webs of relationships. Furthermore, Japan is a wealthy country with a high level of foreign reserves. Its inertia might be due to its past success. Nor was it forced to change by the IMF. The fact that better-performing, stronger Japanese companies have been less likely to sever ties is consistent with the economic rationale for business groups. This finding can be interpreted in various ways: high performers have not encountered a crisis that has forced them to break ties, or well-managed, high-performing firms continue to find value within group relationships. The combination of the tendency for weak groups to break apart and of more peripheral ties to be broken even in stronger groups suggests there might be a greater bifurcation between tightly linked members of surviving groups and more independent firms. Some groups will survive, and others will not.

Korea was the only country among the former newly industrialized countries (NICs) that was directly hit by the crisis. When it became technically bankrupt, the Korean government had to accede to the demands of foreign investors. In the postcrisis restructuring of Korea, the state acted as an agent for foreign capital by following the IMF guidelines closely. Although many groups went bankrupt and dissolved, surviving business groups stayed largely intact. These survivors are, however, under great pressure from both domestic and foreign investors to become less diversified and to focus more on their core businesses.

Taiwan and Singapore were not directly affected by the crisis. Yet each country and its business groups have developed differently. Taiwanese business groups have continued to expand and diversify, especially after deregulation, likely in response to the removal of barriers that prohibited private firms from entering certain markets. Furthermore, because Taiwan was not directly affected by the crisis, there seemed to be no need to curb business groups' expansion. In contrast, the Singapore government emphasized divestment, foreign acquisitions, and professional governance. In Singapore, the distinction between the state and the private sector has been blurry. Many state-owned enterprises (SOEs) formed business groups run by professional managers. When the crisis began, the government sensed the weaknesses of the group structure—weak corporate governance and a lack of market discipline—and initiated restructuring. Yet the pace of divestment by the government-linked groups and banking groups has been gradual at best, reflecting the inertia of government institutions.

Business groups in Malaysia, Thailand, and Indonesia have not exhibited any coherent pattern of restructuring after the crisis. Rather, indigenous business groups that possessed connections with the ruling political powers have generally avoided losses and benefited from the crisis by acquiring failed businesses. The conflict between indigenous people and ethnic Chinese has further distorted the restructuring process and aggravated cronyism and corruption. Despite the crisis, these countries did not capitalize on the opportunity to build institutional infrastructures that might restructure business groups.

For example, in Malaysia, the failure of leading *Bumiputeras* firms created a political crisis. Business groups with better political connections survived, whereas less-connected groups generally did not. Even after the crisis, key political figures maintained their corporate interests and benefited from privatized contracts. Various structural reforms to enhance transparency and accountability in government were not implemented. Similarly, in Thailand, although the government undertook various effective legal measures to remodel the country's institutional environment, the ownership structures of business groups remained intact. Nonetheless, many big Thai business groups lost their financial bases, thus limiting their ability to obtain funds as easily as they used to. In Indonesia, business groups are still struggling to survive. Since the Asian Crisis, some groups have transformed their corporate structures and survived the turmoil. Others have lost control over their companies or struggled to keep control. It is not clear what, if anything, has separated the winners from the losers in this endgame, apart from political connections with the ruling politicians.

Unlike their counterparts in other East Asian countries, Chinese business groups, which have been transformed from SOEs, are still in an early stage of development. When the crisis tested Korean chaebols' resiliency, there were heated debates in China on the government's policy of promoting business groups in China, as Korean chaebols have been one model of business groups for Chinese policymakers. Although Chinese policymakers agree that the business group structure can help develop China's economy, they have discouraged the overly rapid growth and unrelated diversification that characterized many unsuccessful Korean chaebols.

This divergent pattern of development again counters globalization theorists' arguments about rapid global convergence. This argument suggests global competition will encourage all nations to pursue a common set of neoliberal programs to attract liquid capital, and that large corporations should pursue a common structure and strategy because firms, like states, have become more eager to shift capital and operations from one country to another. As Campbell (2004) showed, nations have often not competed to attract foreign capital, and many country-specific institutional arrangements related to organized labor, business, and electoral politics have constrained the predicted effects of globalization. Similarly, Mayer (1998) and La Porta et al. (1998) observed that ownership and control mechanisms still vary greatly throughout the world. This trend refutes the notion of a global convergence towards the Anglo-Saxon model of corporate governance. Instead, there is 'divergent capitalism', which connotes distinct combinations of markets and economic organizations in each country that are adapted to respective institutional environments (Whitley 1999; Guillen 2001).

10.1.3. Changes within Continuity

Although many business groups in each country have remained robust and have continued to develop quite differently, the institutional environments surrounding business groups have undergone important changes. The inflow of foreign capital, which increased consistently throughout the 1990s, was accompanied by demands for accounting transparency and stronger corporate governance. As shown in Table 1.1, the inflow of foreign capital via portfolio investment and foreign direct investment (FDI) in the postcrisis period has been restored to its precrisis level. This inflow remains critical to East Asian countries because many lack the accumulated capital to sustain their future growth. Foreign investors' influence has increased substantially since the crisis, however, as East Asian governments have had to accommodate their demands to keep attracting foreign capital. Governments supervise banks more closely, and have loosened restrictions on mergers and hostile takeovers, further strengthening the discipline of the market. Various entry barriers that had inhibited foreign multinationals from competing in national markets were lifted, exposing business groups to intensified foreign competition. These groups have had to respond to this challenge by focusing on core businesses while divesting unrelated ones. This crisis-induced restructuring is most evident in Korea. In other countries that were directly affected by the crisis, namely Malaysia, Indonesia, and Thailand, the governments have enforced their financial service institutions more stringently and passed laws to strengthen corporate governance. Although it is unclear whether these new arrangements will be effectively implemented, they have the potential to improve capital market functioning in these countries.

There have also been substantial changes in the institutional environments of East Asian nations that were not directly affected by the crisis. For instance, foreign investment into Japan increased sharply. The Japanese government announced financial reforms, including an overhaul of Japanese accounting regulations to make accounting standards consistent with international standards. As part of these reforms, firms were required to report the value of their equity holdings at market value, which resulted in massive sales of bank-owned shares of keiretsu firms. Another reform was a more stringent requirement for consolidation, which made it harder for firms to manage their earnings by allocating gains and losses among group firms. Although these reforms were not directly targeted at keiretsu, they have resulted in weaker ties among poorly performing keiretsu. In Singapore, the government restructured the financial sector and strengthened corporate laws and accountancy practices. It pressured both government-linked corporations and private firms to compete in other nations, divest their noncore assets, and professionalize their corporate governance.

These incremental changes in institutional environments might induce East Asian business groups to restructure in the long run. East Asian business groups might undergo a 'second wave' of restructuring as their nations' capital markets and other institutions develop further and as they compete more intensely with foreign multinationals.

10.2. BUSINESS GROUPS IN OTHER REGIONS

This slow yet divergent evolution in the face of environmental shifts is not isolated to East Asian economies. Similar factors have had similar effects elsewhere. Fligstein (1990) described the US corporate restructuring in the 1980s as a crisis in the market for corporate control, just as the financial crisis in East Asia was a crisis in the governance system. In the 1960s, many US firms grew by diversifying into unrelated areas, mainly through mergers and acquisitions (M&As). These conglomerates performed poorly because it was difficult to manage unrelated diversification and because of intensified competition from Japanese firms. Fligstein argues that this period of restructuring reflected investors' more aggressive use of capital markets to wrest control from the managers of poorly performing firms. Institutional investors such as pension funds and mutual funds became more influential. New financial instruments such as junk bonds helped firms and corporate raiders effect hostile takeovers. Chief executive officers (CEOs) of firms that did not pay attention to institutional investors' demands were replaced. Other managers, paying heed to this trend, restructured their firms, enhanced efficiency, and improved profitability. Overall, increased international competition and active capital market intervention effectively limited US conglomerates' prospects (Chang 1996).

In Europe, the evolution of conglomerates has been affected by country-specific institutions and, more recently, by the formation of the European Union (EU). In postwar Germany, konzern were separated into many individual companies. Groups such as Daimler-Benz and Siemens grew by diversifying their businesses. France has also a long tradition of conglomerates, many of which organized into holding companies. Many new French conglomerates were created during the nationalization and reprivatization by Mitterand's government.[1] Yet, like their US counterparts, these conglomerates have refocused on their core businesses and divested unrelated concerns in the 1990s because of increased competition and greater pressure from capital markets. The introduction of the euro also hastened integration and increased competition.

In the past, European corporations felt little pressure from investors. In Germany, banks have possessed large stakes in big conglomerates and exercised voting rights on behalf of other shareholders. As a consequence, hostile takeovers were almost impossible. In France, cross-shareholding among conglomerates eliminated the possibility of a hostile takeover. Yet cross-shareholding among European companies has been declining. Institutional investors, especially those from the USA, have filled the gap generated by weakened cross-shareholding (Useem 1998). They have initiated higher standards for performance, thereby increasing the pressure on European managers to focus only on core businesses. In addition, European firms are now more willing to attempt hostile takeovers of other firms. The much-publicized case of Vodafone's takeover of Mannesmann is but one prominent example of this trend. Top managers in European firms clearly have strong incentives to enhance their firms' performance.

Consistent with the patterns of divergence emphasized earlier, however, it is premature to announce European conglomerates' demise. European countries have a long tradition of bank-centered financing, and banks still own fairly large shares of industrial firms and maintain tight relations with them. Further, business relationships among banks, industrial firms, and their suppliers and buyers are often reinforced by social and cultural norms. Despite capital market pressures and the increased challenge posed by the Anglo-Saxon version of corporate governance, European business groups appear likely to evolve in a direction rather different from that taken by US conglomerates.

Further, business groups in other developing countries do not show any evidence of decline. *Grupos economicos* in South American countries grew as their home governments pursued import substitution policies (Evans 1979; Guillen 2001). Business groups exploited their political contacts and access to the local markets by forming alliances with foreign multinationals. In fact, these business groups survived the financial crisis that swept Latin American countries such as Chile, Argentina, and Uruguay in the early 1980s. In each of these nations, under pressure from the IMF, the government ignited currency and debt crises by deregulating the economy without establishing an appropriate regulatory framework (Galvez and Tybout 1985). Mexico and Brazil, which also pursued economic liberalization, experienced currency crises in 1994 and 1999, respectively (Fernandez-Jilberto and Mommem 1996; Baer and Love 2000). After years of import substitution development strategies that relied heavily on government intervention, these countries liberalized both by removing controls on prices, trade barriers, and capital flows and by privatizing state-owned firms, including financial service firms. Domestic firms tried to capitalize on the opportunities created by this rapid deregulation and privatization by borrowing from foreign creditors. Business groups in Chile, in particular, acquired banks and used their funds to acquire companies that were being privatized (Tybout 1986). Debt and foreign exchange crises swept these nations when the firms that borrowed from foreign creditors could not pay their loans. The governments had to bail out failed banks by injecting massive public funds. Despite these crises, business groups in Latin American countries continue flourishing.

Moreover, business groups in Eastern Europe have emerged as nations there privatized during the 1990s. For instance, during the rapid privatization in Czechoslovakia, various forms of cross-ownership among banks and investment trust funds were formed, and many of those investment trust companies turned themselves into holding companies (Coffee 1999). Similarly, Stark (1996) showed how previously state-owned firms in Hungary purchased small firms and formed groups on their own. Business groups in each developing country developed idiosyncratically as a function of their nations' respective political, social, and cultural heritages (Whitley 1999).

10.3. CONCLUSION

We believe business groups are creatures of market imperfections, government intervention, and sociocultural environments. We expect that as long as markets, especially capital markets, are imperfect and the East Asian governments influence resource allocation, business groups will continue to exist and even prosper in this region. As markets become more efficient and government intervention subsides, business groups may lose their reason for existence and see their influence decline.

This book provides ample evidence of increases in foreign investors' influence and global competition. Stronger supervision of financial service institutions and enforcement of stronger corporate governance mechanisms will reduce opportunities for business groups to create value. If this trend continues, business groups in East Asia may have to narrow down their business portfolios and focus upon their core businesses.

Business groups will not, however, disband overnight. It takes time to build institutions and for the effects of competition to be felt (North 1990). Furthermore, continued state intervention and the underlying sociocultural environments in East Asian countries may continue to favor business groups in those countries. Each country's history, culture, kinship relations, and ethnic composition will continue providing a strong rationale for affiliates to gather under the umbrella of business groups. Business groups can prosper by focusing on shared resources for which markets are still imperfect, such as managerial talent, brands, and technology, while remaining firmly embedded in their institutional environments. Ethnic tensions and governments' agendas to develop indigenous capitalists in some Southeast Asian countries will continue to aid business groups in those countries.

Business groups in East Asia will also continue expanding overseas. In part, these business groups pursued unrelated diversification to capture the potential rents of access to protected domestic markets. As these markets became more open, East Asian business groups in this region have responded to intensified competition from foreign multinationals by becoming more global. For instance, several Korean companies emerged as strong global contenders. Samsung Electronics has used its prowess in semiconductors, flat panel displays, and mobile phones to command large global market shares and high profitability. Singapore government also urged its business groups to divest unrelated businesses and to undertake global strategies and overseas investment. Several Chinese business groups are pursuing acquisitions of foreign firms to purchase valuable brands and technology, as exemplified by TCL's acquisition of Thomson, Lenovo's acquisition of IBM's PC business, and Shanghai Automobile Industrial Corporation (SAIC)'s acquisition of Ssangyong Motors.

If East Asian business groups continue to expand internationally, they will likely continue to prosper. Yet they will probably also become less diversified than they were before the Asian Crisis. As they become more focused and globally oriented entities, business groups will continue to be important vehicles for the sustained future growth of this region.

NOTE

1. His administration encouraged private French companies to buy shares in reprivatizing companies. For example, CGE (Compagnie Générale des Eaux), a water and waste treatment service company until the mid-1970s that had already diversified into real estate, telecommunications, construction, and hospital management, purchased FFr11 billion worth of shares in other French companies such as Saint-Gobain, Alcatel Alsthom, Accor, Paribas, and Société Générale by mid-1990. At the same time, other companies such as Société Générale, AXA, and Banque Nationale de Paris purchased shares of CGE. CGE then sold unrelated businesses and focused on water management and telecommunications. It changed its name to Vivendi in 1998 to reflect its new strategic focus (Montgomery 1999).

References

Abrahams, P. and Tett, G. I. (1999). 'The Circle is Broken: Japan's Keiretsu Face Collapse as Traditional Corporate Relationships are Undermined by Bank Mergers and a Search for Higher Return on Capital', *Financial Times*, November 9: 26.

Advance Research Group (1995). *Thailand Company Information*. Bangkok: Business and Management Publications.

Ahmadjian, C. L. and Lincoln, J. R. (2001). 'Keiretsu, Governance and Learning: Case Studies in Change from the Japanese Automotive Industry', *Organization Science*, 12/6: 683–701.

—— and Robinson, P. (2001). 'Safety in Numbers: Downsizing and the Deinstitutionalization of Permanent Employment in Japan', *Administrative Science Quarterly*, 46: 622–54.

Amsden, A. (1989). *Asia's Next Giant: South Korea and Late Industrialization*. New York: Oxford University Press.

Amsden, A. H. (1985). 'The State and Taiwan's Economic Development', in B. E. Peter, D. Rueschemeyer, and T. Skocpol (eds.), *Bringing the State Back In*. Cambridge: Cambridge University Press, pp. 78–106.

—— (2001). *The Rise of 'The Rest': Challenges to the West from Late-Industrialization Economies*. New York: Oxford University Press.

—— and Chu, W. W. (2003). *Beyond Late Development—Taiwan's Upgrading Policies*. Cambridge: MIT Press.

—— and Hikino, T. (1994). 'Project Execution Capability, Organizational Know-how and Conglomerate Corporate Growth in Late Industrialization', *Industrial and Corporate Change*, 3: 111–47.

Aoki, M. (1988). *Information, Incentives, and Bargaining in the Japanese Economy*. Cambridge: Cambridge University Press.

—— (2001). *Toward a Comparative Institutional Analysis*. Cambridge, MA: MIT Press.

Asiamoney (1994). Interview. November, 47.

Aunichitworawong, C., Souma, T., and Wiwattanakantang, Y. (2003). Do Families Controlled Banks Prevail after the East Asian Financial Crisis? Evidence from Thailand. Center for Economic Institutions, Institute of Economic Research, Hitotsubashi University, Japan, *Working Paper*, 8.

Baek, J. S., Kang, J. K., and Park, K. S. (2002). 'Economic Shock, Business Group and Determinants of Firm Valve and Restructuring: Evidence from the Korean Financial Crisis', mimeo.

Baer, W. and Love, J. (2000). *Liberalization and Its Consequences*. Cheltenham: Edward Elgar.

Bank of Thailand (2000). *Supervision Report 2000*.

Bebchuk, L. A. and Roe, M. J. (1999). 'A Theory of Path Dependence in Corporate Governance and Ownership', *Stanford Law Review*, 52: 127–70.

Berle, A. A. and Means, G. C. (1967). *The Modern Corporation and Private Property.* New York: Harcourt, Brace & World.

Biggart, N. W. (1991). 'Explaining Asian Economic Organization: Toward a Weberian Institutional Perspective', *Theory and Society*, 20: 199–232.

Borthwick, S. (1988). 'Chinese Education and Identity in Singapore. Chinese Identities in Southeast Asia: Alternative Perspectives', in J. W. Cushman and G. Wang (eds.), *Changing Identities of the Southeast Asian Chinese since World World II.* Hong Kong: Hong Kong University Press, pp. 35–59.

Brooker Group. (2001). *Thai Business Groups: A Unique Guide to Who Owns What.* Bangkok: Brooker Group.

Brown, R. A. (1994). *Capital & Entrepreneurs in South-East Asia.* London: Macmillan.

Bruton, G. D., Ahlstrom, D., and Wan, J. C. C. (2003). 'Turnaround in East Asian Firms: Evidence from Ethnic Overseas Chinese Communities', *Strategic Management Journal*, 24: 519–40.

Bualek, P. (2000). *The Analysis on the Major Owners of Thai Banks during 1932–1973*, 2nd edn. (in Thai). Bangkok: Siam Publisher.

Burt, R. S. (1983). *Corporate Profits and Cooptation: Networks of Market Restraints and Directorate Ties in the American Economy.* New York: Academic Press.

Burt, T. and Ibison, D. (2001). Toyota Trimming Costs in the Nicest Possible Way. *Financial Times*, December 13: 13.

Callen, T. and Reynolds, P. (1997). 'Capital Market Development and the Monetary Transmission Mechanism in Malaysia and Thailand', in J. Hicklin, D. Robinson, and A. Singh (eds.), *Macroeconomic Issues Facing ASEAN Countries.* Washington, DC: International Monetary Fund.

Campbell, J. (2004). *Institutional Change and Globalization.* Princeton, NJ: Princeton University Press.

—— and Lindberg, L. (1990). 'Property Rights and the Organization of Economic Activity by the State', *American Sociological Review*, 55: 634–47.

Carrera, A., Mesquita, L., Perkins, G., and Vassolo, R. (2003). 'Business Groups and Their Corporate Strategies on the Argentine Roller Coaster of Competitive and Anti-Competitive Shocks', *Academy of Management Executive*, 17: 32–44.

Caves, R. E. and Uekusa, M. (1976). *Industrial Organization in Japan.* Washington, DC: Brookings Institution.

CBRD. (2000). Financial Highlights of Companies on the Singapore Exchange 1995–1999, Volume 1 and 2, Centre for Business Research & Development and Faculty of Business Administration, NUS.

Chan, K. B. and Chiang, C. (1994). *Stepping Out: The Making of Chinese Entrepreneurs.* Singapore: Prentice-Hall.

—— and Ng, B. K. (2001). *Singapore. Chinese Business in Southeast Asia.* Surrey: Curzon Press, pp. 38–61.

Chandler, A. (1990). *Scale and Scope.* Cambridge, MA: Harvard University Press.

Chandler, A. D. (1962). *Strategy and Structure: Chapters in the History of Industrial Enterprise.* Cambridge, MA: MIT Press.

Chang, S. J. (1996). 'An Evolutionary Perspective on Diversification and Restructuring', *Strategic Management Journal*, 17/8: 587–611.

—— (2003a). 'Ownership Structure, Expropriation, and Performance of Group-Affiliated Companies in Korea', *Academy of Management Journal*, 46: 238–53.

—— (2003b). *Financial Crisis and Transformation of Korean Business Groups: The Rise and Fall of Chaebols*. New York: Cambridge University Press.

—— and Hong, J. B. (2000). 'Economic Performance of Group-Affiliated Companies in Korea: Intragroup Resource Sharing and Internal Business Transactions', *Academy of Management Journal*, 43: 429–48.

Charumilind, C., Kali, R., and Wiwattanakantang, Y. (forthcoming). 'Connected Lending: Thailand before the Financial Crisis', *Journal of Business*.

Chee, P. L. and Gomez, E. T. (1994). 'Malaysian *Sogoshoshas*: Superficial Cloning, Failed Emulation', in Jomo K. S. (ed.), *Japan and Malaysian Development: In the Shadow of the Rising Sun*. London: Routledge.

Chen, K. P. (1991). 'Chi Tuan Chi Yeh Tsung Kuan Li Chi Kou Kung Neng Yu Tus Chih Chih Yen Chiu [A Study of the Function and Organization of Business Group Headquarters]', in *Department of Business Administration*. Kaohsiung, Taiwan: National Sun Yat-Sen University.

Cheng, T. J. (2001). 'Transformation of Taiwan's Economic Structure in the 20th Century', *China Quarterly*, 165: 19–36.

Chi, S. (1996). *Zhongguo Qiyejituan Yanjiu* [Studies on the China Corporate Group]. Jinan: Jinan Publishing House.

Chin, K. F. and Jomo, K. S. (2001). 'Financial Liberalisation and System Vulnerability', in K. S. Jomo (ed.), *Malaysian Eclipse: Economic Crisis and Recovery*. London: Zed Books.

Chung, C. N. (2001). 'Markets, Culture and Institutions: The Emergence of Large Business Groups in Taiwan, 1950s–1970s', *Journal of Management Studies*, 38: 719–45.

—— (2003). 'Managerial Structure of Business Groups in Taiwan: The Inner Circle System and its Social Organization', *Developing Economies*, 41: 37–64.

—— (2004). 'Institutional Transition and Cultural Inheritance: Network Ownership and Corporate Control of Business Groups in Taiwan, 1970s–1990s', *International Sociology*, 19: 25–50.

—— Mahmood, I. P., and Feng, M. (2004). 'Chandler Revisited: Interface between Strategy and Structure during Institutional Transition'. Paper presented at the annual meeting of the Academy of Management.

Claessens, S., Djankov, S., and Lang, L. H. P. (1999). 'Who Controls East Asian Corporation?', *Financial Economics Unit*, Financial Sector Practice Department, World Bank.

—— Djankov, S., and Lang, L. H. P. (2000). 'The Separation of Ownership and Control in East Asian Corporations', *Journal of Financial Economics*, 58: 81–112.

Clark, E., and Soulsby, A. (1999). 'The Adoption of the Multi-Divisional Form in Large Czech Enterprises: The Role of Economic, Institutional, and Strategic Choice Factors', *Journal of Management Studies*, 36: 535–59.

Clark, K. B. and Fujimoto, T. (1991). *Product Development Performance*. Boston, MA: Harvard Business School Press.

Coffee, J. (1999). 'Privatization and Corporate Governance: The Lessons from Securities Market Failure', *Journal of Corporate Law*, 25(1): 1–39.

Cornell, D. (1993). 'Transferring the "People's Livelihood" to the People: An Evaluation of Taiwan's Privatization Wave', *Law and Policy in International Business*, 24: 943–92.

Corsetti, G., Pesenti, P., and Roubini, N. (1998). 'What Caused the Asian Currency and Financial Crisis?', Working Paper, New York University.

—— G., Pesenti, P., and Roubini, N. (1999). 'Paper Tigers? A Model of the Asian Crisis', *European Economic Review*, 43: 1211–36.

Cotton, J. (1995). 'Interpreting Singapore: Class and Power?', *The Pacific Review*, 8: 558–63.

Dasri, T. (2001). 'Policies and Practices of Corporate Restructuring in East Asia: A case of Thailand', *Quarterly Bulletin: Bank of Thailand*, 39: 1–9.

Denis, D. and Kruse, T. (2000). 'Managerial Discipline and Corporate Restructuring Following Performance Declines', *Joural of Financial Economics*, 55: 391–424.

Department of Foreign Affairs (2000). Transforming Thailand: Choices for the new millennium. the EAAU report, the Australian Government, http://www.dfat.gov.au/publications/trans_thailand/.

Dewenter, K., Novaes, W., and Pettway, R. H. (1999). 'Visibility Versus Complexity in Business Groups: Evidence from Japanese Keiretsu'. *Third Draft.*

DiMaggio, P. and Powell, W. W. (1983). 'The Iron Cage Revisited: Institutional Isomorphism and Collective Rationality in Organizational Fields', *American Sociological Review*, 48/2: 147–60.

Directory of Government-Linked Corporations (1994). Singapore: Temasek Holdings.

Dobbin, F. (1994). *Forging Industrial Policy: The United States, Britain, and France in the Railway Age.* New York: Cambridge University Press.

Dore, R. (2000). *Stock Market Capitalism: Welfare Capitalism: Japan and Germany versus the Anglo-Saxons.* New York: Oxford University Press.

DP Info Network. *Singapore 1000 1998/1999.* Published and ranked by DP Info Network Pte. Compiled by Ernst & Young Consultants Pte.

Evans, P. (1979). *Dependent Development: The Alliance of Multinational, State and Local Capital in Brazil.* Princeton, NJ: Princeton University Press.

—— (1995). *Embedded Autonomy: States and Industrial Transformation.* Princeton, NJ: Princeton University Press.

Fernandez-Jilberto, A. and Mommem, A. (1996). *Liberalization in the Developing World.* London: Routledge.

Fields, K. J. (1995). *Enterprise and the State in Korea and Taiwan.* Ithaca, NY: Cornell University Press.

Flath, D. (1993). 'Shareholding in the Keiretsu: Japan's Corporate Groups', *Review of Economics and Statistics*, 75/2: 249–57.

Flatters, F. (1999). 'Thailand, the IMF and the Economic Crisis: First In, Fast Out?' Brookings Institution/Chung Hua Institute for Economic Research, mimeo.

Fligstein, N. (1990). *The Transformation of Corporate Control.* Cambridge, MA: Harvard University Press.

Fukuyama, F. (1995). *Trust: The Social Virtues and the Creation of Prosperity*. New York: Free Press.

Galvez, J. and Tybout, J. (1985). 'Microeconomic Adjustments in Chile during 1977–81: The Importance of Being a Grupo'. *World Development*, August, 969–94.

Gerlach, M. L. (1992). *Alliance Capitalism: The Social Organization of Japanese Business*. Berkeley, CA: University of California Press.

Gerschenkron, A. (1962). *Economic Backwardness in Historical Perspective: A Book of Essays*. Cambridge: The Belknap Press of Harvard University Press.

Ghemawat, P. and Costa, R. I. (1993). 'The Organizational Tension Between Static and Dynamic Efficiency', *Strategic Management Journal*, 14: 59–73.

—— and Khanna, T. (1998), 'The Nature of Diversified Business Groups: A Research Design and Two Case Studies', *Journal of Industrial Economics*, 46: 35–61.

Gilson, R. J. and Roe, M. J. (1993). 'Understanding Keiretsu Overlaps', *The Yale Law Journal*, 102: 871–906.

Gold, T. B. (1985). *State and Society in the Taiwan Miracle*. Armonk, NY: M. E. Sharpe.

Gomez, E. T. (1990). *Politics in Business: UMNO's Corporate Investments*. Kuala Lumpur: Forum.

—— (1994). *Political Business: Corporate Involvement of Malaysian Political Parties*. Cairns: James Cook University Press.

—— (1999). *Chinese Business in Malaysia: Accumulation, Accommodation and Ascendance*. Honolulu: University of Hawaii Press.

—— (2001). 'Why Mahathir Axed Daim', *Far Eastern Economic Review*, July 5, 164 (26): 50–51.

—— (2002). 'Political Business in Malaysia: Party Factionalism, Corporate Development and Economic Crisis', in Edmund Terence Gomez (ed.), *Political Business in East Asia*. London: Routledge.

Gomez, E. T. and Jomo, K. S. (1999). *Malaysia's Political Economy: Politics, Patronage and Profits*, rev. ed. Cambridge: Cambridge University Press.

—— and Hsiao, H. H. M. (eds.) (2001). *Chinese Business in Southeast Asia*. Surrey: Curzon Press.

Granovetter, M. (1985). 'Economic Action and Social Structure: The Problem of Embeddedness', *American Journal of Sociology*, 91(3): 481–510.

—— (1994). 'Business Groups', in N. J. Smelser and R. Swedberg (eds.), *The Handbook of Economic Sociology*. Princeton, NJ: Princeton University Press, pp. 453–75.

—— (1995). 'Coase Revisited: Business Groups in the Modern Economy', *Industrial and Corporate Change*, 4: 93–140.

—— (2005). 'Business Groups and Social Organization', in N. Smelser and R. Swedberg (eds.), *Handbook of Economic Sociology*. Princeton, NJ: Princeton University Press. pp. 429–450.

Guéhenno, J. M. (1995). *The End of the Nation-State*. Minneapolis, MN: University of Minnesota Press.

Guillen, M. (2001). *The Limits of Convergence*. Princeton, NJ: Princeton University Press.

Guillen, M. F. (2000). 'Business Groups in Emerging Economies: A Resource-Based View', *Academy of Management Journal*, 43: 362–80.

Hadley, E. (1970). *Antitrust in Japan*. Princeton, NJ: Princeton University Press.

Hahn, D. H. (1997). Guanyu zhongguo qiye jituan yu guojia konggu gongsi de yanjiu [A Study on Business Groups and the State Holding Companies in China]. Doctoral dissertation of Peking University (in Chinese).

—— (2002). 'Joonggook giup yinsoo hapbyeongeui baljeon wonyingua yoohyung' [Causes for Development and Types of Business Groups in China]. *Joongso yongu*, Sino-Soviet Affairs, 26(1) (in Korean).

—— and Lee, K. (1998). 'Sijang gyongjaenggua joonggookeui giup jipdan' [Market Competition and Chinese Business Groups]. *Dongbukah gyongje yongu* [Northeast Asian Economic Research], 10(1) (in Korean).

—— —— (1999). 'Joonggook gookyou giupeui yijoongjok damhapgua nebuja tongje moonje' [Dual Collusion and Insider Control Problem in China's State-owned Enterprises]. *Hyundai joonggook yongu* [Study of Modern China], 2 (in Korean).

Hall, P. A. and Soskice, D. (2001). 'An Introduction to Varieties of Capitalism', in A. H. Peter and D. Soskice (eds.), *Varieties of Capitalism: The Institutional Foundations of Comparative Advantage*. New York: Oxford University Press.

Hamilton, G. G. (1997). 'Organization and Market Processes in Taiwan's Capitalist Economy', in M. Orrú, N. W. Biggart, and G. G. Hamilton (eds.), *The Economic Organization of East Asian Capitalism*. Thousand Oaks/London/New Delhi: Sage, pp. 237–96.

—— and Biggart, N. W. (1988). 'Market, Culture, and Authority: A Comparative Analysis of Management and Organization in the Far East', *American Journal of Sociology*, 94 (Suppl.): S52–S94.

—— and Kao, C. S. (1990). 'The Institutional Foundation of Chinese Business: The Family Firm in Taiwan', in C. Calhoun (ed.), *Comparative Social Research*. Greenwich, CT: JAI Press, pp. 135–51.

—— Zeile, W. and Kim, W. J. (1990). 'The Network Structures of East Asian Economics', in S. R. Clegg and S. G. Redding (eds.), *Capitalism in Contrasting Cultures*: 105–29. Berlin: Walter de Gruyter.

Hamilton-Hart, N. (2000). 'The Singapore State Revisited', *The Pacific Review*, 13(2): 195–216.

Hewison, K. (1985). 'The State and Capitalist Development in Thailand', in R. Higgott and R. Robinson (eds.), *Southeast Asia: Essays in Political Economy of Structural Change*: 266–94. London: Routledge & Kegan Paul.

—— (1989). *Bankers and Bureaucrats: Capital and the Role of the State in Thailand*. New Haven, Connecticut: Yale University Southeast Asia Studies.

—— (2000). 'Thailand's Capitalism before and after the Economic Crisis', in R. Robinson, M. Beeson, K. Jayasuriya, and H. R. kim (eds.), *Politics and Markets in the World of the Asian Crisis*. New York: Ruteedge, pp. 193–210.

—— (2001). 'Thailand's Capitalism', in G. Rodan, K. Hewison and R. Robison (eds.), *The Political Economy of South-East Asia*. Melbourne: Oxford University Press, pp. 71–103.

Hirshnan, A. (1958). The Strategy of Economic Development. New Haven: Yale University Press.

Hobday, M. (1995). *Innovation in East Asia: the Challenge to Japan*. Aldershot, Hants, England; Brookfield, VT: E. Elgar

Hoshi, T. and Kashyap, A. (2001). *Corporate Financing and Governance in Japan: The Road to the Future.* Cambridge, MA: MIT Press.

—— ——, and Scharfstein, D. (1990). 'The Role of Banks in Reducing the Costs of Financial Distress in Japan', *Journal of Financial Economics*, 27(1): 67–88.

Hoskisson, R. E., Hill, C. W. L., and Kim, H. C. (1993). 'The Multidivisional Structure: Organizational Fossil or Source of Value?', *Journal of Management*, 19: 269–98.

http://singapore.usembassy.gov/ep/2001/GOVERNMENT-LINKEDCORPORATIONS 2000.html

Huang, J. S. (2000). *1997nian shangshigongsi jianbing feishangshi gongsi anli fenxi* [Analysis of the M&A of Non-listed Firms by Listed Firms in 1997]. Available at: http://www.online-ma.com.cn. April 23 (in Chinese).

Huchet, J. F. (1998). 'Merge & Restructuring SOEs: the Case of Wuhan', Paper presented at the Conference on Chinese Enterprises in Search of a New Corporate Governance System, October 5–6, Beijing.

Ibison, D. (2004). 'MMC Turns to Old Friends in Hour of Need', *Financial Times*, February 4: 18.

IMF (International Monetary Fund) (1997). *Annual Report of the Executive Board for the Financial Year Ended*, April 30. Washington, DC.

—— (1999). *IMF-Supported Programs in Indonesia, Korea and Thailand: A Preliminary Assessment.* IMF, Washington, DC.

——. *International Financial Statistics.* Various issues.

Indonesian Business Data Centre (1997). *Conglomeration Indonesia: Regeneration and Transformation into World Class Corporate Entities.*

IRC (1987). *Jidosha Buhin no 160 Hinmei no Seisan Ryutsu Chosa* [A Survey of Manufacture and Distribution of 160 Auto Parts]. Nagoya.

—— (1996). *Jidosha Buhin no 200 Hinmei no Seisan Ryutsu Chosa* [A Survey of Manufacture and Distribution of 200 Auto Parts]. Nagoya.

Jang, Y. S. (2001). The Expansion of Modern Accounting as a Global and Institutional Practice, Ph.D. dissertation in Sociology, Stanford University.

Japan Fair Trade Commission (2001). *State of Corporate Groups in Japan*, the 7th Survey Report. Tokyo.

Jayasankaran, S. (2001). 'Blueprint for an Asian superbank', *Far Eastern Economic Review*, March 29: 48–51.

Jesudason, J. V. (1989). *Ethnicity and the Economy: The State, Chinese Business and Multinationals in Malaysia.* Singapore: Oxford University Press.

John, K., Lang, L., and Netter, J. (1992). 'The Voluntary Restructuring of Large Firm in Response to Performance Decline', *Journal of Finance*, 47: 891–917.

Johnson, C. (1982). *MITI and the Japanese Miracle.* Stanford, CA: Stanford University Press.

Johnson, S., Boone, P., Breach, A., and Friedman, E. (2000). 'Corporate Governance in the Asian Financial Crisis', *Journal of Financial Economics*, 58: 141–86.

Jomo, K. S. (ed.) (1995). *Privatizing Malaysia: Rents, Rhetoric, Realities.* Boulder, CO: Westview Press.

—— (ed.) (2001). Malaysian Eclipse: Economic Crisis and Recovery. London: Zed Books.

Kang, J. K. and Shivdasani, A. (1997). 'Corporate Restruscturing during Performance Declines in Japan', *Journal of Financial Economics*, 46: 29–65.

—— Lee, I. M., and Na, S. H. (2001). 'Do Chaebol and Non-Chaebol Firms React Differently to Poor Operating Performance? A Test of the Efficiency of Chaebol Governance Structure', *Working Paper*. Michigan State University.

Kang, M. H. (1996). *The Korean Business Conglomerates, Chaebol Then and Now, Institute of Asian Studies*. Berkeley, CA: University of California Press.

Kaplan, S. N. and Minton, B. (1994). 'Appointments of Outsiders to Japanese Corporate Boards: Determinants and Implications for Managers', *Journal of Financial Economics*, 36/2: 225–58.

Kawai, M. and Takayasu, K. I. (2000). 'The Economic Crisis and Banking Sector Restructuring in Thailand', in *Rising to the Challenge in Asia: A Study of Financial Markets*, Vol. 11—Thailand. Asian Development Bank.

Ke, F. C. (1995). *Kung Ssu Fa* [*Company Law*]. Taipei: San Ming.

Keister, L. (1998). 'Engineering Growth: Business Group Structure and Firm Performance in China's Transition Economy', *American Journal of Sociology*, 104(2): 404–40.

—— (2001). 'Exchange Structures in Transition: Lending and Trade Relations in Chinese Business Groups', *American Sociological Review*, 66(3): 336–52.

Khanna, T. (2000). 'Business Groups and Social Welfare in Emerging Markets: Existing Evidence and Unanswered Questions', *European Economic Review*, 44: 748–61.

—— and Palepu, K. (1997). Why Focused Strategies May Be Wrong for Emerging Markets', *Harvard Business Review*, 75(4): 41–8.

—— —— (1999a). 'Policy Shocks, Market Intermediaries, and Corporate Strategy: The Evolution of Business Groups in Chile and India', *Journal of Economics and Management Strategy*, 8: 271–310.

—— —— (1999b). 'Emerging Market Business Groups, Foreign Investors and Corporate Governance'. *NBER Working Paper 6955*, Forthcoming in NBER Volume on *Concentrated Ownership*, ed. R. Morck. Chicago: University of Chicago Press.

—— —— (2000). 'The Future of Business Groups in Emerging Markets: Long-Run Evidence From Chile', *Academy of Management Journal*, 43: 268–85.

—— and Rivkin, J. W. (2001). 'Estimating the Performance Effects of Business Groups in Emerging Markets', *Strategic Management Journal*, 22: 45–74.

—— —— (2002). Strong Ties and Fragile Links: Discerning Business Group Boundaries in an Emerging Economy. *Harvard Business School Working Paper*.

—— and Wu, D. (1998). Empresas CAP, 1994. Harvard Business School Case 9-798-053.

Khantavit, A., Polsiri, P. and Wiwattanakantang, Y. (2003). 'Did Families Lose or Gain Control after the East Asian Financial Crisis? Evidence from Thailand', in J. Fan, M. Hanazaki and J. Teranishi (eds.), *Designing Financial Systems in East Asia and Japan: Toward a Twenty-First Century Paradigm*. New York: Routledge. Forthcoming.

Kim, E. M. (1997). *Big Business, Strong State: Collusion and Conflict in South Korean Developments, 1960–1990*. New York: State University of New York Press.

Kock, C. J. and Guillen, M. F. (2001). 'Strategy and Structure in Developing Countries: Business Groups as an Evolutionary Response to Opportunities for Unrelated Diversification', *Industrial and Corporate Change*, 10: 77–113.

Kogut, B. and Spicer, A. (2002). 'Capital Market Development and Mass Privatization Are Logical Contradictions: Lessons from Russia and the Czech Republic', *Industrial and Corporate Change*, 11(1): 1–37.

Krugman, P. (1998a). *What Happened to Asia?*, Cambridge, MA: MIT. Mimeo.

Krugman, P. (1998b). *Will Asia Bounce Back?* Speech for Credit Suisse First Boston, Hong Kong, March.

Kuroki, F. (2001). *The Present Status of Unwinding of Cross-shareholding: The Fiscal 2000 Survey of Cross Shareholding*. Tokyo: NLI Research Institute.

Kyodo News Service. (2000). *Nissan to Revamp Ties with Parts Suppliers: Ghosn*. April 18.

La Porta, R., Lopez-de-Silanes, F., and Shleifer, A. (1999). 'Corporate Ownership around the World', *The Journal of Finance*, 54: 471–517.

—— —— —— and Vishny, R. W. (1998). 'Law and Finance', *Journal of Political Economy*, 106(6): 1113–55.

Lai, J. and Sudarsanam, S. (1997). 'Corporate Restructuring in Response to Performance Decline: Impact of Ownership, Governance and Lenders', *European Finance Review*, 1: 197–223.

Lawrence, R. Z. (1993). 'Japan's Different Trade Regime: An Analysis with Particular Reference to Keiretsu', *Journal of Economic Perspectives*, 7(3): 3–19.

Lee, C. H. (1992). 'The Government, Financial System, and Large Private Enterprises in the Economic Development of South Korea', *World Development*, 20(2): 187–97.

Lee, K. (1998). '*Joonggook seongnae nakhu jiyeokgwa baldal jiyeok gyongjeeui bigyo yongu*' [Comparative Study on Backward Regions and Developed Regions in Chinese Provinces], *Hyundai Joongguk Yongu* [Study of Modern China], 1 (in Korean).

—— and Hahn, D. H. (2003). 'Why and What Kinds of the Business Groups in China: Market Competition, Plan Constraints, and Hybrid Business Groups'. Paper presented at the International Symposium on Business Groups in East Asia organized by Center for Asian Business, Institute for Enterprise Management, Korea University, September 26.

—— —— (2004). 'From Insider-Outsider Collusion to Insider Control in China's SOEs', *Issues and Studies*, 40(2): 1–45.

—— and Woo, W. (2002). 'Business Groups in China: Compared with Korean Chaebols', in R. Hooley and J. Yoo (eds.), *The post-financial Crisis Challenges for Asian Industrialization*. New York: Elsevier.

—— Lin, J. and Chang, H. J. (2005). 'Late Industrialization and Late Marketization in East Asia: Convergences and Divergences', *Asia-Pacific Journal of Economic Literature*. Forthcoming.

Lee, S. Y. (1990). *The Monetary and Banking Development of Singapore and Malaysia*, 3rd edn. Singapore: Singapore University Press.

Leff, N. (1978). 'Industrial Organization and Entrepreneurship in the Developing Countries: The Economic Group', *Economic Development and Cultural Change*, 26: 661–75.

Lemmon, M. and Lins, K. (2003). 'Ownership Structure, Corporate Governance, and Firm Value: Evidence from the East Asian Financial Crisis', *Journal of Finance*, 58: 1445–68.

Li, K. T. (1988). *Economic Transformation of Taiwan, ROC.* London: Shepheard-Walwyn.

Lieberman, I. and Mako, W. (1998). 'Korea's Corporate Crisis: Its Origins and a Strategy for Financial Restructuring', in M. Yun (ed.), *Korean Economic Restructuring: Evaluation and Prospects.* Seoul: Korea Institute for International Policy.

Lim, M. H. (1981). *Ownership and Control of the One Hundred Largest Corporations in Malaysia.* Kuala Lumpur: Oxford University Press.

Lincoln, J. R. and Gerlach, M. L. (2004). *Structure and Change in Japan's Network Economy: The Form and Consequences of Business Networks.* Cambridge: Cambridge University Press. Forthcoming.

—— —— and Ahmadjian, C. L. (1996). 'Interfirm Networks and Corporate Performance in Japan', *American Sociological Review,* 61(1): 67–88.

—— —— and Takahashi, P. (1992). 'Keiretsu Networks in the Japanese Economy', *American Sociological Review,* 57(5): 561–585.

Lins, K. (2003). 'Equity Ownership and Firm Value in Emerging Markets', *Journal of Financial and Quantitative Analysis,* 38: 159–84.

Loh, G., Goh, C. B. and Tan, T. L. (2000). *Building Bridges, Carving Niches: An Enduring Legacy.* Singapore: Oxford University Press.

Low, C. K. (2000a). 'Corporate Governance in Malaysia', in L. C. Keong (ed.), *Financial Markets in Malaysia.* Kuala Lumpur: Malaysian Law Journal.

—— (2000b). 'Securities Commission', in L. C. Keong (ed.), *Financial Markets in Malaysia.* Kuala Lumpur: Malaysian Law Journal.

Low, L. (1995). 'Privatization in Singapore: The Big Push'. Paper presented to the Symposium on Privatization, Asian Productivity Organization. Bangkok, July 4–6.

—— (2000a). 'State, Politics and Business in Singapore'. *Research Paper Series,* #2000–037. Faculty of Business Administration, National University of Singapore.

—— (2000b). 'Reinventing the Singapore Development Corporate State'. *Research Paper Series,* #2000–042. Faculty of Business Administration Report, National University of Singapore.

—— (2001a). 'The Political Economy of Chinese Banking in Singapore'. *Research Paper Series,* #2001–015. Faculty of Business Administration, National University of Singapore.

—— (2001b). 'The Singapore Developmental State in the New Economy and Polity'. *The Pacific Review,* 14(3): 411–41.

—— (2002). Rethinking Singapore Inc and Government-linked Corporations: From SOE-SOE to SOE-POE. *Research Paper Series,* #2002–005. Faculty of Business Administration, National University of Singapore.

Mahmood, I. P. and Singh, J. (2003). 'Technological Dynamism in Asia', *Research Policy.* Forthcoming.

Mak, Y. T. and Li, Y. (1999). 'Ownership Structure and Board Independence'. *Research Paper Series,* #99–31. Faculty of Business Administration, National University of Singapore.

Malaysia. (1996), *Seventh Malaysia Plan 1996–2000*. Kuala Lumpur: Economic Planning Unit.

—— (2001), *Eight Malaysia Plan 2001–2005*. Kuala Lumpur: Economic Planning Unit.

Mauzy, D. K. and Milne, R. S. (2002). *Singapore Politics Under the People's Action Party*. London/New York: Routledge.

Mayer, C. (1998). 'Financial Systems and Corporate Governance: A Review of the International Evidence', *Journal of Institutional and Theoretical Economics*, 154: 144–65.

McNally, C. A. (1997). 'Shanghai's Way Forward—A Prelude to China's Next Stage of Enterprise Reforms', *China Perspectives*, 14.

McVey, R. (1992). *Southeast Asian Capitalism*. Southeast Asia Program. Ithaca, NY: Cornell University.

Meechai, T. (1983). 'The Effects of the Interactions between Business Groups and Bureaucracy on Thai Politics'. *Master's thesis*. Chulalongkorn University (in Thai).

Ministry of Finance. (1993). *Interim Report of the Committee to Promote Enterprise Overseas*. Singapore Government.

Mitton, T. (2002). 'A Cross-firm Analysis of the Impact of Corporate Governance on the East Asian Financial Crisis', *Journal of Financial Economics*, 64: 215–41.

Miwa, Y. and Ramseyer, M. (2001). 'The Fable of the Keiretsu. Cambridge', *Harvard Law and Economics Discussion Paper*, 316.

Montgomery, C. (1999). 'Vivendi: Revitalizing a French Conglomerate', Harvard Business School Case 9-799-019.

Morck, R. and Nakamura, M. (1999). 'Banks and Corporate Control in Japan', *Journal of Finance*, 54(1): 319–39.

—— —— (2003). 'Been There, Done That: The History of Corporate Ownership in Japan', *Working Paper*. European Corporate Governance Institute.

Nakatani, I. (1984). 'The Economic Role of Financial Corporate Grouping', in M. Aoki (ed.), *The Economic Analysis of the Japanese Firm*. Amsterdam: North-Holland.

Nam, S. W. (1994). 'Financial Reform: Theory and Experience', in G. Caprio Jr., I. Atiyas, and J. Hansen, (eds.), *Korea's Financial Reform since Early 1980s*. New York: Cambridge University Press.

—— (2001). 'Business Groups Looted by Controlling Families, and the Asian Crisis', *Asian Development Bank Institute Research Paper*, 27.

Nihon Keizai Shimbunsha [Japan Economic Journal]. (1987). *Kaisha Sokan* [Company Annual, Unlisted Firms]. Tokyo.

—— [Japan Economic Journal]. (1989). *Kaisha Sokan* [Company Annual, Unlisted Firms]. Tokyo.

—— [Japan Economic Journal]. (1991). *Kaisha Nenkan* [Company Annual, Listed Firms]. Tokyo.

—— [Japan Economic Journal]. (2001). *Kaisha Nenkan* [Company Annual, Listed Firms]. Tokyo.

Nikkei Weekly. (2003). *Mizuho Taps Friends to Get Hands on Fresh Capital*. March 17.

Nishiguchi, T. (1994). *Strategic Industrial Sourcing: The Japanese Advantage*. New York: Oxford University Press.

North, D. (1990). *Institutions, Institutional Change, and Economic Performance.* New York: Cambridge University Press.

Nukul Comission. (1998). *Analysis and Evaluation of Facts behind Thailand's Economic Crisis.* Bangkok: Nation Media Group.

Numazaki, I. (1993). 'The Tainanbang: The Rise and Growth of a Banana-Bunch-Shaped Business Group in Taiwan', *Developing Economies,* 31: 485–510.

Odaka, K., Ono, K., and Adachi, F. (1988). *The Automobile Industry in Japan: A Study of Ancillary Firm Development.* Tokyo: Kinokuniya.

Ofek, E. (1993). 'Capital Structure and Firm Response to Poor Performance', *Journal of Financial Economics,* 34: 3–30.

Ohmae, K. (1990). *The Borderless World: Power, Strategy in the Interlinked Economy.* New York: HarperCollins.

Okabe, M. (2002). *Cross Shareholdings in Japan: A New Unified Perspective of the Economic System.* Cheltenham, UK: Edward Elgar.

Oliver, C. (1992). 'The Antecedents of Deinstitutionalization', *Organization Studies,* 13: 564–88.

Orrù, M., Biggart, N. W., and Hamilton, G. G. (1991). 'Organizational Isomorphism in East Asia', in W. W. Powell and P. J. DiMaggio (eds.), *The New Institutionalism in Organizational Analysis,* Chicago: University of Chicago Press, pp. 361–89.

—— (1997). *The Economic Organization of East Asian Capitalism.* Thousand Oaks, CA: Sage.

Ostrom, D. (2000). 'The Keiretsu System: Cracking or Crumbling?' *Japan Economic Institute,* 14: April 7.

Palepu, K. (1985). 'Diversification Strategy, Profit Performance and the Entropy Measure', *Strategic Management Journal,* 6: 239–55.

Park, Y. C. (1994). 'Korea: Development and Structural Change of the Financial System', in H. Patrick and Y. C. Park (eds.), *The Financial Development of Japan, Korea, and Taiwan: Growth, Repression, and Liberalization.* New York: Oxford University Press.

Peng, M. W. (2003). 'Institutional Transitions and Strategic Choices', *Academy of Management Review,* 28: 275–96.

Phipatseritham, K. (1981). *The Ownership Structure of the Thai Big Business Groups.* Bangkok: Thammasart University Press (in Thai).

—— and Yoshihara, K. (1983). 'Business Groups in Thailand'. *Research Notes and Discussion Paper,* 41. Institute of Southeast Asian Studies.

Phongpaichit, P. and Baker, C. (1995). *Thailand: Economy and Politics.* Kuala Lumpur: Oxford University Press.

Piriyarangsan, S. (1983). *Thai Bureaucratic Capitalism, 1932–1960.* Chulalongkorn University Social Research Institute.

Pistor, K. and Wellons, A. P. (1998). *The Role of law and Legal Institutions in Asian Economic Development: 1960–1995.* New York: Oxford University Press.

Politics and Markets in the Wake of the Asian Crisis. New York: Routledge, pp. 193–210.

Pornavalai, C. (1999). 'Corporate and Debt Restructuring in Thailand', *Newsletter.* Bangkok: Tilleke & Gibbins.

Pornkulwat, S. (1996). 'The Development of Business Strategies of Overseas Chinese: A Case Study of Two Families', *Master's thesis*. Thammasat University (in Thai).

Porter, M., Takeuchi, H. and Sakakibara, M. (2000). *Can Japan Compete?* Boston, MA: Harvard Business School Press.

Powell, W. W. (1990). 'Neither Market nor Hierarchy: Network Forms of Organization', in L. L. Cummings and B. M. Staw (eds.), *Research in Organizational Behavior*, Greenwich, CT: JAI Press, pp. 295–336.

—— and Smith-Doerr, L. (1994). 'Networks and Economic Life', in N. J. Smelser and R. Swedberg (eds.), *Handbook of Economic Sociology*. Princeton, NJ: Princeton University Press, pp. 368–402.

Radelet, S. and Sachs, J. (1998). 'The East Asian Financial Crisis: Diagnostic, Remedies, Prospects', *Brookings Papers on Economic Activity*, 1: 1–90.

Rajan, R. and Zingales, L. (1998). 'Which Capitalism? Lessons from the East Asian Crisis', *Journal of Applied Corporate Finance*, 11(3): 40–8.

Redding, S. G. (1990). *The Spirit of Chinese Capitalism*. New York: W. de Gruyter.

Riggs, F. W. (1966). *Thailand: The Modernization of a Bureaucratic Polity*. Honolow: East-West Center Press.

Rodan, G. (1989). *The Political Economy of Singapore's Industrialization: National State and International Capital*. Basingstoke: Macmillan.

Rumelt, R. P. (1974). *Strategy, Structure, and Economic Performance*. Cambridge, MA: Harvard University Press.

Sappaiboon, T. (2000a). *The Lamsam Family*. Bangkok: Nation Multi Media Group (in Thai).

—— (2000b). *The Fifty-five Most Well-Known Families Version 1*. Bangkok: Nation Multi Media Group (in Thai).

—— (2001). *The Fifty-five Most Well-Known Families Version 2*. Bangkok: Nation Multi Media Group (in Thai).

Saywell, T. and Plott, D. (2002). 'Re-Imaging Singapore', *Far Eastern Economic Review*, 11: 44–7.

Scott, J. (1997). *Corporate Business and Capitalist Classes*. Oxford: Oxford University Press.

Searle, P. (1999). *The Riddle of Malaysian Capitalism: Rent-Seekers or Real Capitalists*. St Leonards/Honolulu: Allen & Unwin/University of Hawaii Press.

Semkow, B. W. (1994). *Taiwan's Capital Market Reform: The Financial and Legal Issues*. Oxford: Oxford University Press.

Shirouzu, N. (1999). 'Toyota is Tightening Control of Key Suppliers in Bid to Block Encroachment by Foreign Firms', *Wall Street Journal*, August 3: A18.

Siamwalla, A. (2001). 'Picking up the Pieces: Bank and Corporate Restructuring in Post-1997 Thailand', in *Governance Re-invented: The Progress, Constraints, and Remaining Agenda in Bank and Corporate Restructuring in East and South-East Asia*. United Nations Economic and Social Commission for Asia and the Pacific.

Sieh, M. L. (1982). *Ownership and Control of Malaysian Manufacturing Corporations*. Kuala Lumpur: UMCB Publications.

Singapore Department of Statistics (2001). *Contribution of Government-Linked Companies to Gross Domestic Product*. March. Singapore: Ministry of Trade and Industry.

Singh, K. and Ang, S. H. (1998). 'The Strategies and Success of Government-linked Corporations in Singapore'. *Research Paper Series*, #98–06. National University of Singapore, Faculty of Business Administration.

Sonsuphap, R. (1996). 'Thai Bureaucratic Capital (1957–1973)', *Master's thesis*. Chulalongkorn University (in Thai).

Stark, D. (1996). 'Recombinant Property in Eastern Europe Capitalism', *American Journal of Sociology*, 101(4): 993–1027.

Strachan, H. (1976). *Family and Other Business Groups in Economic Development: The Case of Nicaragua*. New York: Praeger.

Suehiro, A. (1989). *Capital accumulation in Thailand*, 1855–1985. Tokyo: Yuuki Kikaku.

Suehiro, A. (2000). *The Analysis of Thai Large Companies: State Enterprises, Multinational Companies, and Business Groups*. Institute of Social Science, University of Tokyo, mimeo (in Japanese).

—— (2002). *Reform of the Systems and Restructuring of Firms in Thailand*. Tokyo: Institute of Developing Economies (IDE) (in Japanese).

Sun, Q. (2002). 'The Performance of Singapore Government-Linked Companies', *Pulses*. October 27–29. Singapore: Singapore Exchange.

Suzuki, Y. (1980). 'The Strategy and Structure of Top 100 Japanese Industrial Enterprises 1950–1970', *Strategic Management Journal*, 1: 265–91.

Takao, T. (1989). 'Management in Taiwan: The Case of the Formosa Plastics Group', *East Asian Cultural Studies*, 28: 63–90.

Tamney, J. B. (1995). *The Struggle Over Singapore's Soul: Western Modernization and Asian Culture*. Berlin: Walter de Gruyter.

Tee, M. S. (1995). *'The Singapore Successful Business Elites'*, trans. by Huang, S. Singapore: Cross Century Creative City.

Temasek Holdings. (2002). The Temasek Charter. www.temasekholdings.com.sg

The Central Committee of the Chinese Communist Party. (1993). 'Zhonggong zhongyang guanyu jianli shehuizhuyi shichangjingji ruogan wenti de jueding' [Decisions of the Central Committee of the Chinese Communist Party on Several Issues Regarding the Establishment of the Socialist Market Economy] (in Chinese).

The Federation of Chinese Enterprises and the Association of Chinese Entrepreneurs. (2002). 'Zhongguo qiye fazhan baogao', [A Report on the Development of Chinese Enterprises]. Beijing: Enterprise Management Publishing House (in Chinese).

The State Council of China, (1997). 'Guanyu shenhua daxing qiye jituan shidian gongzuo de yijian' [A Suggestion on Deepening Experiment of Promoting Big Business Groups], *Gazette of the State Council*, 15 (in Chinese).

Thompson, J. D. (1967). *Organizations in Action: Social Science Bases of Administrative Theory*. New York: McGraw-Hill.

Tien, H. M. (1989). *The Great Transition: Political and Social Change in the Republic of China*. Stanford, CA: Hoover Institution Press, Stanford University.

Tokyo Stock Exchange. (2002). *Share Ownership Survey*. Tokyo.

Toyo Keizai. (2000). *Kigyo Keiretsu Soran* [Guide to Corporate Groupings]. Tokyo.

Tsui-Auch, L. S. (2004). 'The Professionally Managed Family-ruled Business: Ethnic Chinese Business in Singapore', *Journal of Management Studies*, 41(4): 693–723. Sage Publications.

—— (2005). 'Unpacking Regional Ethnicity and the Strength of Ties in Shaping Ethnic Entrepreneurship', *Organization Studies*, 26(8): 1189–1216.

—— and Lee, Y. J. (2003). 'The State Matters: Management Models of Singaporean Chinese and Korean business groups', *Organizational Studies*, 24(4): 507–34. Sage Publications.

Tybout, J. (1986). 'A Firm-level Chronicle of Financial Crises in the Southern Cone', *Journal of Development Economics*, 24: 371–400.

United Nations Conference on Trade and Development. (1997). *World Investment Report 1997: Trans-national Corporations, Market Structure and Competition Policy*. Switzerland: United Nations.

US Embassy of Singapore (2001). *Government-linked Corporations Face the Future*. March.

Useem, M. (1998). 'Corporate Leadership in a Globalizing Equity Market', *Academy of Management Executive*, 12(4): 43–59.

Vasil, R. (1995). *Asianising Singapore: The PAP's Management of Ethnicity*. Singapore: Heinemann Asia.

Wade, R. (1990). *Governing the Market: Economic Theory and the Role of Government in East Asian Industrialization*. Princeton, NJ: Princeton University Press.

Wang, W. and Kang, R. (eds.) (2001). 'Zhongguo binggou baogao' [Report on M&A in China]. Beijing: China Material Publishing House (in Chinese).

Webb, S. and Saywell, T. (2002). 'Untangling Temasek', *Far Eastern Economic Review*, November 7: 42–6.

Weinstein, D. E. and Yafeh, Y. (1995). 'Japan's Corporate Groups: Collusive or Competitive? An Empirical Investigation of Keiretsu Behavior', *Journal of Industrial Economics*, 43(4): 359–77.

Whitley, R. (1992). *Business Systems in East Asia: Firms, Markets and Societies*. London: Sage Publications.

Whitley, R. (1999). *Divergent Capitalisms: The Social Structuring and Change of Business Systems*. Oxford: Oxford University Press.

Whittington, R. and Mayer, M. (2000). *The European Corporation: Strategy, Structure, and Social Science*. New York: Oxford University Press.

Wiwattanakantang, Y. (2001). 'Controlling Shareholders and Corporate Value: Evidence from Thailand', *Pacific Basin Finance Journal*, 9: 323–62.

Wong, K., Phunsunthorn, C. and Sucharitkul, T. (2000). 'Problems and Promises: the Reform of Thai Bankruptcy Law in the Wake of the Asian Financial Crisis', *Harvard Asia Quarterly*, 4 (Winter).

Wong, S. L. (1985). 'The Chinese Family Firm: A model', *The British Journal of Sociology*, 36(1): 58–72.

Woo, J. E. (1991). *Race to the Swift: State and Finance in Korean Industrialization*. New York: Columbia University Press.

World Bank (1998). *East Asia: Road to Recovery*.

—— (2000). *East Asia: Recovery and Beyond*.

—— (2000). *Thailand Economic Monitor, February 2000*. www.worldbank.or.th/monitor.

Worthington, R. (2003). *Governance in Singapore.* New York: RoutledgeCurzon.

Yafeh, Y. (2002). *An International Perspective of Japan's Corporate Groups and their Prospects.* NBER Working Paper W9386.

Yeh, Y. H., Ko C. E. and Su Y. H. (2003). 'Ultimate Control and Expropriation of Minority Shareholders: New Evidence from Taiwan', *Academia Economic Papers,* 31: 263–99.

Yeung, H. W. (2000). 'State Intervention and Neoliberalism in the Globalizing Era', *The Pacific Review,* 7(3): 399–432.

—— (2003). 'Managing Economic (in)security in the Global Economy: Institutional Capacity and Singapore's Developmental State'. A revised paper presented at the conference on 'Globalization and Economic Security in East Asia: Governance and Institutions', September 11–12. Institution of Defense and Strategic Studies, Nanyang Technological University, Singapore.

Zucker, L. G. (1983). 'Organizations as Institutions', *Research in the Sociology of Organizations,* 2: 1–47.

Index

Chang: Business Groups in East Asia